BEYOND ADJUSTMENT
THE ASIAN EXPERIENCE

BEYOND ADJUSTMENT
THE ASIAN EXPERIENCE

Edited by
Paul Streeten

International Monetary Fund
February 1988

© 1988 International Monetary Fund
Reprinted March 1990

Library of Congress Cataloging-in-Publication Data

Beyond adjustment: the Asian experience.

"February 1988."
Proceedings of a conference sponsored by the Indian Council for Research on International Economic Relations and the International Monetary Fund.
Bibliography: p.
1. Asia—Economic policy—Congresses. 2. Economic stabilization—Asia—Congresses. 3. Asia—Foreign economic relations—Congresses. 4. Economic stabilization—Congresses. I. Streeten, Paul. II. International Monetary Fund. III. Indian Council for Research on International Economic Relations.
HC412.B444   1988   338.95   87-36163
ISBN 1-55775-000-9 (pbk.)

Price: US$15.00

Address orders to:
External Relations Department, Publication Services
International Monetary Fund, Washington, D.C. 20431
Telephone: (202) 623-7430

Contents

	Page
Foreword *Michel Camdessus*	ix
Acknowledgments	xi
Introduction and Discussion Summary	1
Opening Remarks *R. N. Malhotra*	18
1. Growth and Adjustment: Experiences of Selected Subcontinent Countries *Bijan B. Aghevli, Insu Kim, and Hubert Neiss*	30
Comments *K. M. Matin*	54
2. Alternative Growth and Adjustment Strategies of Newly Industrializing Countries in Southeast Asia *Sang-Woo Nam*	68
Comments *Arshad Zaman*	95
3. Contrasting External Debt Experience: Asia and Latin America *Azizali F. Mohammed*	106
Comments *Sunanda Sen*	113

		Page
4.	Trade Regimes and Export Strategies with Reference to South Asia *Ehtisham Ahmad*	117
	Comments *Wilhelm G. Ortaliz* *Charan D. Wadhva*	160 165
5.	Structural Adaptation and Public Enterprise Performance *V. V. Bhatt*	174
	Comments *Muzaffer Ahmad* *T.L. Sankar*	203 208
6.	Institutional Framework for Decision Making in Korean Public Enterprises: Some Implications for Developing Countries *Hyung-Ki Kim*	212
7.	The Asian Experience and the Role of Multilateral Institutions, Foreign Aid, and Other Financial Sources *C. Rangarajan*	227
	Comments *Nimal Sanderatne*	249
8.	Surpluses for a Capital-Hungry World *Paul Streeten*	256
	Biographical Sketches	263
	Seminar Participants and Observers	269

The following symbols have been used throughout this book:
... to indicate that data are not available.
— to indicate that the figure is zero or less than half the final digit shown, or that the item does not exist;
– between years or months (e.g., 1983–84 or January–June) to indicate the years or months covered, including the beginning and ending years or months;
/ between years (e.g., 1983/84) to indicate a crop or fiscal (financial) year.

"Billion" means a thousand million.

Details may not add to totals shown because of rounding.

The term "country," as used in this book, does not in all cases refer to a territorial entity which is a state as understood by international law and practice; the term also covers some territorial entities that are not states but for which statistical data are maintained and provided internationally on a separate and independent basis.

Foreword

I am delighted that the Indian Council for Research on International Economic Relations was able to join with the International Monetary Fund in sponsoring a seminar on Adjustment and Economic Growth: The Asian Experience. The seminar, which was held in Bombay in December 1986, was attended by economists from universities, central banks, governments, corporations, research institutions, and other organizations; other government officials; corporate executives; and journalists representing a broad spectrum of views on the issues discussed. Participants, who attended in a personal capacity, came from Bangladesh, India, Indonesia, the Republic of Korea, Malaysia, Maldives, Nepal, Pakistan, the Philippines, Sri Lanka, and Thailand. Staff members of the Fund and the World Bank also participated.

The relevance and immediacy of the topics discussed provided an opportunity to have a frank and constructive exchange of views and experiences which, I believe, has improved understanding of the issues and has helped to focus the search for appropriate solutions. This, of course, is a major objective of promoting a better understanding of the work of the Fund and of improving the Fund's knowledge of thinking in academic, business, and other nongovernmental circles.

This book represents the continuation of the Fund's effort to publish a wide variety of views about its role and activities in the developing world. While all the views expressed are not necessarily shared by the Fund, it is our hope that their dissemination can contribute to a more informed discussion of the issues.

MICHEL CAMDESSUS
Managing Director
International Monetary Fund

Acknowledgments

It is tempting to mistake enjoyment for achievement. In the case of the Bombay seminar on Adjustment and Growth: the Asian Experience, however, enjoyment and productivity went together. The seminar was jointly sponsored by the International Monetary Fund and the Indian Council for Research on International Economic Relations (ICRIER). Much of the success was due to the hard work put into organizing it by the Fund and ICRIER, and to the splendid setting of the Taj Mahal Intercontinental Hotel. Governor Malhotra of the Reserve Bank of India opened the proceedings with an inspiring speech, to whose themes we returned again and again in the subsequent days. Dr. K.B. Lall presided with just the right combination of firmness, gentleness, and wit, adding to our deliberations from the great store of his experience and wisdom. Azizali Mohammed and Ahmed Abushadi of the Fund not only contributed during the seminar, preventing us from going off the rails, but also put a vast amount of work into designing, planning, and organizing it.

The Fund does not always have a good press, and its critics abound. But the spirit of this seminar showed no trace of confrontation, acrimony, or hostility. The staff members of the Fund were entirely open-minded and willing to listen, which is sometimes more difficult to do than talking. And the participants voiced none of the ill-informed complaints and grudges so often heard and read. I am convinced that we all learned from each other. At a minimum, my criterion for a good seminar is to meet again one old friend and to make one new friend. This seminar exceeded vastly this minimum requirement, not only for me but for all participants, and not only in terms of old and new friendships but also in terms of clarification of the difficult issues of adjustment. I should like to express my particular thanks to Azizali Mohammed and Ahmed Abushadi for their continual support through the stages of planning the seminar and editing this book. Finally, I should like to thank Sylvia Holmes for typing several drafts and Paul Gleason and Jennie Lee Carter of the Editorial Division of the International Monetary Fund for seeing this volume through its final stages.

Paul Streeten
Boston

Introduction and Discussion Summary

Paul Streeten

I. Introduction

In discussing structural adjustment, we may ask the following questions: Adjustment for what? To what? Of what? By whom? and How? The first question is adjustment *for what* purpose? Any adjustment must have some end in view. Sometimes constraints are considered as if they were objectives of policy, and, of course, they can take the form of intermediate objectives. Thus the elimination of a deficit in the balance of payments or in the budget or in public enterprises, though a constraint, can become an overriding short-term objective. Or we may wish to adjust from a strategy of import substitution to one of export orientation, or to growing debt service, or to more food production. Or we may wish to correct other distortions in order to improve the allocation of resources. Or we may wish to reduce high rates of inflation. These are, at best, intermediate objectives.

Among the objectives of structural adjustment are usually cited (1) the reduction or elimination of a balance of payments deficit, (2) the resumption of higher rates of economic growth, and (3) the achievement of structural changes that would prevent future payments and stabilization problems. One of the most important purposes of structural adjustment is to make the economy less vulnerable to future shocks. This can be done by increasing flexibility and adaptability. The success of a structural adjustment program depends largely on the absence of rigidities. But it may also be its aim to reduce such rigidities. Unless they can be removed, structural adjustment can be very costly, or altogether out of reach. Growing flexibility is therefore both a condition for and an objective of adjustment policy.

Flexibility can be applied to the market for products or the market for factors of production. If it is confined to products, but factors remain inflexible, large rents would arise which have no economic function.

There are more fundamental objectives, such as the elimination of hunger and malnutrition; the alleviation of poverty; or development of cultural autonomy, self-reliance, or greater national strength and military power. Some would say that accelerating economic growth is also such a fundamental objective, although growth is simply the time dimension of other goals of policy such as consumption, or poverty alleviation, or reduced inequality, or more employment. Whatever the technical intricacies of the adjustment process, it is useful to bear its purpose in mind, if only because some of these objectives may conflict with one another.

The next question to be asked is adjustment *to what?* Adjustments may be to an unexpectedly favorable turn of events, or, more normally, to an unfavorable turn of events. Adjustments to a favorable turn may be to an exceptionally good harvest; to an improvement in the terms of trade; to a rise in export prices, such as that experienced by oil exporting countries in the seventies or in response to a rise in the price of coffee of the Côte d'Ivoire or Colombia; to unexpected inflows of financial resources; or to a sharp drop in the price of oil for oil importing countries, such as occurred in 1986. Inability to adjust to such favorable turns can lead to opportunity losses and can be almost as important as inability to adjust to unfavorable turns of events.

The large literature on the "Dutch disease" that arose from the bonanza of natural gas discoveries in the Netherlands testifies to the fact that a large rise in the supply of foreign exchange can be, at best, a mixed blessing, and, at worst, a curse. The exchange rate appreciates; exports of goods and services other than the one whose price has risen, decline; competitive imports flood into the country; domestic employment declines while inflation rises, as the demand for non-tradables increases. The removal of the foreign exchange and savings constraints can bring to the fore other obstacles. Adjustment policies should then be devoted to their identification and removal. Among these will be promotion of exports other than the commodity whose price has risen; some control of imports, possibly through a dual exchange rate; sterilization of some of the inflowing foreign exchange; control of domestic inflation; and creation of alternative productive assets. Even a favorable turn of events can cause serious adjustment problems.

Much more common, unfortunately, is the need to adjust to an unfavorable turn of events. Adjustments may have to be made in response to shocks that are expected to last a long time or a short time, and they may have their origins in macroeconomic or in microeconomic factors.

A widely accepted distinction is that between the need to adjust to shocks caused by external factors, or exogenous shocks, such as a drastic deterioration of the international terms of trade; a reduction in the demand for export volumes, resulting, for example, from a world recession, or a rise in interest rates for countries with large debts, and those caused by domestic events or policies, or endogenous shocks, such as an excessively lax fiscal and monetary policy, price distortions, losses of public enterprises, excessive protection, excess foreign borrowing, or domestic upheavals, including revolutions. On the face of it, the distinction is clear enough. Foreign reductions in demand, owing to a new technology, to a change in tastes, to rising competitors, or to a recession abroad, or a sudden and large rise in the prices of essential imports are very different phenomena from domestic harvest failures, strikes, corrupt policies, mismanagement, or political change. Yet, on closer inspection, the distinction becomes blurred. If prices of a country's exports drop and its terms of trade deteriorate, it is a matter of good policy to have foreseen this event, or at least its possibility, and to be ready to move out of the declining export trade into more profitable lines. Thailand, Malaysia, and the Philippines diversified their crops and raised productivity in existing crops in response to declining price prospects (for example, rubber in Malaysia), while other countries failed to do this (for example, Tanzania for sisal).

Alertness to expected future changes in comparative advantage and new opportunities in technology and demand, and flexibility and mobility in response to unexpected changes are domestic responses to international influences. To get stuck producing goods in declining export lines can be, at least partly, attributed to a failure of domestic policy. In this case, deteriorating terms of trade, apparently owing to external forces, must be attributed to deficiencies in domestic policy. The distinction between exogenous and endogenous causes gives no clue to the source of the fault and the allocation of blame or entitlements to foreign aid. Events originating in the domestic economy may be just as much beyond policy control as some outside events. A failure of the domestic harvest, a flood, a hurricane, or an earthquake cannot be attributed to domestic mismanagement, though provision for such emergencies—like provision against shocks from abroad, such as ample foreign exchange reserves, inventories, or spare capacity—is prudent. The exogenous/endogenous distinction is sometimes taken as a basis for the justification of international assistance. External shocks, beyond the control of the country, should entitle a country to foreign aid, but not economic problems with internal causes. But some events entirely within the domestic economy are beyond the control of policymakers, such as a prolonged drought, whereas some external causes could, and perhaps should, have been anticipated and planned for. The external-internal distinction is not a useful guide for allocating fault or blame or entitlements to finance.

In addition, the use of the words "exogenous" and "endogenous" can be misleading. Though they are applied in this context as meaning originating outside or inside the country in question, they normally mean in economic analysis originating outside or inside the variables of an analytical model. And this model could comprise external variables as parts of its interdependent system, in which case they would be endogenous, and domestic determinants could be assumed to be outside its system, and they would then be exogenous.

Even if the distinction between external and internal origins were helpful in allocating blame or fault, unless more external assistance were forthcoming in one case than in the other, it would not be helpful in determining what measures to adopt. For even faults that lie entirely outside the country have to be ajusted to, just as if they originated in the country.

Some of the major changes arising mainly from the world economy which call for adjustments by the developing countries are these:

(1) growing debt service, combined with fewer loans and higher interest rates;
(2) deteriorating terms of trade, whether resulting from rises in import prices, such as that of oil, or drops in export prices, such as those of major export crops;
(3) high levels of inflation in the world;
(4) slower growth in the Organization for Economic Cooperation and Development (OECD) countries; and
(5) technical innovations, such as those in electronics, that change the location of industries.

In addition, the following factors may also necessitate adjustment:

(6) continuing high rates of population growth;
(7) urbanization;
(8) scarcities of land and certain raw materials;
(9) scarcities of foodgrains;
(10) policies adopted by the developed countries to protect their industry, agriculture, and services;
(11) environmental pollution;
(12) international migration;
(13) natural disasters, such as prolonged droughts; and
(14) man-made disasters, such as the arms race or wars.

Adjustment may be made to disturbances caused by domestic policies or by the policies of other countries. With regard to domestic policies, a good deal of attention has recently been paid to the losses of public enterprises, whose pricing policies are one of the most common sources of budget deficits in many developing countries. There are clearly some cases where the losses of a public enterprise benefit a particular vulnerable group or achieve a social objective, either of which may be part of the reason for the enterprise's existence.

In some cases, keeping the prices of the products and services supplied by public enterprises low helps to combat cost-push inflation. Policymakers have to weigh the demand-inflationary impact of budget deficits to finance public enterprise losses against the cost-inflationary impact of permitting their prices, and with them wages, to rise.

Public enterprises should also be judged by their ability to contribute, directly and indirectly, to foreign exchange earnings or savings, to the introduction of appropriate technologies, and to the protection of the natural environment. But, in fact, the losses of these enterprises far exceed the costs of achieving these social objectives, and in many instances do not achieve them at all. Far from subsidizing poor consumers, they subsidize fairly-well-off consumers and private enterprises. The losses can be understood mainly in terms of political pressures. Structural adjustment loans by the World Bank can help to exercise counterpressures for more rational policies of these enterprises.

A particular type of adjustment, often very difficult, is that to the policies of the advanced industrial countries. It is of the essence of interdependence that single nation-states are, by unilateral action, capable of inflicting considerable harm on other countries. The main danger here arises from beggar-my-neighbor protectionist policies. Disguised as regional or industrial policies, even policies that go under the name of adjustment *assistance* often can amount to adjustment *resistance*. Such measures affect most directly the newly industrializing countries (NICs), which are in search of markets for their growing manufactured exports. But the low-income countries, also, can be harmed by these measures.

Exchange rate flexibility on the part of developed countries has trade-reducing effects on developing countries and, if the latter peg their rates to one major trading country, trade-diverting effects from the rest of the world. Both represent costs for countries attempting to increase and diversify their trade.

A difficult problem is presented to the developing countries by the impact of the U.S. mix of monetary and fiscal policies on other industrial countries. The recent combination of loose fiscal and tight monetary policies combines the burden of high interest rates with depressed demand for exports from developing countries, as other developed countries have to put up their interest rates to avoid excessive capital outflows. What is needed is a higher degree of North-North coordination in government policies, as well as North-South and South-South cooperation. The best scenario would be a continuing U.S. expansion while the U.S. budget deficit was brought under control. U.S. interest rates would drop, easing the debt burden, Europe and Japan would expand with easier monetary policies, and demand for the exports of the developing countries would grow. A higher degree of North-North cooperation and coordination of policies would be a great help to the developing countries. Structural adjustment for the advanced countries, like charity, begins at home.

So far we have discussed adjustments as mainly responses to shocks, whether external or internal. But adjustments may be required as a result of more active initiatives for a change in strategy. A government may wish to change from import-substituting industrialization to export orientation, or to change from a conventional concentrated growth strategy to a more egalitarian one, or to institute a land reform or a tax reform, or to make poverty eradication one of its principal targets. The adjustment problems that such transitions create are therefore often inadequately treated and sometimes misunderstood. These will include sectoral imbalances in supply and demand, manifesting themselves in unemployment combined with inflation, and disturbances in the balance of payments, and will increase the time period for financing adjustments. Some of these adjustment problems are mistaken for manifestations of mismanagement, which, of course, especially for inexperienced reformist governments, may independently add to their difficulties.

Economists have been better in analyzing comparative statics and comparative dynamics than at determining the optimal transition path from one type of strategy to another. We completely lack a handbook for reform-minded prime ministers and presidents who would like to know how to manage the transition to a better society. The international community, in turn, should be ready to assist such reform-minded leaders with Radical (or Reformist) Adjustment Loans (RALs) to ease the transition, to help overcome the dislocations, and to provide more flexibility and elbow room.

Next there are the questions as to adjustment *of what* and *by whom*. In developed countries adjustment sometimes means the revival, with new technology, of old industries, which rise like phoenixes from the ashes, and at other times it means the creation of new industries at the frontiers of technological knowledge. And the question then often posed is whether labor should move to the industries or whether capital and entrepreneurs should move to the labor. Developing countries have a much smaller industrial base and the question is normally a different one: Should there be adjustment of *policies*, particularly pricing policies, say from protection to freer trade or from keeping food prices down to raising them to the level of world prices, or should there be adjustment of *institutions*? These may refer to a land reform, or to population control, or to the administrative system, or to education and training. Whatever the adjustment, the distribution of benefits and losses will be different for different arrangements, and some groups will bear the brunt of the adjustment. This, in turn, will often be a function of the power distribution in the country. Proper pricing policies often work best in conjunction with certain actions in the public sector. It is of little use to have high agricultural incentive prices if there are no roads to get the crops to the market, or no irrigation systems to water the crops.

It is often claimed that a prime candidate for a source of switching expenditure is military and defense expenditure. How many village pharmacies could we have for one tank? Many men and women of good will see in the large and rising military expenditures a source that should be tapped for better purposes. But the presentation of more attractive alternatives has no impact on the military establishment. If we wish to make an impact on the military establishment, we shall have to convince it that growing defense expenditure can be counterproductive in terms of its own objective: security. It is probably one of the areas in which the Laffer curve applies. Beyond a certain point, more defense expenditure reduces, rather than increases, national security. If this point can be established, and we can show that we have transgressed it, for multilateral and for unilateral disarmament, resources would be freed for social and other objectives.

Other candidates for expenditure cuts are found under various headings in the budget and include the losses of public enterprises. As we have seen, these losses constitute a major element in the budget deficits of many developing countries. The purported social purposes of many public enterprises appear to legitimize their losses. Before this conclusion is accepted, though, two questions should be asked. First, are these social purposes actually achieved, or are the public subsidies to these enterprises not, in fact, counterproductive in terms of the claimed objectives? Second, even where the social purposes are achieved, could this not be done at lower costs, more efficiently, and therefore with smaller losses or, possibly, with surpluses? One way of testing this hypothesis is to calculate the precise amount of the cost of any "social objective," to hand this amount of subsidy to the enterprise, and to then ask it to cover its total costs.

When we consider the question of adjustment *by whom,* the candidates are labor or capitalists, the rich or the poor, men or women and children. How can we bring about the required adjustment with the minimum harm to the most vulnerable groups? Some cuts in expenditure are required. Much investment is productive investment and we do not want to cut this, for it would undermine long-term growth. In low-income countries the rich are few, and some consumption cuts are bound to fall on the poor. But it is possible to prevent the poorest and most vulnerable groups, such as children and women, from suffering cuts in their consumption.

The last question is closely linked to the question *how?* What means are to be employed to bring about the adjustment? Adjustment policies generally comprise measures additional to stabilization, such as the reduction of tariffs, trade liberalization, the elimination of controls on wages and prices, the creation of institutions to facilitate export credits, and the improvement in infrastructure.

The analysis can be conducted by determining the answers to three questions:

(1) How severe will be the adjustment problem—the disease—as registered in the balance of payments deficit? (A secondary and, more important, but more difficult, calculation to make would be that of the costs imposed by alternative corrective measures, such as deflation, devaluation, import restrictions, tariffs, etc.)

(2) What range of medicines is available? For example, exchange rate flexibility increases the number of medicines, while pegging exchange rates reduces the number of medicines in the cupboard by one; forswearing increases in tariffs reduces it by another. The possibility of retaliation complicates matters.

(3) How effective is any given medicine? For example, when the volume of trade is growing more slowly, demand elasticities will be lower and exchange rate adjustments less effective. Within a free trade area or common market, elasticities may be expected to be higher than elsewhere.

The task of policy is to combine the financing of deficits with steps to bring about their eventual elimination in such a way as to minimize reductions in employment, output, and the standard of living of the poor (as well as the sacrificing of any other objectives, such as income distribution). Appropriate methods of financing deficits, combined with the right type of conditionality, do not frustrate the process of adjustment but instead can facilitate it and reduce its costs.

II. Discussion Summary

Chart 1 shows the adjustment process for a number of countries between 1981 and 1985. According to our textbooks, adjustment should take the form of raising exports and reducing imports, a movement from southeast to northwest. Only Colombia, Mexico, and Brazil conform to this pattern. Most countries reduced both exports and imports (but imports by more), while Turkey and the

Chart 1. Developments in the Merchandise Trade of 16 Indebted Countries: 1985 Compared with 1981

(Billion U.S. dollars)

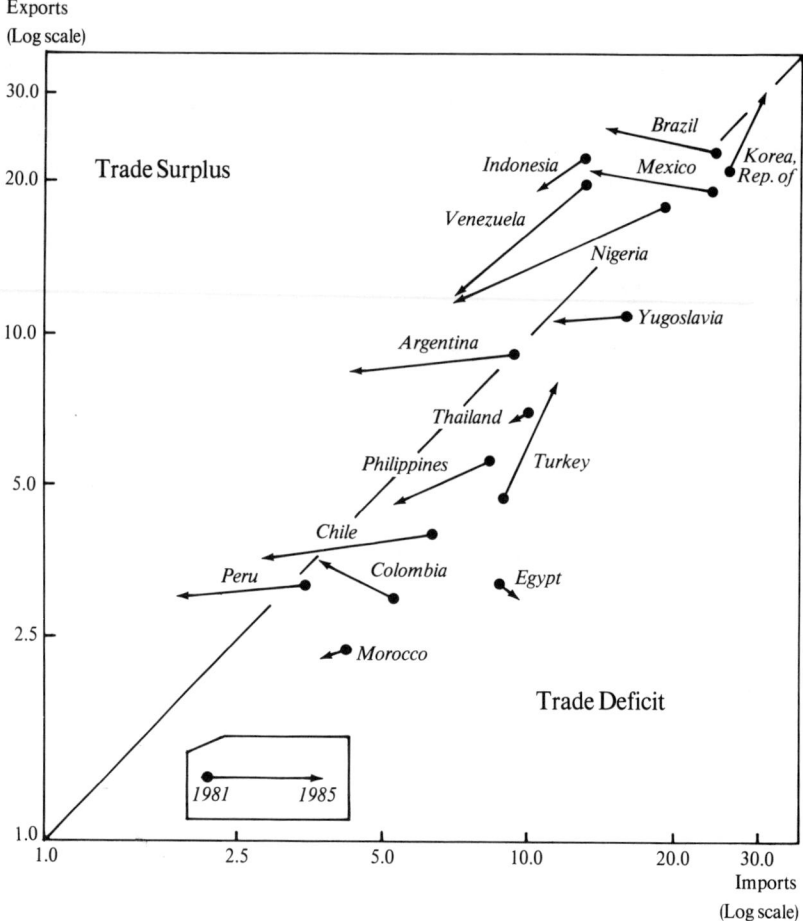

Source: Giovanni Andrea Cornia and others, eds., *Adjustment with a Human Face: Protecting the Vulnerable and Promoting Growth*, Vol. 1 (Oxford, England: Clarendon Press, 1987), p. 64.

Note: Points on the diagonal line correspond to balanced trade: exports (f.o.b.) equal imports (c.i.f.), based on customs returns.

Republic of Korea increased both imports and exports (but exports by more). (The fact that Korea did not register a surplus during this period shows that it could borrow.) Since we know that many of the export prices of these countries declined for independent reasons, it would be quite illegitimate to attribute the whole of this process to the adjustment policies. Nevertheless, the result has a bearing on any discussion of how to "adjust with growth." A decline over five years of both exports and imports is not an indicator of vigorous growth.

A question that occupied the seminar was why did Latin America fare so much worse in the early 1980s than East Asia? Professor Jeffrey Sachs's study throws some light on this question.[1] The Latin American economies shrank in that period, whereas the East Asian ones grew almost as fast as they did in the 1970s. Among the factors explaining the difference, the following have been mentioned: (1) greater external economic shocks (e.g., oil prices and interest rates); (2) higher debt service; (3) higher burden of taxation; and (4) higher government-expenditure ratios. Sachs shows that none of these can explain the difference in performance. The biggest difference is, as Azizali Mohammed pointed out, the rapid rises in the shares of exports in gross domestic product (GDP) in East Asia, compared with much smaller rises in Latin America. As a result the ratio of debt service to exports averaged 153.8 percent for six Latin American countries and only 61.7 percent for four East Asian ones. Latin America had therefore to slash imports and thereby brought on the recession of the early 1980s. Those who believe in exchange rates will find comfort in the fact that in 1982–83 the black market discount on the currencies of the Latin American countries averaged 40.4 percent, compared with 6.9 percent for the East Asian countries. The explanation of why East Asia was so much more successful in exporting may lie in the area of political economy. Whereas in 1980, 72 percent of the population of Latin America lived in towns, in East Asia the proportion was only 32 percent. The strength of agricultural and rural interests in East Asia who benefit from devaluation and exports may explain its success in exporting. Today the rural-urban proportions in the two regions are not nearly so different.

---

[1] Jeffrey D. Sachs, "External Debt and Macroeconomic Performance in Latin America and East Asia," *Brookings Papers on Economic Activity*: 2 (1985) (Washington), pp. 523–64.

On the other hand, we have been taught by Mancur Olson that large interest groups often lack the cohesion (as a result of too many free riders) to pursue their interests successfully, and that smaller groups are more effective in mobilizing government action in their interest. It is the small rural interests in high-income countries and the small urban interests in low-income countries that dominate policy.

One of the participants pointed to the greater capital flight from countries more severely hit by the debt crisis. But capital flight is a function of lack of confidence and as much a consequence as a cause of mismanagement and difficulties.

Insofar as the Latin American situation has to be attributed to the wrong policies, perhaps inspired by urban bias, there was apprehension lest the ways of dealing with the debt crisis reward greedy lenders and profligate borrowers at the expense of financial flows to the sober, prudent, and careful countries of South Asia, which avoided inflation, borrowed wisely, and made good use of the loans.

There was much concern about "negative resource transfers" and the relation between new capital inflows and debt service. In a dynamic setting, as long as the rate of new lending and investment exceeds the rate of interest and amortization payments, no foreign exchange leaves the borrowing country. But the current situation, in which a "negative transfer" has occurred, could be described as one in which the borrowing countries are investing in order to restore creditors' confidence, so that the required net inflow can be resumed. At the same time, the advice to the South Asian countries to go to the commercial capital markets may be premature, in view of their still-low incomes and high interest rates. We should avoid breeding a Latin American situation in India in ten years. By almost any set of criteria, whether poverty, ability to make good use, democratic government, political stability, good past performance, or strategic location, India deserves more concessional development aid.

There was, at the seminar, a clear presentation of the theory of comparative advantage and the analytical basis for advocating liberal trade policies. At the same time some qualifications were introduced. Some of the assumptions of the doctrine of comparative advantage may not be realistic.

(1) If production is subject to increasing returns, neither the Ricardo nor the Heckscher-Ohlin version of the doctrine applies.

Adam Smith said that the division of labor is limited by the (geographical) extent of the market. Allyn Young added that the extent of the market (determined also by the size of incomes) is limited by the division of labor (including cost-reducing innovations). On the interaction between these two causal chains hinges economic progress. But it has to be analyzed along lines very different from conventional trade theory. There would, for example, be no tendency toward factor-price equalization.

(2) The doctrine must assume an efficient mechanism by which comparative real advantages (and disadvantages) are translated into absolute price advantages (and disadvantages). For it is not the doctrine, but market prices, that guide the behavior of businessmen. This mechanism can be domestic monetary policy or exchange rates. If this mechanism does not work, because massive speculative capital movements interfere with the process of translation, the doctrine no longer applies. The recent volatility of exchange rates is not reassuring on this score.

(3) In the old days comparative advantage was regarded as God-given, or at least given by nature. Economists spoke of "factor endowments" as if they were inherited genes. Today, comparative advantage has become increasingly the result of the direction of research efforts and research and development expenditure. And it changes continually. The benefits from extra output and income have therefore to be weighed against these repeated adjustment costs. Particularly for an affluent society, free trade may therefore not be the best way of advancing its national self-interest, disregarding any obligations to low-income exporters in developing countries. On the other hand, many countries probably protect their agriculture and industry far beyond the point where the marginal costs of disruption equal the marginal benefits from further international division of labor.

In the discussion of public enterprises, much attention was paid to the impact of their losses on macropolicies and social objectives. There is, above all, the contribution of public enterprises, positive or negative, to the surplus available for reinvestment. There is the conflict between encouraging cost inflation by raising prices and encouraging demand inflation by running budget deficits to finance the losses. There is the impact of the losses on income distribution. There is the impact on employment. There is the contribution to foreign exchange earnings and foreign exchange savings, as well as the impact on the natural environment and on the use of appropriate technology. In none of the these areas have public enterprises been particularly successful in achieving the social objectives. On the other hand, it was pointed out that there are other forms of enterprise than either private or centrally run public ones; cooperatives; self-managed enterprises; and various hybrid forms, including enterprises with profit sharing, workers' councils, and management participation, many of which might be explored.

There was an unexpectedly high degree of consensus on most fundamental policy issues, although many participants expressed a strong desire for more financial resources for their countries, on easier terms. The Indians said that the design of their own policies, quite independently, completely coincided with the conditions of the Fund loan.

Much of the discussion concerned the limitations of outward-looking trade strategies. The following points were made:

(1) There is no sharp line of demarcation between import substitution and export industries and firms. Often a phase of import substitution precedes a phase of export, laying the foundations for successful export performance. This is true of both firms and countries. Volkswagen Brazil started as an import-substituting firm and has become a very successful exporter. Bharat Heavy Electricals in India is now exporting — after having been denounced as a high-cost "white elephant." (The rate of time discount that might have to be applied to the investment may, however, be very low or negative.) Brazil laid the foundations for its export capacity in the years of the Depression and World War II, when it was cut off from world trade. China, Turkey, Taiwan Province of China in the 1950s; South Korea in the 1960s; Japan; and even England are examples of phases of "breathing in" preceding phases of "breathing out."

(2) Even analytically, the distinction between inward- and outward-looking is untenable. Much of development consists in substituting domestic inputs for imported inputs into exports. Is this import substitution, because it substitutes domestic production for imports, or is it export promotion, because it adds more value to export earnings?

(3) Clearly, not all import substitution provides a good foundation for subsequent export. The skill consists in efficient import

substitution. The success of the successful exporters lies not in export promotion and looking exclusively outward, but in doing both import substitution and export promotion efficiently. Economic doctrine has habituated us to looking at movements on the production frontier in the direction of comparative advantage. Formal theory has much less to say about improving incentives, institutions, organization, and the provision of information so that we can move nearer to the production frontier. The market has an allocative and creative function. Success has to be sought much more in the creative function, in pushing production feasibilities outward, than in the allocative function, reallocating resources between import substitutes and exports.

(4) What matters for investment decisions in manufacturing and agriculture is not past or current prices and opportunities, but future prices and market opportunities. These are uncertain. The world market for exports may be different in the late 1980s and 1990s from the buoyant markets of the 1960s and 1970s. It is, of course, true that action on gloomy prophecies can be self-justifying. But the appropriate way to meet an uncertain future is to attempt to calculate and compare the high costs of import substitution if export opportunities are lost, with the costs of excess capacity or deteriorating terms of trade or unsold stocks of potential exports if markets do not materialize. The answer to planning in conditions of uncertainty is to provide for flexibility between import substitution and exports (and adequate foreign exchange reserves), even at some increase in average costs for the most probable outcome.

(5) Next, there is the fallacy of generalizing from a few countries to all developing countries. If all developing countries matched Taiwan Province of China's proportion of the labor force or gross domestic product (GDP) in exports, the need to absorb a vastly larger volume of exports would run into difficulties. Formally, of course, it is true that the extra revenue earned by these exports would be spent on extra imports. The phasing of trade liberalization will be different for different countries, and not all exports will be dumped simultaneously. The commodity composition and the export/GDP ratios will also be different for different countries and at different times. Many developing countries will continue to export primary products. Since labor-rich, resource-poor developing economies like the Republic of Korea, Taiwan Province of China, Singapore, and Hong

Kong are likely to have a larger proportion of their labor force in exports than are resource-rich, labor-poor countries like Brazil and Argentina, the impact on world markets will be reduced. Some exports will be directed to other Third World countries whose vested interests in clamoring for protection are less strong. And, as a result of trade liberalization, counter-protectionist pressure groups in the developed countries, such as farmers in the United States, may gain in strength.

In spite of these mitigating circumstances, there are bound to be adjustment problems in the importing countries. If growth rates are sluggish and unemployment is high, protectionist barriers are likely to worsen, or the terms of trade are likely to deteriorate for exports of manufactured products.

(6) In making recommendations about trade liberalization, it would be useful to distinguish according to a set of criteria for a country typology. Important among these would be the size of the economy. Taiwan Province of China, Singapore, and Hong Kong can create jobs by producing labor-intensive exports; but India and China are bound to devote the bulk of their efforts to designing products and technologies for their vast domestic markets.

(7) The Republic of Korea and Taiwan Province of China have not promoted exports solely by means of the "invisible hand." This "invisible hand" was supported by the highly visible and strong arm of the state. The issue is not government intervention versus laissez-faire, but efficient forms of intervention versus crippling ones. The countries that are often cited as shining examples of free markets have powerfully and efficiently intervened in the allocation of investment (steering the private sector by differential interest rates and other interventions), have used a battery of import controls and export incentives, and have had large public sectors.

(8) Finally, two points of political economy were made. More liberal economic policies (and in spite of and through state intervention, some policies are more market-oriented) do not often go with liberal political policies.

(9) Rousseau said: "Man is born free, and everywhere he is in chains." Similarly, we might say: "All economists recommend free trade, and everywhere there is protection." Why? It was argued that we should replace the notion of political will with that of political base—through an analysis of the constituencies, the pressure groups,

and the political leverage that could be mobilized for trade liberalization. Independent retailers, consumer organizations, and bankers each have an interest in freer trade, and their power and influence could be harnessed to the cause. By and large, people are quite good at pursuing their self-interest without the support of political scientists and political economists, but there may be obstacles, inhibitions, and ignorance—to whose removal political analysis could contribute.

Perhaps the most important general lesson that emerged was that there are no general lessons, and that each case has to be treated separately and on its merits. This pragmatic approach made it possible to discuss policies without getting bogged down in ideological or dogmatic positions.

Opening Remarks

R. N. Malhotra

(1) I am happy that the Indian Council for Research on International Economic Relations (ICRIER) and the International Monetary Fund (the Fund) have jointly sponsored this Seminar on "Adjustment and Economic Growth: The Asian Experience." I am thankful to the organizers for affording me this opportunity to share my thoughts with you on this important subject. May I also extend a hearty welcome to all those who have come here to participate in the seminar. I trust they would find the discussions useful and would have a pleasant stay in Bombay.

(2) The policies and operations of the Fund have generated wide interest not only among government and central bank officials but also among business communities, academicians, and the general public. It is only appropriate that the Fund and various organizations interested in it should seek to explain to all concerned the role of the Fund and the evolution and implementation of its policies, and I regard this seminar, which will concentrate on the Asian experience with Fund programs, as a commendable effort in that direction. My involvement in Fund matters in recent years has convinced me that the question of how to combine adjustment with healthy growth is one of the major issues which the Fund and its membership must resolve expeditiously in a satisfactory manner.

(3) The international economic environment continues to cause concern despite some improvements over the last three years. The world economy has, no doubt, emerged from the deep and prolonged recession of the early 1980s. Inflation rates have declined significantly and there has also been a desirable realignment in exchange rates of major currencies, though instability in exchange markets persists. However, overall world economic activity seems to be settling down to a low level of income and trade growth, with adverse repercussions on developing countries, many of whom have a large overhang of external debt. These developments have affected unfavorably the financial flows to developing countries and their growth prospects. In fact, in 1985, there was a reverse net transfer

of resources of US$22 billion from developing countries. The decline in international interest rates in nominal terms is a favorable factor, but the real interest rates still remain high, with adverse effects on investment activity. The combined current account deficit of developing countries, which had contracted to US$19 billion in 1985, is estimated to rise threefold, to nearly US$58 billion, this year–an occurrence that calls for effective responses.

(4) The Fund's Articles of Agreement, as adopted at Bretton Woods in 1944, prescribed six major objectives. First, the Fund would promote cooperation on international monetary issues. Second, it would facilitate balanced growth of trade and, through this, contribute to high levels of employment and real income and the development of productive capacity. Third, it would promote exchange stability and orderly exchange arrangements. Fourth, it would foster a multilateral system of payments and current transfers and seek elimination of exchange restrictions that hindered growth of world trade. Fifth, the Fund would make financial resources available to members for correction of payments imbalances without their having to resort to measures destructive of national or international prosperity. Last, it was to seek reduction of both the duration and magnitude of payments imbalances. I would like to concentrate my remarks on the objective of the Fund that stresses the need for contributing to high levels of employment and real income and the development of productive capacity as well as on its role of providing financial resources to members, since financing is crucial for successful adjustment with growth.

(5) It follows from the Fund's objective of promoting high employment, growth, and investment in productive capacity that its balance of payments financing should aim at achieving adjustment with growth. However, it would appear that for several years, Fund programs have tended to emphasize "adjustment" rather than "growth." This is probably due to a restrictive interpretation of the Fund's Articles of Agreement, as well as the inadequacy of resources available to it. Developing countries have long advocated strongly the maintenance of a proper balance between adjustment and growth. It is only after the severe recession of the early 1980s and the persistence of the debt crisis, threatening the international financial system, that the policy of "adjustment with growth" has received broader acceptance. Clearly, the policy is of general

application, even though it has been emphasized recently mainly with reference to the highly indebted countries. This policy, to be meaningful, must be seen as an advance on the past perceptions, and it is essential to discuss and grasp its implications for the design and implementation of the Fund programs, especially when they relate to developing countries. If, however, the view were to be taken that the Fund programs already strike the right balance between adjustment and growth, a complacent approach in favor of the status quo could develop and the search for new initiatives and advances could be undermined.

(6) Developing countries constitute a majority of the Fund membership and, over the years, the Fund staff has gained considerable knowledge and experience of conditions in the developing world. Since there is a great diversity between developing countries, it is difficult to generalize their situation. It would nevertheless be right to say that most of these countries have common problems. They are all striving to achieve higher growth to improve the living standards of their people. With some notable exceptions, their per capita incomes are low, as are their savings and investment. Their infrastructures are inadequate. While there are wide variations in the degree of diversification of their economies, most of them are nowhere near developing their full potential. Typically, again with some exceptions, their balances of payments tend to be fragile. The inflow of finance is uncertain and insufficient. Their populations are growing fast, as are the political, social, and economic aspirations of their people. Income distribution is generally skewed and the incidence of poverty is still high. The development process over the last few decades has, no doubt, improved matters considerably in many developing countries. Some of them have graduated to the middle-income group and are producers and exporters of manufactures of varying degrees of sophistication. There have been considerable advances in agriculture, with some large and medium-sized countries attaining food self-sufficiency. Still, the developing world has a long way to go, and its future path of progress will by no means be easy. Insufficiency of resources relative to requirements and the growing demands of vast masses of people could be a source of social friction and strife. Add to this the uncertainty of the international environment and recurrent adverseness in their terms of trade, and it is easy to see why the

growth objective is so crucial and all-absorbing for the developing world.

(7) It is against this background that most Fund country programs have to be evolved. It is well known that since the problems of developing countries are structural in nature, they do not lend themselves to easy and speedy solutions. The overemphasis in some quarters on the temporary nature of Fund financing and the revolving character of its resources has historically been responsible for a restrictive view as to the period of Fund programs and the time over which financing should be available. Perhaps underlying this approach is the experience of developed industrialized economies, which have the capacity to respond relatively quickly to policy changes with a view to correcting imbalances. However, the response lag to policy changes in developing economies is much slower. Diversification requires substantial investment. Directing production to the external sector is not always easy in the face of rising domestic requirements. It is, therefore, not surprising that many Fund programs for developing countries with short time frames tend to fail or, even when they succeed for the time being, are prone to recur. In many cases, insufficiency of quotas and the consequent inadequacy of financing dictate that adjustment be made far too fast, which can often result in import compression, slackening of economic activity, and general deflation. A view has been expressed, particularly with regard to sub-Saharan African countries, that since their problems are structural, Fund financing can, at best, be catalytic and that it is for an institution like the World Bank to take care of their problems. This raises some fundamental issues about the Fund's policies vis-à-vis such countries, especially the latter's rights as members of the Fund. In my view, the policy of adjustment and growth, if it is to be effectively pursued, has important implications for the resource base of the Fund, its financing policies, the length of Fund programs, and Fund conditionality. Also, at the international level, the policy of adjustment and growth would dictate adoption of measures aimed at raising economic activity and international trade, reducing protectionism, and fostering a greater appreciation of the imperatives of interdependence of nations.

(8) The main source of financing by the Fund is its quotas, more particularly its holdings of usable currencies. Apart from the

near-permanent General Arrangements to Borrow (GAB), the Fund has augmented its resources through borrowings from time to time. However, quota increases remain the major source of additional net financing by the Fund. Unfortunately, Fund quotas, judged by their relationship to world trade, have lagged behind requirements.

(9) It is true that over the years, the Fund has developed quite a large number of financing facilities in response to evolving situations. For instance, in 1963, it established the compensatory financing facility to enable members to meet temporary setbacks to export earnings, mostly arising for cyclical reasons. As such developments are reversible and normally beyond a member's control, it was conceded that in these circumstances it would not normally be necessary for countries to "adjust." Accordingly, the compensatory financing facility was developed as a low-conditionality facility. In the 1970s, several other facilities were evolved as major imbalances developed in the balances of payments of several member countries owing to oil crisis and high inflation. There were two oil facilities. Since the oil facilities carried high charges, an interest-subsidy account was instituted. Further, as many countries could not, on account of their structural problems, adjust within the short time horizon of the Fund programs, the extended Fund facility was established. Later, since the Fund quota resources were inadequate, the supplementary financing facility, based partly on the Fund's own resources and partly on borrowed resources, was set up, and this was followed by the enlarged access policy. Despite these developments, in view of the reluctance to increase "quotas" adequately, the Fund's contribution to external financing has continued to be quite modest. At the end of 1985, developing countries' use of the Fund credit outstanding was less than US$40 billion, which amounted to just 4 percent of their total external debt.

(10) In view of the large current account imbalances that had continued since the early seventies, one would have thought, the situation was tailor-made for the Fund to play a central role in balance of payments financing. Through ad hoc initiatives mentioned earlier, together with the Trust Fund assistance, the Fund did try to meet the challenge, but it fell far too short of requirements. In 1982, of the combined current account deficit of developing

countries, which reached a peak of US$84 billion, the net credit provided by the Fund was barely 7.5 percent.

(11) The Fund should be enabled to live up to its objectives and obligations regarding balance of payments financing, and adequate increases in quotas need to be agreed upon well in advance of emerging needs. Though the current account deficits of developing countries have narrowed considerably from the peak of 1982, this partly reflects the undue compression of imports at the cost of growth. The import requirements of developing countries that are consistent with satisfactory growth in their incomes are greater than current levels of imports and would entail larger external financing. However, the decline in commercial financing of many hitherto creditworthy countries has become steeper. The flow of concessional finance to low-income countries is also stagnant, if not falling.

(12) With the recent decline in the terms of trade of developing countries, there has been a massive transfer of resources from the Third World to industrial countries. The figure for the current year is estimated at US$80 billion. Despite these developments, there have been relentless pressures for reducing the maximum and actual access of members to Fund resources. This has resulted in substantial and repeated reductions in the maximum potential access under the enlarged access policy. Actual access has been much lower. In fact, at a time when the need for finance is so large, we have a situation in which even the readily available resources of the Fund are not being made available in adequate measure.

(13) It is sometimes argued that given the burden of debt servicing experienced by many developing countries, there is only a limited scope for their reliance on financing of the "debt-creating" type, which would add to already-high debt service. To be realistic, the ability of many developing countries in need of adjustment to attract non-debt-creating flows is limited. Besides, foreign equities also tend to be highly geared by way of loan finance. Therefore, external financing needs of these countries to strengthen their growth prospects and servicing capabilities will be required to be met through "debt-creating" flows on appropriate terms and conditions. The easier the terms, the larger the finance that could be made available within the safe limits of debt servicing. Further,

the servicing burden on existing debt could be reduced among others through rescheduling, as is happening in several cases, and even through renegotiation of the terms in appropriate cases. In respect of the Fund repurchases, for some hard cases, the period over which these are required to be effected can be elongated. The relevant provision in the Fund's Articles, however, has not been used so far, though it may have to be rather than allowing accumulation of overdue obligations.

(14) Experience has shown that despite earnest efforts, achieving adjustment in developing economies requires a fairly long period. The time frame has widened, since the order of adjustment required has become enormous. Besides, many economies of limited diversification have had to adjust simultaneously. The supportive actions by large economies, particularly those having large and sustained surpluses, have been inadequate and in some cases they have added significantly to the burden of adjustment on poor developing countries.

(15) The revolving character of the Fund's resources is often cited as the reason why short-term financing is provided by the Fund. The establishment of the extended Fund facility was at least a recognition that the adjustment period could be longer. Recently, however, the use of the extended facility has, regrettably, declined sharply, with only one country currently having such an arrangement in force. This disenchantment with the extended facility in the face of the need for financing over longer periods may have something to do with the stiff conditionality that is being attached to such programs.

(16) A special feature of the Fund's lending is its conditionality, which has been the subject of great controversy and criticism, especially in the developing world. As you all know, conditionality relates to a set of policies a member should follow in order to bring its balance of payments into a viable situation without tightening further its restrictions regarding current payments. On certain assumptions relating to the international environment, the Fund staff negotiates with the national authorities requesting the use of the Fund resources, a set of policies and measures which, according to the Fund staff's experience and judgment, would lead to a viable balance of payments position within a specified period. The countries often find that the speed of adjustment demanded under the

program is far too rapid, requiring tough policies for which peoples' cooperation may not be forthcoming. Besides, several basic assumptions and the linkages between policies and their impact may go significantly wrong. While every country admits the need for better resource allocation and improved efficiency in the use of resources, perceptions differ regarding appropriate policies and strategies to be pursued to achieve adjustment and growth. The stress placed on import liberalization and export promotion, which has become a standard prescription in almost all programs supported by the Fund, does not have universal validity under all circumstances. During negotiations of programs, much greater awareness of what policies and measures would be feasible and acceptable within a given time frame is necessary for their success. Besides, any worsening in the international situation as compared with what has been assumed as the basis for the program need to be offset by extending the period of adjustment or providing larger financing rather than encouraging even stronger adjustment. The contingency mechanisms envisaged in the stand-by arrangement for Mexico, which involve automatic adjustments of performance criteria and the availability of external financing in response to developments in commodity prices, are indeed a good beginning. Such features should become the rule rather than the exception. Heavy dependence on demand management policies, which have frequently led to deflation, has been a point of strong criticism. If the policy of adjustment with growth were implemented effectively, it would remove the sting of this criticism. It has also been stressed that often conditionality aims at large devaluations, mostly in developing countries, and that this is not always appropriate or productive of expected results, given the structural nature of their problems. The long period it has taken for the recent realignment in exchange rates of some major currencies to show a visible impact on their external balances should have a sobering effect on assessment of what can be achieved over a specific period through exchange rate policy.

(17) It is also necessary to review in depth the design of Fund programs. There has been a growing tendency to multiply performance criteria and to define them with ever-increasing precision. The conditions in developing countries, however, call for greater flexibility and more elbow room rather than a straitjacket metic-

ulously tailored to take care of numerous concerns. Breaches of such performance criteria occasion frequent interruptions of financial flows, which can be highly disruptive.

(18) National policies for reduction of poverty are important for promoting social equity and political stability. These policies often involve subsidization through price and interest rate mechanisms. While subsidies should remain within reasonable limits and need to be sensibly administered, their relevance in developing countries deserves greater recognition. The larger role of the public sector units and their needs for capital, often provided through the budget, have important implications for Fund conditionality. A more balanced approach to the public sector-private sector controversy is also called for.

(19) One way of gearing adjustment programs to growth would be to link them to development plans of countries making use of Fund resources. This would raise the level of commitment of the authorities concerned to Fund adjustment programs. Simultaneously, it would be necessary for the Fund to adjust its approach so as to make its programs compatible with the growth objectives of the country concerned. This approach has already been found useful in a few cases and needs to be extended.

(20) The preoccupation with conditionality resulted some time ago in tightening the requirements for financing under the compensatory financing facility. This and the reduction in access under that facility relative to quotas were unfortunate developments. There is an urgent need to review these decisions. Instead, a view has been expressed that the relevance of the facility itself needs re-examination, as the prolonged decline in commodity prices might represent a fundamental change in demand for commodities. This is a matter of considerable concern.

(21) The Fund can provide assistance through conditional finance and through allocation of SDRs, which are an unconditional form of liquidity. It is desirable to have a balanced growth between conditional and unconditional liquidity through substantial and regular allocation of SDRs. The steady increase in international transactions calls for a rise in reserves of individual members. Allocation of SDRs would help meet this need and also improve the composition of their reserves. It is unfortunate that for several years now, there has been no allocation of SDRs despite a strong

perception in all developing, and many developed, countries that it is long overdue.

(22) Effective surveillance of the policies of major industrial countries by the Fund would promote "adjustment with growth" of countries in current account deficit. It should encourage industrial countries to achieve the maximum feasible growth rates consistent with reasonable price stability and to open up their markets to imports from developing countries. Such developments would improve the export performance of developing countries, ease their debt-servicing problems, and raise their creditworthiness. Though the need for surveillance is accepted, and indeed is a requirement of the Fund's Articles, there are strong differences as to policy recommendations arising from the surveillance exercise and as to the need, manner, and timing of their implementation. Greater cooperation among Fund members is needed to resolve these issues. Of late, there is some evidence of a heightened awareness, on the part of major industrial countries, of the need to improve coordination of policies among themselves. To help this process, some ideas regarding performance indicators are being discussed. Recent concerted actions by the Group of Five countries on exchange rates and interest rates have demonstrated that, given the political will, it is possible to concert and coordinate policies effectively. Further developments would doubtless be watched with interest. Here the Fund has a crucial role to play through its World Economic Outlook reports and Article IV consultations. This role could be strengthened with the cooperation of large-economy countries.

(23) The need for adjustment has rarely been disputed by developing countries. There have, however, been strong differences regarding the path and speed of adjustment, and the appropriate policies and the timing of their implementation. For developing countries, adjustment without growth is unthinkable in view of the need to improve the living conditions of large segments of their populations. At the same time, many developing countries have demonstrated their will to take strong measures and to pursue their objective of growth with reasonable price stability. This is not surprising, as high inflation has specially harmful effects on the weaker sections of society. In India we have consistently followed a policy framework which emphasizes increased domestic savings, enlarged investment, restraint in fiscal deficits, and prudence in

incurring external debt. The plan strategy aims at strengthening the infrastructure, modernization, and diversification of agriculture, industries, and services sectors and at maximizing the growth potential in both public and private sectors. It lays great stress on improving the lot of the poor by enlarging the scope for gainful self-employment. We are currently engaged in giving a new and dynamic thrust to our policies with a view to raising the productivity and competitiveness of the economy. I find that the Asian Department of the Fund has produced for this seminar a paper on experiences of selected subcontinental countries with Fund programs. Among others, India entered into an extended arrangement with the Fund (1981/82 to 1983/84). The paper shows that the program was successfully concluded with achievements regarding the rate of growth, restraint of inflation, and reduction of the current account deficit exceeding the program targets, though export performance was below expectations. The experience of Pakistan was also somewhat similar. In my view, two important reasons for our success were our commitment to growth objectives with reasonable price stability and the linkage of the Fund program to our Sixth Five-Year Plan aims.

(24) Developing countries need development, as well as balance of payments, finance. Coordination between the World Bank and the Fund, the two premier international financial institutions, is, therefore, desirable, so that both long-term and balance of payments needs can be met. It is the expectation of developing countries that this cooperation between the two will lead to greater financial and technical assistance which otherwise would not have been possible. The possibility of cross-conditionality as a result of closer coordination between the two institutions has been officially denied, and I hope the experience of the countries concerned will not be different.

(25) The Fund has been playing a crucial role as an international monetary institution. It showed remarkable skill and resilience in moderating the impact of the recent debt crisis. The time gained has been utilized by international banks in strengthening their capital bases with a view to avoiding failures, though the debt problem will linger for quite some time. Within its constraints, the Fund has shown willingness to help and has tried to adjust programs to different country conditions. The appropriate emphasis

on adjustment and growth objectives, however, remains a matter for further exploration and calls for new initiatives.

(26) The deliberations in the seminar with participation of experts from the Fund and from different Asian countries with a wide range of experience regarding successful and not-so-successful adjustment programs should be rewarding. I have great pleasure in inaugurating the seminar.

1
Growth and Adjustment: Experiences of Selected Subcontinent Countries
Bijan B. Aghevli, Insu Kim, and Hubert Neiss

I. Introduction

During the late 1970s and early 1980s, there was a re-emergence of serious payments imbalances in the international community, primarily reflecting the sharp increases in oil prices and the concomitant decline in commodity prices. These imbalances were particularly pronounced in the non-oil developing countries, which suffered not only from the marked deterioration in their terms of trade but also from the ensuing recession in the industrial countries and the sharp rise in international interest rates. The total current account deficit of non-oil developing countries widened from about SDR 100 billion during 1976–78 to SDR 260 billion during the subsequent three years. The severe external payments difficulties facing these countries led to a substantial increase in the number of adjustment programs supported by Fund resources.[1]

An important accompanying development to the increase in Fund-supported programs was the growing emphasis on the need for structural adjustment to strengthen productive capacity and foster growth potential. In view of the substantial size of payments imbalances and the apparent persistence of the shift in the terms of trade, the adjustment strategy in the non-oil developing countries was reoriented such that demand-oriented policies were supplemented by more comprehensive structural or supply-oriented policies that were aimed at improving resource allocation, promoting

---

[1]The number of Fund-supported programs (under upper-credit-tranche stand-by and extended arrangements) increased from 54 (a total commitment of SDR 8 billion) during 1976–78 to 88 (SDR 24 billion) during 1979–81.

domestic investment and savings, and strengthening external competitiveness.[2] This shift in the adjustment strategy was reflected in a marked increase in member countries' recourse to extended arrangements with the Fund, which were designed to provide medium-term assistance to cope with structural imbalances.[3] Among the countries that entered into such arrangements were four subcontinent countries—India, Pakistan, Sri Lanka, and Bangladesh—which together accounted for more than half of the total commitment of Fund resources under the extended facility during 1979–81 (Table 1).

This paper focuses on the design and implementation of the growth-oriented adjustment programs adopted by these four countries. It examines the effectiveness of the programs in achievement of key domestic and external objectives both during and after the program period. The performance of key economic and financial variables is discussed mainly in terms of targets set under the programs, and an attempt is made to analyze the impact of both policy and exogenous variables on actual developments.

The first section of the paper provides a brief overview of economic difficulties faced by the subcontinent countries prior to the adoption of the adjustment programs, and the second section discusses the objectives and policy design of these programs. The third section reviews the extent of policy implementation and the performance of key economic variables in the countries during the program period, and then a brief overview of economic and policy developments during the postprogram period is presented. The concluding section provides a summary of major findings and issues for discussion.

---

[2]The distinction between demand-oriented policies and supply-oriented policies is made for presentational convenience. In reality, major policy measures—such as fiscal, monetary, pricing, and exchange rate policies—cut across the distinction between demand and supply.

[3]The extended Fund facility was established in 1974 to help member countries to overcome balance of payments problems caused by structural rigidities which are associated primarily with cost and price distortions. The key thrust of programs under extended arrangements is to promote the efficient use and allocation of resources and expand capacity output through structural measures, such as the reduction in price distortions and the increase in domestic investment and savings. In view of a much longer time period required for the implementation of structural measures, the extended arrangements cover a period of up to three years, with financial support amounting to the equivalent of 140 percent of a member's current quota. This compares with maximum financial support of up to 100 percent of quota and a program period of only up to one year under standard stand-by arrangements.

Table 1. Four Subcontinent Countries: Arrangements Under Extended Fund Facility, 1979–81
(In millions of SDRs)

Country	Date of Agreement	Original Expiration Date	Date of Cancellation	Committed	As percentage of quota	Drawn
Sri Lanka	January 1979	December 1981	—	260	219	260
Pakistan	November 1980	November 1983	—	1,268	445	1,079
Bangladesh	December 1980	December 1983	June 1982	800	351	220
India	November 1981	November 1984	May 1984	5,000	291	3,900

II. Background to Extended Adjustment Programs

The adjustment effort of the four subcontinent countries was initiated in the late 1970s and prior to the introduction of the extended arrangements with the Fund. Except for India, these efforts, which had been designed to counter poor economic performance and a deteriorating external position, were supported by stand-by arrangements with the Fund. In Sri Lanka, significant policy reforms were implemented in 1977 to revitalize the economy, which had suffered from pervasive government controls and cost-price distortions. Major corrective measures included the reduction of administrative controls, establishment of realistic relative prices through reduction of consumer subsidies, introduction of major tax and interest rate reforms, and unification of the exchange rate system at a depreciated level. In Pakistan, adjustment efforts were initiated in 1977/78 to narrow the fiscal imbalance and reduce cost-price distortions that had led to inefficiency in key economic sectors and depressed private sector confidence and investment. In Bangladesh, a stabilization program was adopted during 1979/80 to promote price stability, improve the financial position of the public sector, and strengthen production, particularly through adequate producer prices for key agricultural products.

Notwithstanding the progress made in achieving economic adjustment, the four subcontinent countries continued to be plagued by a number of deep-rooted structural problems that required sustained reform efforts over the medium term. While the extent of these problems varied across the countries, a number of common factors are identifiable. Economic growth was still hampered by inefficiencies in key economic sectors, severe industrial and infrastructure bottlenecks, and pervasive cost-price distortions arising from infrequent adjustments in both administered prices and the exchange rate in the face of domestic inflation. These impediments to growth were compounded by adverse weather, which disrupted agricultural production and, in India, also interfered with power generation. Fiscal conditions remained structurally weak because of low and inelastic revenue in the face of rapidly rising government expenditure that was propelled by increasing social and development needs. The fragile fiscal position was a primary source of excessive monetary expansion, which placed the four countries under inflationary pressure. Weak production bases, together with inadequate producer incentives, continued to constrain the countries' export capacities. At the same time, domestic demand pressures gave rise to strong import demand, which was suppressed through tight exchange and import controls at the expense of economic efficiency. These strains on the economy and the balance of payments position were intensified by the marked deterioration in the terms of trade and the subsequent slowdown in export markets.

III. Policy Design of Extended Adjustment Programs

The principal adjustment strategy adopted by the subcontinent countries was to strengthen productive capacity and promote economic expansion in a context of financial and external stability. Higher economic growth was envisioned to be realized through measures to raise both domestic investment and savings and to improve the efficiency of production and resource allocation; the latter was to be achieved primarily through the correction of cost-price distortions, the relaxation of restrictive industrial regulations, and the liberalization of trade policies. These policies were to be accompanied by restrained financial policies aimed at maintaining price stability and thus facilitating structural adjustment.

In view of the relatively long gestation period of structural programs, the improvement in the external current account position was expected to materialize only over the medium term. Underlying the supply-oriented adjustment strategy was the recognition that there was substantial scope for export growth and import substitution in these economies through the removal of structural imbalances and bottlenecks. The strategy was also in conformity with the urgent developmental needs to provide employment for the growing labor forces and to alleviate poverty. All the adjustment programs were incorporated into comprehensive economic development plans.

The adjustment programs envisaged a substantial step-up in domestic investment. In view of the major role of the public sector in the subcontinent countries, the governments were expected to take the lead in expanding investment. In general, public sector investment programs were to be reviewed and reoriented in close consultation with the World Bank with the objectives of improving infrastructure, exploiting opportunities for comparative advantage, and avoiding projects with excessively long gestation periods. Substantial resources were to be allocated to the agricultural sector, to the energy sector (in India and Pakistan), and to the industrial sector. Most programs foresaw a broadened role for private investment through the adoption of policies conducive to liberal industrial and import-licensing arrangements and to foreign collaboration.

The step-up in domestic investment was to be financed mainly by an increase in domestic resource mobilization so as to avoid disruption in financial stability and excessive recourse to external finance. The major burden for resource mobilization was placed on the public sector. The government budget was expected to generate larger savings through tax reforms, reductions in subsidies (particularly on food, fertilizer, and petroleum products), and restraint in wage outlays. Substantial savings were also to be generated by nonfinancial public enterprises, primarily through flexible pricing policies and the rationalization of their operations, including privatization in some cases. The programs also stressed the need for encouraging private savings through flexible interest rate policy, widening the range of financial instruments, and strengthening financial intermediation.

The programs recognized that the alleviation of cost-price distortions was essential for improving resource allocation and stimulating production. Substantial upward adjustments were to be made in procurement prices, particularly for those agricultural commodities that were considered to have potential for export and for import substitution. More flexible adjustment of administered prices for industrial outputs was also perceived to be important for reducing cost-price distortions. Furthermore, increased financial incentives were deemed necessary to improve the profitability and external competitiveness of the export sector, which had been adversely affected by heavy indirect taxes and inflationary pressures. To this end, exchange rate policy was expected to be used actively in accordance with developments in domestic and external prices.

Crucial elements of the adjustment programs were the deregulation of industry and liberalization of import controls. The programs called for the easing of regulatory restraints on capacity utilization and expansion and for the simplification of licensing approval procedures in order to encourage private sector production and facilitate modernization. The liberalization of import policy was aimed primarily at ensuring increased access to raw materials and intermediate goods so as to alleviate supply bottlenecks and improve international competitiveness. Imports of capital goods were also to be liberalized in order to improve the efficiency of domestic production and investment. Several programs envisaged a shift from quantitative restrictions to tariffs for regulating imports and protecting domestic industry.

Notwithstanding the emphasis on structural measures, prudent demand management remained a principal element of the adjustment programs, as financial and price stability was viewed as the fundamental prerequisite for successful economic adjustment. A major policy objective was the strengthening of the budgetary position through measures to increase revenue and restrain expenditure. The programs envisaged a substantial reduction in the overall budget deficit and a corresponding decline in government recourse to bank borrowing. At the same time, the growth of liquidity and domestic credit was to be contained to moderate inflationary pressures while supporting economic growth and private sector activity.

IV. Performance Under Adjustment Programs

1. Overview

The performance of the four economies with respect to growth, inflation, and external adjustment was uneven: India and Pakistan broadly achieved the original objectives of the programs, while Sri Lanka and Bangladesh were less successful. In most cases, the average economic growth during the program period was broadly in line with program targets (Tables 2 and 3). In India and Pakistan, a favorable growth outcome was accompanied by relative financial and price stability and a larger-than-anticipated improvement in the external current account deficit. In contrast, Sri Lanka suffered from both intensified inflationary pressures and a marked deterioration in its current account balance. In Bangladesh, program objectives in terms of both growth and inflation were not met and the current account deficit was reduced only through a drastic cut in the issuance of import licenses. The extended arrangement with Bangladesh became inoperative during its first year, as it became clear that the situation

Table 2. Four Subcontinent Countries: Indicators of Performance Under Adjustment Programs[1]

Targets	India 1981/82–1983/84	Pakistan 1980/81–1982/83	Sri Lanka 1979–81	Bangladesh 1980/81–1981/82
Growth	A	A	A	U
Inflation	A	A	U	U
Current account	O	O	U	O
Savings	U	U[2]	U	...
Public	U	...	U	...
Private	U	...	U	...
Investment	U	U	A	...
Public	U	...	A	...
Private	U	...	A	...
Export volume growth	U	U[3]	U[3]	U
Import volume growth	O	O[3]	U[3]	O
Overall balance	O	O	U	A
Official reserves	O	O	...	...
Effective exchange rate	R	R	R	D
Fiscal deficit	A	A	U	A
Expenditure	A	A	U	...
Revenue	A	A	A	...
Credit expansion	O	A	U	A

[1] A = broadly achieved
O = overachieved
U = underachieved
R = appreciated
D = depreciated
[2] For gross domestic savings.
[3] Based on broad judgment.

was not conducive to undertaking fundamental structural reforms; the authorities renewed their adjustment efforts in 1982/83 when they entered into another financial arrangement with the Fund.

The path and pace of economic adjustment in the subcontinent countries were influenced significantly by unanticipated deviations of exogenous variables and of policy implementation from the programs' original assumptions. Recurrent droughts adversely affected growth performance in India (1982/83), Sri Lanka (1979), and Bangladesh (1980/81). The task of adjustment was further complicated by the prolonged international recession and by a precipitous

Table 3. Four Subcontinent Countries: Selected Economic Indicators[1]
(*In percent*)

	Preprogram Average	Program Average Targets	Program Average Outcome	Postprogram Average[2]
India				
Real GDP	7.8	4.8	5.3	4.0
Inflation (WPI)	18.2	9.3	6.1	6.4
External current account/GDP	−1.6	−2.1	−1.6	−1.4
Pakistan				
Real GDP growth	7.3	5.7	6.5	5.3
Inflation (CPI)	10.7	10.0	8.4	8.0
External current account/GDP	−4.5	−4.6	−3.3	−4.2
Sri Lanka				
Real GDP growth	5.8	6.0	6.0	5.1
Inflation (GDP deflator)	7.8	11.7	18.1	15.5
External current account/GDP	−5.5	−10.8	−14.9	−10.4
Bangladesh				
Real GDP growth	3.5	7.2	3.7	3.1
Inflation (CPI)	18.5	11.5	14.4	10.2
External current account/GDP	−11.5	−12.9	−10.6	−8.1

[1] Dates for preprogram, program, and postprogram periods are defined as follows:

Country	Preprogram Period	Program Period	Postprogram Period
India	1980/81	1981/82–1983/84	1984/85–1985/86
Pakistan	1979/80	1980/81–1982/83	1983/84–1984/85
Sri Lanka	1978	1979–1981	1982–1984
Bangladesh	1979/80	1980/81–1981/82	1982/83–1984/85

GDP denotes gross domestic product, WPI the wholesale price index, and CPI the consumer price index.

[2] Partly preliminary.

decline in export prices that reinforced emerging fiscal difficulties (Sri Lanka and Bangladesh). On the other hand, all the subcontinent countries benefited from stronger-than-expected private transfers, particularly from oil exporting countries; also, adjustment in India and Pakistan was facilitated by more moderate increases in oil prices.

The extent of policy implementation also varied across the four programs. On average, implementation with regard to structural measures, especially those related to the strengthening of tax revenue, mobilization of private savings, and relaxation of industrial and import controls, was weaker than envisaged. Also, measures taken to promote exports were generally modest, with exchange rate policy playing little role in improving the profitability and international competitiveness of the export sector. On the positive side, important progress was made in pricing policy: incentives to agricultural producers were raised; excessive subsidies were reduced; and the financial position of public enterprises was improved. The extent of price adjustments, however, fell short of eliminating the subsidy burden on certain items and mobilizing sufficient resources for investment in some cases. Financial policies were generally restrained in India and Pakistan, but they turned out to be expansionary in Sri Lanka and Bangladesh.

2. Implementation of Structural Policies

a. *Public Sector Investment and Savings*

Public investment in India, Pakistan, and Bangladesh was constrained by lower-than-expected public sector resources. In India, revenue shortfalls limited the scope for investment in a number of important sectors, including electric power, irrigation, coal, and the railways. Nevertheless, substantial progress was made in expanding capacity in these economic sectors. Both India and Pakistan achieved a notable expansion in investment in the oil and gas sectors. Pakistan and Bangladesh also reoriented their public investment toward more quick-yielding projects, although the magnitude of the reallocation was less than originally planned. Sri Lanka also attempted to reorient the pattern of its public investment, but it was less successful, as priority continued to be accorded to capital-intensive and import-intensive projects with long gestation periods (particularly housing and urban development programs) at the expense of more efficient and quick-yielding projects (tree crops). More generally, inadequate control over public investment in Sri Lanka resulted in excessive investment, which proved to be unsustainable.

Progress in public sector resource mobilization was below expectations in all the countries. The generation of higher budgetary savings was thwarted by the continued low buoyancy of the tax system and increases in current expenditure. The intended tax reform to broaden the tax base did not materialize in Pakistan, Sri Lanka, and Bangladesh, and tax exemption remained pervasive. Efforts to contain the subsidy burden were strengthened in most countries. The rising import cost of petroleum products was mostly passed on to consumers, and the issue prices of food and fertilizer were raised substantially. In Sri Lanka, a large increase in key issue prices (wheat flour and rice) led to a reduction in government subsidies.[4] However, the extent of price adjustment with respect to food and fertilizer was relatively limited in India, Pakistan, and Bangladesh, and the budgetary burden remained substantial in these countries.[5] In Sri Lanka, much of the reduction in government subsidies was offset by a sharp increase in wages and salaries and interest payments.

Resource mobilization by public enterprises was mixed across the countries. In India, sizable adjustments of administered prices for industrial outputs and public services were implemented, providing a large portion of the additional resources required for public investment.[6] However, limited adjustments made to electricity tariffs and irrigation charges constrained resource mobilization at the state government level. In both India and Pakistan, the oil sector played a major role in mobilizing domestic resources through a substantial increase in the prices of domestically produced crude oil and gas,[7] although their prices still remained below international prices during the program period. In Sri Lanka and Bangladesh, resource mobilization by public enterprises was constrained by inadequate price adjustments. In general, the financial position of public enterprises remained weak in most countries, because of limited progress in the rationalization of their management and operations.

b. *Pricing Policy*

Pricing policy was an integral element of structural adjustment. Procurement prices for key crops were raised substantially in most

---

[4] A significant reduction in food subsidies was partly offset by an increase in subsidies under a food stamp system, which replaced a food ration system.

[5] Total subsidies on food and fertilizer in India and Pakistan amounted to 12 percent of central government revenue and 6 percent of consolidated central and provincial government revenue, respectively, in the last year of the program period. The fertilizer subsidy also rose substantially in Sri Lanka during the third year of the program period.

[6] The size of price adjustment over the mid-1980 level amounted to about 45 percent for coal, 18–38 percent for steel and iron, 20 percent for aluminum, 16 percent for cement, and 60 percent for fertilizer. Also, railway and postal tariffs were raised substantially. Most of these adjustments were introduced in the first year of the program period.

[7] The price of domestically produced crude oil was tripled in India and doubled in Pakistan over the program period.

countries to offset increases in production costs and to strengthen financial incentives for producers. As already mentioned, flexible pricing policies were also pursued with respect to major consumer commodities and industrial outputs, resulting in a reduction in subsidies. In India, progress was made in strengthening the market mechanism for price determination: official control on steel prices was lifted and a dual pricing system was introduced for the cement industry. While the degree of price adjustment in certain commodities was limited, the increased flexibility in pricing policy marked an important step toward reducing cost-price distortions in the subcontinent countries.

c. *Industrial and Import Policies*

Liberalization of industrial regulations was relatively slow in most of the subcontinent countries. In India, a number of measures were taken to ease industrial regulations, but their immediate impact was limited. These measures included a relaxation of constraints on capacity utilization; an easing of restrictions on industrial location; the exemption of investment in export capacity from industrial licensing requirements, antimonopoly regulations, and reservation policies for small-scale industry; an extension of various concessions to 100 percent export-oriented units and industries with high export potential; and liberal access to foreign collaboration. In Pakistan, the intended deregulation of industrial policies and labor reforms was postponed.

A central feature of the adjustment programs, particularly those adopted by India and Pakistan, was the liberalization of the import system. In both countries, import liberalization was largely implemented as envisaged in the programs, but its overall effect was generally modest. In India, liberalization measures focused on easing exporters' access to imports, including imports of capital goods and foreign technology. Preliminary appraisals of these measures suggest that the effective restriction of licensing on access to imports under the least restrictive licensing category was virtually eliminated. However, licensing continued to impose an effective constraint on imports under the more restricted import categories. In Pakistan, major measures included the abolishment of licensing ceilings on most nonconsumer goods, an increase in the ceilings on items that continued to be subject to licensing, and a reduction of import bans to protect domestic industry. Some steps were also taken to rationalize the tariff system, but a comprehensive tariff reform envisaged in the program was not implemented. In Bangladesh, import controls were tightened in response to a sharp deterioration in the trade deficit and an intensification of foreign exchange shortage.

d. *Export Promotion*

In most programs, the objective of promoting exports was pursued primarily through the liberalization of industrial regulations and import controls. In addition, steps were taken to offset the incidence of heavy indirect taxes and improve the profitability and external competitiveness of the export sector. Major measures taken to this end included special tax benefits for export-oriented industries, the improvement and extension of cash compensation and duty drawbacks (India and Pakistan), and the increased provision of export rebates (Pakistan); the latter almost tripled over the program period.

Exchange rate policy was conducted more flexibly in most of the countries in order to improve external competitiveness. After a sharp appreciation during the first year of the program, Pakistan severed the link between its currency and the U.S. dollar during the second year in an effort to restore export competitiveness. Sri Lanka also allowed a substantial depreciation of its currency in the second year of the program to offset an appreciation that had occurred in the first year. Notwithstanding the increased flexibility, however, the overall outturn of exchange rate policy proved to be less than satisfactory in most countries. Over the program period, the currencies of India and Pakistan appreciated by about 5 percent in real effective terms. In Sri Lanka, despite a relatively large nominal depreciation, the rupee appreciated by 28 percent in real effective terms because of high domestic inflation. Only Bangladesh was successful in achieving a moderate depreciation in real effective terms.

3. Financial Policies

a. *Fiscal Policy*

The extent of fiscal adjustment among the four countries varied. In India and Pakistan, the overall budget deficit in relation to gross domestic product (GDP) was relatively close to target, although fiscal restraint faltered during the latter part of the program (Table 4). In

Table 4. Four Subcontinent Countries: Financial Indicators[1]
(*In percent*)

	Preprogram Average	Program Average Targets	Program Average Outcome	Postprogram Average[2]
India				
Overall budget deficit/GDP	6.6	6.5	6.8	8.8
Revenue (including grants)/GDP	10.0	11.0	10.7	11.6
Expenditure/GDP	16.5	17.5	17.6	20.4
Current expenditure/GDP	*10.6*	*11.9*	*11.4*	*13.5*
Credit expansion	22.3	18.3	17.5	16.9
Liquidity growth	18.3	14.7	15.6	17.2
Real effective exchange rate	2.9	...	1.7	−5.6
Pakistan				
Overall budget deficit/GDP[3]	6.2	4.8	5.8	7.0
Revenue (including grants)/GDP[4]	16.3	16.6	16.3	16.8
Expenditure/GDP	23.1	22.6	22.7	24.3
Current expenditure/GDP	*15.0*	*14.0*	*15.0*	*17.9*
Credit expansion	15.1	17.2	16.1	18.6
Liquidity growth	17.6	14.1	15.6	11.8
Real effective exchange rate	−2.7	...	0.7	−2.1
Sri Lanka				
Overall budget deficit/GDP	13.8	10.9	17.5	13.4
Revenue (excluding grants)/GDP	26.2	20.0	20.1	19.0
Expenditure/GDP	40.0	31.0	37.6	32.4
Current expenditure/GDP	*27.6*	*18.1*	*21.2*	*17.3*
Credit expansion	18.4	36.0	39.4	7.3
Liquidity growth	27.5	25.8	31.0	20.7
Real effective exchange rate	—	...	8.9	6.3
Bangladesh				
Overall budget deficit/GDP	12.2	10.6	9.0	9.8
Revenue (including grants)/GDP	9.8	...	9.0	8.6
Expenditure/GDP	22.0	...	18.0	18.4
Current expenditure/GDP	*6.2*	...	*5.6*	*6.7*
Credit expansion	39.7	28.7	28.3	23.2
Liquidity growth	34.3	15.7	15.7	33.5
Real effective exchange rate	2.6	...	−7.4	4.7

[1] GDP denotes gross domestic product.
[2] Partly preliminary.
[3] For a consolidated public sector.
[4] Excludes surpluses of autonomous public enterprises.

Sri Lanka, however, fiscal policy was quite expansionary, reflecting expenditure overruns and revenue shortfalls. The overall deficit was contained below target in Bangladesh, at the expense of a large cut in development expenditure. The deterioration in the fiscal position in these latter two countries diverted the authorities' attention from structural adjustment to demand management.

Revenue performance came close to target in most countries, although progress toward broadening the tax bases, reducing tax exemptions, and improving tax administration was limited. In Pakistan and Bangladesh, the continued heavy dependence on import duties, together with a sluggish expansion in imports, resulted in a low buoyancy of revenues. In India, increased tax concessions designed to stimulate industrial activity and private savings weakened tax buoyancy. In Sri Lanka, progress in reducing dependence on export taxes was relatively modest.

Total expenditure was also broadly in line with targets in most countries, reflecting a reduction in excessive subsidies and an anticipated retrenchment in capital expenditure. In both Pakistan and Bangladesh, development outlays had to be curtailed substantially in order to limit the overall deficit in the face of a stagnation in revenues. However, pressure on expenditure remained strong in most countries, owing partly to still-large subsidies on food and fertilizer (India, Pakistan, and Bangladesh) and continued increases in wages/salaries and interest payments (Sri Lanka). In Sri Lanka, capital expenditure registered a notable expansion in the second year of the program as a result of ambitious investment programs and a lack of effective fiscal control.

b. *Credit and Interest Rate Policies*

Monetary conditions in the subcontinent countries were critically affected by fiscal developments. India and Pakistan were generally successful in limiting the growth of domestic credit to program targets, although in Pakistan the credit ceiling for the third year was exceeded as a result of the widening fiscal deficit. Credit to the private sector grew roughly in line with program targets in both countries. In Sri Lanka and Bangladesh, the deterioration of fiscal operations led to a strong expansion of credit; in Bangladesh, an excessive credit growth during the first year of the program was offset by a significant tightening of credit policy in the subsequent year. In both countries, credit to the private sector was sharply reduced during the course of the program so as to restore monetary stability. The average growth of liquidity for the program period as a whole was generally higher than envisaged in all four countries. In India and Pakistan, the rapid expansion was attributable partly to external sector developments, particularly during the third year, that were more favorable than expected.

Interest rate policy was used more actively in most countries to encourage private financial savings. Key deposit rates at commercial banks were raised by 5 percentage points, to 20 percent, in Sri Lanka; by 5–6 percentage points, to 12–15 percent, in Bangladesh; and by 1.5 percentage points, to 8–11 percent, in India. Despite these adjustments, interest rates remained below or barely higher than the domestic inflation rate in these countries. In India, the interest rate measures were supplemented by a number of other measures, including an increase in the rates of return on debentures and government securities, tax concessions on interest income, and a widening of financial instruments. Interest rate policy was inactive in Pakistan, reflecting the pursuit of an interest-free financial system in accordance with Islamic principle.

4. Economic Outturn

a. *Production, Investment, and Prices*

The favorable growth performance achieved by India, Pakistan, and Sri Lanka was generally associated with an increasing resilience in agricultural production. This reflected the effect of policies to increase the area under irrigation and to stimulate the spread of modern production techniques and inputs, particularly fertilizer; the use of the latter was encouraged by low pricing policy and strengthening of field service support (India and Pakistan). Notwithstanding recurrent adverse weather, substantial progress was made in India, Pakistan, and Bangladesh toward self-sufficiency in foodgrain production, which contributed to import substitution.

Industrial developments were also generally encouraging. Manufacturing registered a strong expansion in Pakistan, owing to the coming on stream of new capacity for import substitution, fuller capacity utilization, and improved import availabilities. The growth of India's manufacturing sector remained well below program targets, reflecting the impact of the world recession and continued domestic controls. However, performance in basic industries and infrastructure generally improved, and bottlenecks were reduced substantially. The production of crude oil and gas increased robustly in both India and Pakistan, leading to a substantial reduction in oil imports.[8]

Domestic investment relative to GDP was below target in both India and Pakistan (Table 5). The less-favorable-than-targeted performance of public investment in these countries reflected limited resource mobilization by the public sector; in addition, private investment was constrained by weak domestic and external demand in the aftermath of the oil price increases and by uncertainties over the relaxation of industrial regulations and import controls. Sri Lanka was successful in achieving the program target, but at the expense of excessive expansion in public sector investment. Private investment in the country also remained buoyant, aided by monetary and fiscal concessions and a low pricing policy for imported capital goods.

Despite the importance attached to domestic resource mobilization, savings performance fell short of program targets in all four countries. The shortfalls were registered by both the public and private sectors in India and Sri Lanka; private savings fell in relation to GDP during the program period in these countries, because of drought-induced declines in agricultural income, a sharp fall in the terms of trade (Sri Lanka), the lingering adverse income effect of higher energy prices, and weak policy initiatives. In most of the subcontinent countries, workers' remittances continued to be an important factor contributing to national savings.

Inflation subsided broadly in line with program targets in India and Pakistan, as restrained financial policies, improved supply availability, and a substantial moderation in international inflation more than offset the upward adjustment of administered prices. In Sri Lanka, however, the rapid expansion in domestic credit, combined with a sharp increase in international oil prices, gave rise to strong inflationary pressures, and the program targets were exceeded by a wide margin. Inflationary pressures were also strong in Bangladesh.

---

[8] In India, crude oil production rose by 150 percent over the preprogram level. This significant increase, however, was attributable partly to a low production level in the base year owing to unrest in Assam. In Pakistan, the production of crude oil and gas increased by 26 percent and 20 percent, respectively, over the program period.

Table 5. Four Subcontinent Countries: Savings and Investment[1]
(In percent)

	Preprogram Average	Program Average Targets	Program Average Outcome	Postprogram Average[2]
India				
Gross national savings/GDP	22.2	24.0	22.3	22.9
Public	4.0	4.8	4.5	3.6
Private	18.2	19.2	17.8	19.3
Gross capital formation/GDP	23.8	26.1	23.9	23.7
Public	11.4	12.9	11.7	12.5
Private	12.4	13.2	12.2	11.2
Pakistan				
Gross national savings/GNP	11.9	12.8	12.8	12.0
Gross domestic savings/GNP	5.9	7.6	5.9	4.9
Gross fixed capital formation/GNP	15.6	16.0	14.3	14.3
Public	10.5	...	8.9	8.6
Private	5.1	...	5.4	5.7
Sri Lanka				
Gross domestic savings/GDP	15.5	16.8	14.2	17.8
Public	−1.3	1.1	−1.7	...[3]
Private	16.8	15.7	15.9	...[3]
Gross fixed capital formation/GDP	20.0	28.3	29.0	28.4
Public	7.2	14.7	16.0	...[3]
Private	12.8	13.6	13.5	...[3]
Bangladesh				
Gross national savings/GDP	4.5	...	2.4	4.9
Gross domestic savings/GDP	3.0	...	—	1.0
Gross capital formation/GDP	13.6	...	13.0	13.0
Public	7.8	...	7.3	6.4
Private	5.8	...	5.8	6.6

[1]GDP denotes gross domestic product, GNP gross national product.
[2]Partly preliminary.
[3]Because of changes in the classification of the public and private sectors, no consistent data series are available.

b. *External Developments*

The cumulative current account deficit over the program period was substantially smaller than targeted in India and Pakistan (Table 6). The current account deficit was also kept below target in Bangladesh, primarily through a substantial tightening of import-license issues. In contrast, the payments deficit target was exceeded in Sri Lanka as a result of higher imports and poor exports.

Table 6. Four Subcontinent Countries: Balance of Payments

	Preprogram Average	Program Average Targets	Program Average Outcome	Postprogram Average[1]
		billion SDRs		
India				
Exports	6.6	9.5	7.6	8.6
Imports	12.3	15.4	13.2	13.3
Services and private transfers	3.0	2.3	3.1	2.2
Current account	−2.7	−3.6	−2.5	2.5
Overall balance	−0.4	−2.1	−1.4	0.3
Official reserves	6.1	...	4.9	5.4
Export volume growth (*in percent*)	−0.4	6.3	1.2	3.1
Import volume growth (*in percent*)	15.6	2.3	1.3	1.4
Sri Lanka				
Exports	0.7	0.9	0.8	1.1
Imports	0.8	1.2	1.4	1.8
Services and private transfers	—	—	0.1	0.2
Current account	−0.1	−0.3	−0.5	−0.5
Overall balance	0.1	—	−0.1	0.1
Official reserves	0.3	...	0.3	0.5
Export volume growth (*in percent*)	...	...	−1.6	5.3
Import volume growth (*in percent*)	...	...	5.7	6.5
		billion U.S. dollars		
Pakistan				
Exports	2.4	3.2	2.6	2.5
Imports	4.9	6.2	5.6	6.0
Services and private transfers	1.4	1.5	2.0	2.1
Current account	−1.1	−1.5	−1.0	−1.4
Overall balance	0.2	−0.4	—	−0.5
Official reserves	0.6	...	1.9	0.8
Export volume growth (*in percent*)	...	...	3.5	−3.2
Import volume growth (*in percent*)	...	...	0.9	6.8
Bangladesh				
Exports	0.7	0.9	0.7	0.8
Imports	2.4	2.8	2.5	2.4
Services and private transfers	0.2	0.1	0.4	0.5
Current account	−1.5	−1.8	−1.4	−1.1
Overall balance	−0.2	−0.3	−0.2	0.1
Official reserves	0.3	...	0.4	0.4
Export volume growth (*in percent*)	...	12.2	9.4	1.0
Import volume growth (*in percent*)	...	−1.5	2.2	5.7

[1] Partly preliminary.

The smaller-than-expected current account deficits in India and Pakistan were due to a significant reduction in imports and stronger net services and private transfers. Oil imports accounted for about 60 percent of the import savings over program projections in India, while they remained roughly unchanged at the 1980/81 level in Pakistan. These developments were aided by smaller increases in world oil prices and, more importantly, by reduced import requirements. The growth of non-oil imports was also more sluggish than expected in these countries, largely because of the improved availability of key agricultural commodities and industrial inputs. The increase in workers' remittances in India accounted for three fourths of the improvement in the current account deficit over the program projections. In Pakistan, the combined contribution made by private transfers and net services was more than the improvement in the current account. Sri Lanka also experienced larger-than-expected private transfers.

Exports were considerably below expectations in all four countries. The cumulative shortfall in export earnings largely offset the gains in imports in India and Pakistan. In most countries, the average growth rate of export volume was below that achieved by non-oil developing countries (of about 4 percent) during the corresponding period. This disappointing export development reflected the severe international recession, the limited progress made in alleviating domestic impediments to export development, and a deterioration in external competitiveness.

V. Developments in Postprogram Period

Despite stepped-up efforts under the adjustment programs, the extent of structural adjustment achieved during the program period was limited in most of the subcontinent countries. This was attributable not only to the intensity of structural imbalances prior to the inception of the programs but also to the gradual approach adopted by the countries and to possible lags before certain adjustment policies became effective. However, further follow-up measures were introduced by most countries during the postprogram period to sustain the momentum of structural adjustment.

In India, significant liberalization measures were taken during 1985 in industrial licensing, import policy, tax reform, and the financial system. The coverage of the antimonopoly legislation was reduced considerably through a substantial increase in the asset limit and the exemption of a large number of industrial groups from restrictions on capacity expansion. In addition, most of the exempted industries were delicensed and large companies were permitted to diversify their operations. Import policy was liberalized to allow improved access to industrial machinery through the removal of licensing requirements, simplification of procedures, and the reduction or elimination of tariffs. For a wide range of materials and components, monopoly imports by public corporations were terminated. The structure of direct tax was rationalized, with a substantial reduction in tax rates and an increase in the exemption limit for personal income tax, in order to foster private sector growth and reduce tax evasion. Steps were also taken to alleviate rigidities in the interest rate structure through an increase in interest rates on government securities.

In Bangladesh, an adjustment program was reinstated in 1982/83 and supported by a new stand-by arrangement with the Fund. Under the program, progress was made in strengthening the fiscal position through an increase in taxes, reduction of subsidies (particularly on fertilizer and foodgrains), and adjustment of key administered prices (electricity, natural gas, and petroleum products). At the same time, exchange rate policy was conducted more flexibly, and a more liberal import policy was pursued with a view to improving the efficiency of the economy, especially that of the export sector.

In Pakistan, the authorities continued to pursue flexible pricing policies with respect to petroleum and gas, which contributed to a significant increase in petroleum production and to the containment of petroleum subsidies. The import regime was further liberalized with the adoption of a negative list scheme. However, progress toward structural adjustment in key areas—including tax reform, liberalization of import controls, and export promotion—was sluggish. Also, little progress was made in Sri Lanka in alleviating underlying weaknesses in public finance and promoting the development of exports, particularly dynamic manufacturing exports.

Economic performance during the postprogram period was relatively favorable in all four countries. Economic growth remained robust, if allowance is made for the adverse impact of droughts on agricultural production in India and Bangladesh. Gross capital formation was sustained broadly at the program period level, and savings performance improved with the exception of Pakistan. Inflation subsided further, partly aided by a decline in international prices. The external current account deficit narrowed in relation to GDP, except in Pakistan. In India and Sri Lanka, the reduction in the current account deficit was accompanied by an improvement in export growth performance. However, the fiscal deficit widened, with the exception of Sri Lanka, as expenditure rose rapidly in the face of stagnant revenues. In Sri Lanka, a substantial decline in the fiscal deficit resulted from a large cutback in current expenditure. Notwithstanding the widening fiscal deficit, domestic credit expansion slowed in most of the subcontinent countries, partly because of increased nonbank financing.

VI. Conclusions

The principal objective of the adjustment programs adopted by the four subcontinent countries was to seek external adjustment through the strengthening of production and investment with the support of restrained demand management. Under the programs, most countries were successful in achieving robust economic growth, despite the deepening of the international recession and recurrent adverse weather. In India and Pakistan, satisfactory growth performance was accompanied by a moderation in inflation and a substantial improvement in the balance of payments. In Sri Lanka and Bangladesh, however, progress toward price stability and external viability was thwarted by expansionary financial policies and the marked deterioration in the terms of trade.

Notwithstanding the robust economic growth, the extent of structural adjustment achieved in key areas during the program period was below expectations. Public sector resource mobilization was constrained by modest progress in improving the tax buoyancy and by rising current expenditure. The smaller-than-expected resource availability limited public investment below targets in India, Pakistan, and Bangladesh, and the reorientation of public investment was less than satisfactory in Sri Lanka. The response of private investment and savings to a number of initiatives offered by the governments was less encouraging in most countries.

The most disappointing development for all the subcontinent countries was the continued weakness in export performance. The growth of exports remained heavily constrained by low productivity and inadequate financial incentives. Although there appears to be further scope for external adjustment through efficient import substitution, the strong development of the export sector will be crucial for achieving external viability over the medium term. This suggests that the focus of further structural adjustment be placed particularly on liberalizing industrial and import controls and on improving the profitability and external competitiveness of the export sector.

The experience of the subcontinent countries shows that restrained financial management plays a major role not only in improving the balance of payments but also in facilitating structural adjustment. As indicated by the experiences of Bangladesh and Sri Lanka, the lack of financial stability made it difficult to extend the authorities' policy attention to structural adjustment. In addition, financial instability tended to nullify the effect of structural measures and to reinforce distortions, especially in investment patterns, savings, and relative prices. These experiences reaffirm that the sustainment of cautious demand management is essential for the effective pursuit of structural adjustment. In view of the dominant role of fiscal operations in affecting financial stability in the subcontinent countries, success in demand-management policy will require bold action to reform the tax system and limit the excessive expansion in current expenditure.

In most countries, weakness in political commitment was the ultimate factor constraining the pace and extent of structural adjustment. This points to the importance of groundwork to explore the degree of political commitment. Such groundwork will involve comprehensive assessment of economic, political, and social priorities in an economy and of the possible incidence of adjustment burden among key economic groups. It will be only through such groundwork that a realistic policy framework for structural adjustment backed by strong political commitment can be firmly established.

Another generalization to be made on the basis of experience of the subcontinent countries is the importance of adopting a comprehensive, rather than piecemeal, approach in undertaking structural adjustment. Policy measures aimed at alleviating only part of pervasive distortions tend to be relatively ineffective and, at times, even counterproductive. Progress toward structural adjustment would be successful only if major constraints are removed through continuous adjustment efforts. This underscores the importance of sustaining the momentum of economic adjustment that was initiated under the adjustment programs. In this context, it is encouraging that continued efforts were made by most of the subcontinent countries during the postprogram period.

Comments
K. M. Matin

The continuing debate on the costs and benefits of Fund conditionality has generated a substantial empirical literature on Fund-supported stabilization programs. The paper by Aghevli, Kim, and Neiss constitutes an important contribution to that literature, especially because it addresses extended Fund facility programs. It is not only timely[1] but also insightful and informative, providing a wealth of analysis and data that had hitherto not been available.

Of the four countries examined by the paper, only Bangladesh's program was suspended and cancelled prematurely, because of a breach in credit ceilings. The latter was by no means an isolated case. More than half of the 30 extended arrangements initiated up to June 1983 were suspended and/or cancelled due to noncompliance with demand-based performance criteria, notwithstanding the proclaimed emphasis on structural adjustment. This raises questions about the Fund's ability to protect growth, even in medium-term adjustment programs. The use of a pinpointed quarterly credit ceiling as the chief performance criterion can, and has, led to suspension of extended Fund facility programs, even when the mode of expenditure management and implementation of structural measures are quite satisfactory. This was the case in Bangladesh. Using the paper's framework for evaluation, my comments will attempt to establish that contention.

To assess the success of extended arrangements in the four countries, Aghevli, Kim, and Neiss look at the degree of policy implementation and the actual performance of key macrovariables over the program period, relative to that expected in the program. If policies are implemented and targets met, the program is judged successful, notwithstanding the possibility that an alternative set of policies might have achieved the same objectives at lower cost.[2]

---

[1] In view of the new structural adjustment facility for low-income countries.
[2] Comparing program performance with what could have happened under alternative sets of policies would be more apt. However, to simulate the effects of alternative packages, an econometric model with estimated parameters would be needed for each country.

On that basis, my comments will endeavor to

  (i) point out the difficulties of assessing the extent of policy implementation;
 (ii) indicate the problems with the Fund's response to those difficulties, when that response was to continue using a credit ceiling as the main performance criterion; and
(iii) show that the paper's conclusions about Bangladesh's experience are certainly misleading, if not incorrect, and that Bangladesh's process of adjustment was adversely affected because of the use of inappropriate performance criteria.

I. Assessing Policy Implementation

Problems of monitoring or assessing the extent of policy implementation in a program that combines stabilization and structural adjustment are inherent in the present state of knowledge. These problems exist because there is no unified, well-articulated analytical framework for designing consistent demand- and supply-oriented policies.[3] Performance on the supply side can no doubt be gauged by looking at changes in the share of domestic investment and savings in gross domestic product (GDP), in the growth of export volume (or share of exports in output), in the share of revenue in GDP, and so on, as the paper has done. However, the link between multiple structural policy instruments and the total effect on the quantity and composition of aggregate supply is much less direct. Some measures (e.g., privatization vs. liberalization of interest rates) have conflicting effects, and the trade-offs are seldom articulated in a coherent model. It is conceivable, therefore, that, even if all policies are implemented as envisaged, performance, in terms of structural change, may not be as expected. Thus, the degree of implementation of structural measures must be assessed by examining movements in the policy variables themselves. Conclusions about the degree of overall policy implementation become problematic only if some structural measures are better

---

[3] On the demand side, relationships between policy instruments (e.g., fiscal deficit reduction or lowering rate of domestic credit), aggregate demand, and policy objectives are fully articulated in the Fund's monetary model of the balance of payments. The effects of changes in domestic credit on prices, output, and external balance may be distributed differently, based on differences in the structural characteristics of countries.

implemented than others, or if some are implemented and others are not. In Bangladesh's case, all supply-side policies were implemented, even though all indicators of structural change did not move favorably or equally favorably. The Aghevli, Kim, and Neiss paper substantiates the latter conclusion.

II. Fund's Implementation of Extended Fund Facility

In the implementation of extended facility programs, the Fund has tended to rely mainly on the traditional criterion of policy implementation—that is, the degree to which the country has met domestic credit targets. The use of credit ceilings as the chief performance criterion in extended programs means that a breach in a ceiling automatically triggers suspension of the program, irrespective of the degree of implementation of structural measures. More importantly, even when the breach is caused by a government's efforts to protect public investment in the face of an unanticipated adverse shock—efforts that are conducive to structural adjustment—the program can be suspended. Bangladesh's experience bears testimony to this fact.

III. Experience of Bangladesh

Of the four countries examined, Bangladesh's experience with the extended Fund facility is distinctive in many ways. Foremost of these is that the extended Fund facility was suspended in the first year (June 1981) because of a breach of a single quarter's credit ceiling, and was canceled in the second year without further disbursements. The paper lumps together 1980/81 and 1981/82 as the program period. This obscures more than it clarifies. For example, overexpansionary financial policy is said to have wrecked the program (page 51), yet, as shown in Table 2 of the Aghevli, Kim, and Neiss paper, Bangladesh appears to have broadly achieved the credit expansion targets. Also, the program specified targets for credit, inflation, growth, and the balance of payments for the first year only. In addition, since suspension occurred in July 1981, and cancellation in July 1982, actual performance in 1980/81 and expectations for 1981/82 and 1982/83 must have played an important role in the Fund's decision to withhold reactivation. Moreover, the drastic credit squeeze that followed suspension and the subsequent absence of expected facility disbursements over 1981/82 altered performance in that year relative to an uninterrupted program. It is, therefore, more appropriate and less confusing to look at 1980/81 and 1981/82 separately, with the first being the effective program period.

Aghevli, Kim, and Neiss conclude that "progress toward price stability and external viability was thwarted by expansionary financial policies . . ." (page 51) because of "stagnation in revenues" (page 44) and rising current expenditure resulting from "still-large subsidies on food and fertilizer" (page 44) and continued financial weakness of public enterprises. The implementation of structural adjustment is claimed to be inadequate, except for successful import substitution in foodgrains and moderate depreciation of the real exchange rate. Inadequacies described by the paper relate to tightening of import controls (page 42), insufficient public sector price adjustments (page 40), poor incentives for exports, reduced availability of credit to the private sector, and reduced public investment.

Table 1. Bangladesh: Macroeconomic Performance[1]

Variables	1979/80	Program Targets	1980/81	1981/82	1982/83
			Percent		
Growth					
Real GDP	1.2	7.2	6.2	1.4	3.2
Real agricultural GDP	0.2		5.4	0.9	4.6
Real non-agricultural GDP	2.5		8.2	0.7	3.0
Industrial production	0.4		8.3	0.5	−4.0
			Million U.S. dollars		
Inflation					
CPI (middle class)	18.5	11.5	12.5	16.2	9.9
CPI (industrial)	16.0		8.9	17.4	2.6
GDP deflator	13.1		10.3	12.7	4.8
Basic balance	−253	−300	−291	−394	164

Source: Computed from International Bank for Reconstruction and Development, *Bangladesh: Economic and Social Development Prospects* (Washington, April 1985).

[1] GDP denotes gross domestic product, and CPI denotes consumer price index.

Yet a more detailed scrutiny of facts fails to support those contentions. Instead, it suggests the following:

(i) financial policies were expansionary in 1980/81, but they resulted from an unanticipated shortfall in foreign aid,[4] not from unplanned budget deficits;

(ii) implementation of structural measures were significantly greater than is suggested by Aghevli, Kim, and Neiss and could easily be deemed as satisfactory, if low investment were attributed to the aid shortfall, as it should be;

(iii) performance in 1981/82 would, in any case, have been adversely affected by drought and the collapse of jute export prices, but the drastic retrenchment of credit to meet the original September 1981 ceilings and the lack of extended Fund facility arrangements made it worse;

(iv) conclusions (i), (ii), and (iii) suggest that the probability of achieving the objectives of the program might have been increased if there had been no suspension; if it had been quickly reactivated; or, better still, if quarterly credit ceilings had not been used as the main performance criterion.

1. Credit and Fiscal Policy

Bangladesh breached the credit ceiling for only the quarter ended June 1981 (Table 2). Table 3 below shows that government borrowing from the banking system to finance its fiscal deficit was the main cause of this breach, which occurred notwithstanding good fiscal performance. Revenues did not stagnate; instead, they rose by 25.7 percent in 1980/81 (exceeding the program target of 25 percent). Current expenditure (inclusive of the food subsidy) did rise by more than was envisaged in the budget (8.5 percent instead of 1.5 percent)[5] even though the subsidy was lower, and public enterprises as a whole made a net profit for the first time in

---

[4] Receipt of a lower-than-expected level of aid than had been projected in the Fund program was surprising, considering the claim that Fund-supported adjustment efforts "encourage donor countries to provide funds for members that have limited resource bases and are at low levels of development," which is made in Manuel Guitián, *Fund Conditionality: Evolution of Principles and Practices,* IMF Pamphlet Series, No. 38 (Washington: International Monetary Fund, 1981), p. 41.

[5] The current surplus was lower than the projected level by only one billion taka.

Table 2. Bangladesh: Extended Fund Facility Performance Criteria and Outturn
(In millions of taka)

	Total Domestic Credit Expansion		Gross Credit to Government and Public Sector	
	Ceiling	Actual	Ceiling	Actual
September 1980	—	—	—	—
December 1980	47,000	45,019	29,100	28,744
March 1981	48,900	47,506	30,300	30,127
June 1981	49,480	54,888	30,450	35,862
September 1981	54,000	54,043	33,200	35,016

Source: Table XXI in K. M. Matin, *Bangladesh and the IMF: An Exploratory Study* (Dhaka: Bangladesh Institute of Development Studies, January 1986), p. 100.

Table 3. Bangladesh: Sources of Quarterly Changes in Total Domestic Credit
(In millions of taka)

	Sept.–Dec. 1980	Dec.–Mar. 1981	Mar.–June 1981	June–Sept. 1981
Total quarterly change	4,320.6	2,487.1	7,382.7	−845.2
Sources of change[1]				
Fiscal operations[2]	1,054.6 (24.4)	891.0 (35.8)	3,354.3 (45.4)	−149.0
Public sector	1,575.5 (35.5)	492.6 (19.8)	2,380.4 (32.2)	−846.3
Private sector	1,690.5 (39.1)	1,103.5 (44.4)	1,684.0 (22.4)	1.1

Source: Same as Table 2.

[1] Data in parentheses are the percentage changes in total domestic credit that are contributed by that source.

[2] These are not identical to figures for net credit outstanding to the Government, since commercial banks' borrowing from the Government is not deducted from total claims on the Government to derive figures for fiscal operations.

1980/81.[6] The reason for government recourse to the banking system is to be found partly in the financing of larger-than-usual food stocks necessitated by a bumper harvest. Price supports and higher procurement prices constituted an integral element of the program, and the excess outlay was not avoidable. The most significant factor was still the unanticipated fall in total foreign assistance of 12.7 percent instead of the rise of 21 percent that had been projected in the program.[7] In short, credit ceilings for June 1981 were breached because foreign assistance was 5.9 billion taka lower than had been expected in the program (Table 4).

2. Implementation of Structural Measures

Table 5 shows the supply-side measures and policy objectives that were part of the program. Table 6 shows the behavior of several supply-side indicators, not only for the program period (1980/81) but also beyond, since a year is in any case too short a period in which to expect noteworthy structural changes to occur. Except for domestic savings, a sustained positive performance is evident. The actual extent of implementation of structural measures in the four major areas is examined below.

a. *Export Promotion*

Nominal devaluations were undertaken frequently in 1980/81 and after, such that the price-deflated real exchange rate for Bangladesh's exports experienced real depreciation over the entire three-year period (Table 7, Row I.3). This constituted a departure from earlier trends. Commercial policies were used in line with those envisaged by the program. Export duties on traditional items were reduced (Row II.1), and some subsidies were provided to leather exports. However, the major attempt at increasing export subsidies was directed at nontraditional exports. The coverage of export performance licensing (XPL) was expanded, and the enti-

---

[6] Public enterprises as a whole made losses of Tk 709 million in 1979/80 and Tk 840 million in 1981/82. Only in 1980/81 did they make a profit (Tk 209 million). See International Bank for Reconstruction and Development, "Bangladesh: Recent Economic Developments and Selected Development Issues" (unpublished, Washington, March 1982).

[7] If special food assistance of Tk 2 billion is subtracted from the 1979/80 figures, aid can be shown to have risen by 4 percent instead of the projected 2 percent.

Table 4. Bangladesh: Government Budgetary Operations
(In millions of taka)

	1979/80 Actual	1980/81 Budget	1980/81 Actual
Total revenue	17,400	21,930	21,880
Current expenditure (excluding food subsidy)	10,820	11,910	13,000
Loss on food trading	2,910	2,020	1,900
Current surplus	3,670	8,000	6,980
Food stocks	2,410	1,470	2,750
Other capital expenditure	770	320	400
Surplus	490	6,200	3,830
Development expenditure	21,720	28,190	24,960
ADP (Annual Development Program)	20,820	27,000	23,690
FFW (Food-for-work)	900	1,190	1,050
Deficit	21,230	21,990	21,130
Financed by:			
Domestic resources			
Banking system	2,920	—	5,000
Other	860	730	900
Foreign resources (net)	17,450	21,190	15,230
Of which: project aid plus commodity aid	*11,830*	*17,600*	*13,640*

Source: Table 1.10 in International Bank for Reconstruction and Development, "Bangladesh: Recent Economic Developments and Selected Development Issues" (unpublished, Washington, March 1982), p. 30.

tlement rates were enhanced. This increased the level of subsidy, but by not as much as had been expected. The market premium on XPL certificates fell sharply in the second year as a result of the credit squeeze-induced recession in demand and the larger supply of remittances.[8] Nevertheless the effective subsidy rate increased over 1980/81 and 1981/82. The policies, despite the setback, helped exporters to receive a greater taka return per dollar of export earnings than before. This is evident from the real effective exchange rates for nontraditional exports, shown in Row III.4 of Table 7. Real effective rates for traditional exports depreciated continuously,

---

[8] The XPL certificates and remittances are sold to potential importers at market-determined rates.

Table 5. Bangladesh: Program's Supply-Side Policies and Objectives

Area	Objectives	Policy Measures
Export promotion	Raise exports—in particular the shares of exports in manufacturing output, nontraditional items in total exports, and free foreign exchange market.	Change exchange rate to offset inflation differentials. Raise export subsidies to offset bias. Reduce restrictions on wage earners' scheme imports; improve export performance licensing and merge it with the wage earners' scheme to raise subsidy.
Import substitution	Increase foodgrain production. Raise share of domestic gas in consumption of total energy.	Raise procurement prices for rice. Raise share of agriculture in Annual Development Program. Raise price of imported oil to reflect foreign prices (weighted average rise of 46 percent). Raise investment in gas production and distribution.
Resource mobilization	Increase revenue and elasticity of tax system. Increase domestic and national savings.	Implement new tax measures. Raise prices of public enterprises to improve their financial situation. Raise nominal interest rates to ensure positive real interest rates. Reduce restrictions in wage earners' scheme to increase demand and thus rates for remittances. Reduce subsidies on food and fertilizer.
Investment	Raise share of total domestic investment in gross domestic product. Promote faster growth of private investment relative to public investment.	Reorient and step up public investment. Liberalize industrial regulations and provide easier credit and imports for private investors. Provide foreign investors with increased incentives.

Table 6. Bangladesh: Selected Supply-Side Indicators, 1979/80–1982/83[1]
(In percent)

	1979/80	1980/81	1981/82	1982/83
Aggregate domestic savings/GDP	2.0	2.3	−3.5	1.7
Aggregate national savings/GDP	4.0	5.3	−0.7	5.9
Aggregate domestic investment/GDP	16.7	17.2	13.9	16.4
Revenue/GDP	9.2	10.1	9.6	9.4
Fiscal deficit/GDP	9.8	7.0	8.4	8.9
Share of agriculture in Annual Development Program	28.5	31.8	32.5	30.6
Foodgrain production (*million tons*)	13.3	14.7	14.3	15.1
Share of nontraditional exports in total exports[2]	12.3	13.8	18.2	26.9
Share of manufactured exports in total manufactured output[2]	—	12.2	12.3	14.9
Share of wage earners' scheme in total imports[3]	7.6	12.5	12.7	20.7
Change in real non-foodgrain imports	5.0	26.5	2.3	−11.9

Source: Same as Table 1.
[1] GDP denotes gross domestic product.
[2] K. M. Matin, "Effective Devaluation as an Export Incentive" (unpublished, Bangladesh, Planning Commission, June 1984).
[3] Computed from Bangladesh Bank, *Economic Trends* (Dhaka), various issues.

even though not as much as those for the nontraditional ones. Export volume grew, with growth of nontraditional exports exceeding that of traditional items. The share of nontraditional exports in total exports rose significantly, as a result (Table 6).

b. *Import Substitution*

Policies aimed at raising farmers' profitability and at encouraging shifts in domestic energy demand toward domestic gas were put in place exactly as expected. Foodgrain production rose from 13.3 million tons in 1979/80 to 15.1 million tons in 1982/83, notwithstanding the severe drought of 1981/82. Increased domestic-currency prices of imported energy and higher public expenditures

Table 7. Bangladesh: Real Effective Exchange Rates for Exports, 1975/76–1982/83
(Taka per U.S. dollar)

	1975/76	1976/77	1977/78	1978/79	1979/80	1980/81	1981/82	1982/83
I. Exchange rate								
1. Official exchange rate[1]	14.50	15.50	15.00	15.00	15.00	16.00	19.50	23.76
2. Export-weighted nominal exchange rate	13.92	14.42	14.40	14.85	14.85	15.22	16.56	17.94
3. Price-deflated, export-weighted real rate[2]	13.92	16.66	15.26	14.99	14.85	15.07	16.23	17.58
II. Effective exchange rate: traditional[3]					*Million taka*			
1. Export duties[4]	71.1	162.6	213.9	302.4	424.0	418.9	220.9	108.7
2. Export subsidy[5]	—	—	—	—	101.5	82.6	87.9	12.9
3. Net duty (II.1 minus II.2)	71.1	162.6	213.9	302.4	322.5	336.3	133.0	95.8
4. Traditional exports	5,022	6,006	6,494	8,445	9,649	9,897	10,130	13,162
5. Effective net duty *(percent)*	1.42	2.70	3.29	3.58	3.34	3.40	1.31	0.73
6. **Real effective exchange rate** *(Taka per U.S. dollar)*	13.72	16.20	14.76	14.45	14.35	14.56	16.02	17.45
III. Effective exchange rate: nontraditional[6]								
1. Export subsidy	—	—	—	—	63.8	52.6	97.9	39.2
2. Nontraditional exports	530	664	684	1,187	1,348	1,587	2,257	4,854
3. Effective subsidy rate *(percent)*	—	—	—	—	4.73	3.31	4.34	0.81
4. **Real effective exchange rate** *(Taka per U.S. dollar)*	13.92	16.66	15.26	14.99	15.55	15.57	16.93	17.72

[1] Taken from Bangladesh, Ministry of Finance and Planning, *Economic Survey: 1982/83*.
[2] Export shares of the top 16 trading partners (excluding countries with which barter trade occurs) over 1979–82 were taken from Bangladesh, Bureau of Statistics, *Yearbook of Trade Statistics, 1983*, and were used as weights. Prices and exchange rates of trading partners were taken from International Monetary Fund, *International Financial Statistics*.
[3] The following exports, whose Standard International Trade Classifications appear in parentheses, were treated as traditional: tea (074), hides and skins (211), raw jute (264), unmanufactured leather (611), jute yarn (65198), jute fabrics (6545), and jute bags (6581). Data were taken from computer printouts supplied by Bangladesh's Bureau of Statistics.
[4] Taken from records of Bangladesh's Directorate of Research and Statistics, National Board of Revenue.
[5] The level of subsidy received by different items through the Export Performance Licensing Scheme was estimated in Bangladesh, Tariff Commission, "Industrial Assistance Effect of Export Performance Licensing," (Dhaka, March 1984).
[6] Nontraditional export value is a residual: total exports minus traditional exports.

on production and distribution of indigenous gas led to a 58 percent rise in production over the three-year period.[9]

c. *Domestic Investment*

Growth in gross domestic investment in the actual program period, though considerable, was lower than planned because of an unanticipated shortfall in aid inflows. A fall in revenue owing to a low level of dutiable imports led to an absolute decline in investment in 1981/82. It recovered sufficiently in the following year to regain the high share in GDP it had commanded in 1980/81. Private investment fluctuated, too, but the dip in 1981/82 was largely caused by a fall in private industrial investment induced by the severe credit squeeze early that year.

d. *Resource Mobilization*

Though all policies envisaged for the purpose of raising national savings were implemented, overall results were disappointing. This was due mostly to stagnant gross domestic savings. Public savings rose in the program period, but could not be sustained; data on private savings are poor, but indications are that they fared no better. Liberalization of the wage earner's scheme (WES) market did, however, lead to a substantial increase of remittance inflows; this contributed to national savings.

3. Performance of Key Macrovariables

Over the actual program period, targets for growth, inflation, and the basic balance of payments were broadly achieved (Table 1), notwithstanding the breach of credit ceilings in June 1981. This is perhaps not surprising. (In a country with institutional and structural characteristics like those of Bangladesh and, more importantly, one with frequent changes in its exchange rate, it is difficult to ascertain the precise level of domestic credit that would be consistent with a target balance of payments position[10] in a

---

[9] International Bank for Reconstruction and Development, *Bangladesh: Economic and Social Development Prospects* (Washington, April 1985).

[10] I have tried to compute the annual level of credit expansion consistent with payments equilibrium, on the basis of an estimated model for Bangladesh—along the lines of Polak

given year. In fact, for most developing countries, the information necessary to fine-tune domestic credit every quarter is not usually available.)[11] Macroeconomic performance did, however, deteriorate in 1981/82. The monetary overhang no doubt contributed to inflation; the drought-induced crop failure was, however, a bigger factor in raising the inflation rate. Agricultural growth was lower because of weather, but the fall in industrial output (Table 1) was policy-induced.

At the insistence of the Fund, Bangladesh instituted draconian credit control measures in order to meet the original September 1981 ceilings. This necessitated a fall in the absolute level of domestic credit, instead of only in its rate of expansion. Table 3 shows the magnitude of the absolute fall required to stay within the ceiling. The fall affected the output of public enterprises adversely. While there was no absolute reduction in private sector credit, there was no growth either.[12] Nevertheless, the credit squeeze led to expectations of poor credit conditions, reducing both private sector production and industrial investment.

In addition, withholding of extended Fund facility disbursements worsened an already difficult economic situation. In anticipation of balance of payments pressures arising from drought-induced imports of foodgrains and from reduced export volume and prices, the Bangladesh Government raised import deposits and increased import controls in early 1981/82. When actual domestic demand for imports turned out to be lower than expected, largely owing to recessionary conditions, restrictions on imports were gradually reduced. No tightening of import controls occurred, however, in the actual program period.

---

and Argy (J.J. Polak and Victor Argy, "Credit Policy and the Balance of Payments," *Staff Papers,* International Monetary Fund (Washington), Vol. 18 (March 1971), pp. 1–24)—to see if *actual* payments disequilibrium was consistent with the direction of deviations of actual domestic credit from their computed levels. In nearly 7 out of 10 years, it was not. See details in K. M. Matin, "IMF's Stabilization Programmes in Bangladesh," *Bangladesh Development Studies* (Dhaka) (forthcoming).

[11] This has been demonstrated by the use of a dynamic balance of payments model in Mohsin S. Khan and Malcolm D. Knight, "Stabilization Programs in Developing Countries: A Formal Framework," *Staff Papers,* International Monetary Fund (Washington), Vol. 28 (March 1981), pp. 1–53.

[12] The actual level of credit to the public sector was higher than had been envisaged in the program in all quarters up to June 1981.

It is obvious that 1981/82 performance was affected adversely by exogenous factors. Bangladesh's ability to deal with the situation was significantly handicapped by the suspension of expected disbursements and by the Fund's insistence on drastic credit controls. Failure to reactivate the extended Fund facility further weakened ongoing efforts to achieve structural change.

IV. Conclusion

There can be no doubt that sustained expansionary financial policies do thwart price stability and external viability. Thus, monitoring domestic credit expansion remains important in supply-oriented programs, such as those under the extended Fund facility. However, the use of quarterly credit ceilings as the chief performance criterion is clearly inappropriate for such programs. This is so because such use implies that a breach in any quarter, whatever the cause, must trigger automatic suspension, even if fiscal performance is good and the implementation of structural measures is as envisaged. The resulting interruption can (and has in the case of Bangladesh) undermine the process of structural adjustment initiated under the program.

It is therefore most unfortunate that the Fund has continued to rely overwhelmingly on credit ceilings, despite their obvious inadequacies in a supply-oriented program. After more than a decade, the Fund has made only limited progress in developing and using supplementary indicators to monitor overall implementation of extended arrangements. Still, in order to permit a better and more balanced *review* of overall program performance, which is what should happen after a breach, such indicators should be used. The new structural adjustment facility makes such use imperative. Many low-income countries that depend heavily on concessional foreign assistance could face a situation like the one that Bangladesh faced if the present Fund practice of using credit ceilings as the main performance criterion continues.

2
Alternative Growth and Adjustment Strategies of Newly Industrializing Countries in Southeast Asia

Sang-Woo Nam

I. Introduction

Probably most notable in the development history of the last quarter century is the emergence of newly industrializing countries (NICs) in Southeast Asia. The remarkable export and growth performance of these countries is widely viewed as a successful case of export-oriented development strategies. However, frequently overshadowed by the outstanding growth record is the fact that even these economies are not free from structural adjustments.

A most obvious case in point was the economy of the Republic of Korea in the later years of the 1970s, with accelerating inflation, real appreciation of the exchange rate, and a complicated and differentiated industrial incentive structure. Koreans were relatively quick to tackle these problems with a comprehensive stabilization program and various structural reforms. What makes the Korean adjustment efforts more interesting is that the adjustments, as manifested in the deceleration of inflation and improved balance of payments, were, unlike those made in Latin American countries, made at the minimum sacrifice of growth.

This paper, in the next section, briefly reviews the growth performance of the Southeast Asian newly industrializing countries in connection with their export-oriented strategies. From their experiences, an attempt has been made to derive conditions critical for a successful export-oriented strategy. Then, macroeconomic developments in the 1970s in Taiwan Province of China and the Republic of Korea are compared to highlight the consequences of macropolicies that are inconsistent with export orientation.

In the following section, major features of the Korean adjustment efforts in the 1980s are presented, with an emphasis on stabilization policies—the centerpiece of the whole adjustment program. Some lessons from the experiences of the Republic of Korea, as well as the other Southeast Asian newly industrializing countries, are presented in the concluding section.

II. Strategies and Performance

1. Export Orientation and Growth

It is well known that four newly industrializing economies in Southeast Asia—the Republic of Korea, Taiwan Province of China, Singapore, and Hong Kong—have achieved remarkable economic growth through the successful implementation of export-oriented development strategies. The average annual growth rate of per capita gross national product (GNP) for these countries ranged between 6.2 percent (Hong Kong) and 7.8 percent (Singapore) over the 1966–84 period. This growth performance was exceeded only by Botswana and Malta.[1]

Identifying the major factors that contributed to this outstanding growth performance is certainly not an easy task. Frequently suggested factors include export-oriented development strategies, a favorable world trade environment, a high level of education or a critical mass of educated members of an elite, political stability, and a Chinese cultural background, which tends to produce people who are hard-working, thrifty, disciplined, and respectful to authority. Even though it seems almost impossible to assess the relative importance of these factors in accounting for the growth of these economies, convincing arguments have been given why higher growth could be expected for countries pursuing export-oriented strategies.

Export-oriented development means the division of labor and specialization—a more efficient use of productive resources. For relatively small countries, economies of scale cannot be attained without relying on overseas markets. Exposure to, and competition

---

[1] See International Bank for Reconstruction and Development, *World Development Report, 1986* (Washington, 1986).

in, the world market also drives firms to be more efficient and tends to produce a more competitive domestic market structure. In addition, policies centered on export promotion tend to be less distortive than alternative strategies. For instance, there has been ample evidence that import-substitution regimes generally lead to a complex incentive structure involving differential tax treatment and direct controls over prices, credit allocation, and imports. Export-oriented strategies, however, usually provide fairly uniform incentives among export industries and make it possible to pursue consistent macroeconomic policies over time without succumbing to the stop-and-go pattern associated with periodic foreign exchange crises.

Empirical studies have shown a significant positive correlation between the openness of an economy to world trade and its growth rate.[2] Although one may argue that the direction of the association is ambiguous, the experiences of the Southeast Asian newly industrializing countries seem to indicate that the causality runs from openness to high growth.

In these countries, the high growth since the mid-1960s has been accompanied by rapid export expansion and growth of the manufacturing sector. Especially pronounced is the case of the Republic of Korea, where commodity exports grew 3.2 and 2.1 times as fast as gross domestic product (GDP) during 1966–73 and 1974–84, respectively, to increase the GDP share of exports of goods and nonfactor services from 9 percent to 37 percent between 1965 and 1984. Even in Hong Kong and Singapore, where commodity exports have not grown particularly faster than GDP, trade-related services seem to have contributed greatly to the overall growth.

It has frequently been argued that export-oriented economies are more vulnerable to external shocks and will suffer more under an unfavorable external environment. Table 1 shows that this claim is not valid, at least for the growth of the Southeast Asian countries under study, since the first oil price shock. The average annual growth of these economies dropped by 2.5 percentage points, from 10.5 percent during 1966–73 to 8 percent during 1974–84, which

---

[2] See Michalopoulos and Jai (1973), Michaely (1977), Balassa (1978), and Krueger (1978).

Table 1. Real Growth of Production and Exports
(In percent)

	GDP[1]		Manufacturing		Commodity Exports	
	1966–73	1974–84	1966–73	1974–84	1966–73	1974–84
Republic of Korea	10.0	7.2	21.1	11.5	31.7	15.1
Taiwan Province of China	11.0	7.6	18.7	9.0	26.3	12.1
Singapore	13.0	8.2	19.5	7.6	11.0	7.1
Hong Kong	7.9	9.1	—	—	11.7	12.9
Middle-income group	7.4	4.4	9.2	5.5	6.3	0.8

Sources: International Bank for Reconstruction and Development, *World Development Report, 1986* (Washington, 1986); Taiwan Province of China, Council for Economic Planning and Development, *Taiwan Statistical Data Book, 1985* (Taipei); Directorate-General of Budget, *National Income in Taiwan Area, The Republic of China* (Taipei, 1985).

[1] Gross domestic product.

compares favorably with a 3 percentage point drop for all middle-income countries. Export-oriented economies, typically with a high import/GDP ratio and a more flexible and innovative business sector, may be in a better position to adapt themselves to changes in world market conditions.

2. Ingredients of a Successful Export-Oriented Strategy

What was the major momentum forcing these industrializing economies to be oriented toward manufacturing exports? For Hong Kong and Singapore, their small size and lack of natural resources almost dictated the choice of an export-oriented strategy. Under British rule, they had grown as the commercial and financial entrepôts for South China and British Malaya, respectively, and inherited economic liberalism as well as modern infrastructures.

With the United Nations embargo on trade with China after the outbreak of the Korean war, and the resulting flush of Chinese refugees, including capitalists and skilled workers, Hong Kong had no alternative to developing manufacturing for export during the 1950s. The success of Singapore as a manufacturing exporter came a little late, after its independence in 1965. Increased demand related to the Viet Nam war, oil exploration in the region, and an active role by multinational corporations, together with a boom in world trade, helped in the transformation of the Singapore economy.

Table 2. Structure of Production and Demand
(In percent of nominal GDP[1])

	Agriculture 1965	Agriculture 1984	Manufacturing 1965	Manufacturing 1984	Exports[2] 1965	Exports[2] 1984	Domestic Savings 1965	Domestic Savings 1984
Republic of Korea	38	14	18	28	9	37	8	30
Taiwan Province of China	24	6	26	42	19	58	21	34
Singapore	3	1	15	25	123	—	10	43
Hong Kong	2	1	24	—	71	107	29	29
Middle-income group	21	14	20	22	18	25	21	22

Sources: Same as Table 1.
[1] Gross domestic product.
[2] Exports of goods and nonfactor services.

In Taiwan Province of China and the Republic of Korea, however, the choice of development strategy was not that obvious. Not only were their domestic markets much larger than those of the other two economies, but their policymakers were influenced by the popular postwar belief in the import-substitution policy. Both had maintained highly overvalued currencies and strict quantitative import controls, as well as a high tariff wall. With the relatively small domestic markets and the noncompetitive environment, economic growth was slow, not to mention the development of export industries. Foreign aid was an important source of funds to cover the deficit in the balance of payments.

It was in the spring of 1958 that, after some debate, Taiwan Province of China switched to an export-oriented strategy. The currency was devalued substantially, and the complicated multiple exchange rate system was unified in the following year. Import restrictions were also relaxed gradually. For the Republic of Korea, it was not until 1964 that similar reorientation was made. By then, the country had almost exhausted easy import substitution, and further import substitution of capital goods and durable consumer goods was not considered feasible owing to the small domestic market and large capital requirement. Furthermore, U.S. assistance programs were being phased out, which made foreign exchange earnings through export promotion an imminent task.

For both of these industrializing economies, an export-oriented development strategy was more than just removing previously existing disincentives to export activities. It included various export promotion measures: subsidized export credit, tax exemption or remission on export-related activities, allowing the use of export earnings for imports, and support of overseas marketing through information services. Although the complicated incentive structures defy any precise quantification of the subsidy, it has been estimated to be well over 10 percent of gross export earnings.[3]

What can be said about any prerequisites or conditions for a successful export-oriented strategy, given the above brief description of motivations and economic transformation? Above all, strong government commitment to, and consistent pursuance of, an export-oriented strategy is critical.

More specifically, there should be no institutional barriers for exporters to overseas intermediate inputs, technology, and export-related services. Reducing physical barriers by adequate communication and transport infrastructure is also important. Furthermore, macroeconomic policies, particularly those related to the exchange rate and wages, should be consistent with an export-oriented strategy.

Since the exchange rate directly affects export profitability, maintaining an adequate and stable real exchange rate is critical for the smooth and sufficient allocation of resources into the export sector. Under an inflationary environment, however, keeping the real exchange rate stable is not, practically speaking, an easy task. Thus, an export-oriented strategy frequently involves price stabilization efforts. The labor market should also be allowed, without any major institutional rigidity, to adjust in response to market forces, to ensure not only adequate export profitability but also flexible and resilient adaptation of the economy to world economic changes.

---

[3] See Balassa and others (1982).

3. Macroeconomic Imbalance in Export-Oriented Economies

The success of export-oriented strategies for Southeast Asian newly industrializing countries, as manifested in their outstanding export and growth performances, seems to have been possible because, by and large, they met the above conditions. Nevertheless, not all the countries have been equally successful; nor has one country done equally well over time. In this section, macroeconomic developments in these countries since the early 1970s will be more closely reviewed in relation to their macropolicies. Such comparisons as are made, mainly between the Republic of Korea and Taiwan Province of China, depend very much on their unique geographies and histories, and are less relevant for most developing economies.

Table 3 shows the economic performance of the two countries since the latter half of the 1960s. During 1966–73, Korean export growth surpassed that of Taiwan Province of China, though Korean GNP growth was slightly lower. That reflects mainly the small

Table 3. Republic of Korea and Taiwan Province of China: Economic Performance, 1966–85

	1966–73	1974–75	1976–78	1979–80	1981–85
Real GNP growth (*percent*)					
Republic of Korea	10.0	7.3	12.2	−0.2	7.5
Taiwan Province of China	11.0	2.7	12.5	7.8	6.4
Export growth[1] (*percent*)					
Republic of Korea	43.9	25.5	35.7	17.4	11.6
Taiwan Province of China	33.3	8.8	33.7	25.0	9.2
Foreign savings (*percent of GNP*)					
Republic of Korea	7.5	11.0	2.1	9.5	5.3
Taiwan Province of China	−2.0	5.8	−4.3	0.2	−9.0
Inflation[2] (*percent*)					
Republic of Korea	13.9	27.7	19.4	23.0	6.6
Taiwan Province of China	5.9	16.3	5.7	13.7	3.7

Sources: Republic of Korea, Economic Planning Board, *Major Statistics of Korean Economy 1986* (Seoul) and Taiwan Province of China, Council for Economic Planning and Development, *Taiwan Statistical Data Book 1985* (Taipei); Directorate-General of Budget, *National Income in Taiwan Area, the Republic of China* (Taipei, 1985).

Note: GDP denotes gross domestic product, GNP gross national product.
[1] Measured in nominal U.S. dollars.
[2] As measured by the GDP deflator.

Korean export base; Taiwan Province of China's GDP share of exports was more than twice that of the Republic of Korea in 1965.

A striking contrast between the two countries can be seen by examining their growth and export performance during the two oil price crises. During 1974–75, Korean GNP and export growth rates were much higher, while during 1979–80 the Korean GNP growth rate was negative, compared with annual growth of 7.8 percent for Taiwan Province of China.

Sharp differences also lie in their balances of payments and inflation rates. While foreign savings have constituted a substantial portion of GNP in the Republic of Korea, foreign savings (net lending and transfers to the rest of the world) in Taiwan Province of China have been negative since the early 1970s, except for the oil shock periods. During 1981–85, negative foreign savings reached as high as 9 percent of GDP. The annual inflation rate measured in terms of the GDP deflator had been about 10 percentage points higher for the Republic of Korea, until the gap narrowed to 3 percentage points during 1981–85. Compared with inflation in Taiwan Province of China, Korean inflation was particularly bad during the boom years after the first oil price shock.

As will be elaborated in the next section, the Korean economy started to show a macroeconomic imbalance from the early 1970s. Noteworthy is how differently the two countries reacted to the first oil price shock. In Taiwan Province of China, there was a sharp deceleration of the money supply ($M1B$) growth to below 12 percent in 1974 and upward adjustment of the rediscount rate from 8.5 percent to 12 percent during 1973–74. The Korean money supply ($M1$) growth was almost 30 percent in 1974, and the bank lending rate (15.5 percent per annum, which was much lower than the inflation rate) was not changed during 1973–75. To ease the slowdown of exports, the Korean authorities devalued the currency by 20 percent in December 1974.

These differential policy responses resulted in a wider gap in the inflation rates of the two countries and a deterioration of Korean export competitiveness in the following years.[4] The Korean mac-

---

[4] The annual growth rate of commodity exports dropped sharply, from 41 percent during 1976–77 to 22 percent during 1978–79, for the Republic of Korea, while that of Taiwan Province of China declined only marginally, from 33 percent to 31 percent, during the same period.

Table 4. Nominal and Real Exchange Rates
(Indices: 1975 = 100)

	Nominal (*per U.S. dollar*)			Real[1]		
Year	Republic of Korea	Taiwan Province of China[2]	Singapore	Republic of Korea	Taiwan Province of China	Singapore
1965	55.0	105.4	129.1	73.9	90.1	91.9[3]
1970	64.2	105.4	129.1	79.2	93.7	99.2[3]
1973	82.3	102.7	103.6	111.9	103.5	94.0[3]
1975	100.0	100.0	100.0	100.0	100.0	100.0
1978	100.0	97.4	95.9	90.5	109.7	104.6
1979	100.0	94.8	91.7	88.4	108.9	101.6
1980	125.5	94.8	90.3	91.9	103.2	96.1
1981	140.7	97.2	89.1	84.6	97.2	90.3
1982	151.0	102.3	90.2	82.9	97.8	91.3
1983	160.3	105.5	89.1	86.0	100.2	91.6
1984	166.5	104.9	90.0	87.1	97.2	91.5
1985	179.8	104.4	92.8	91.9	97.9	95.0

Source: International Monetary Fund, *International Financial Statistics* Yearbook, 1986 (Washington, August 1986).

[1] Adjusted for not only the relative wholesale price index (WPI) inflation (against the United States) but also the U.S. dollar/SDR exchange rate.

[2] Average of the two year-end values.

[3] The WPI was calculated from the consumer price index (CPI) using the ratio of average WPI inflation rate to CPI inflation rate during 1975–85.

roeconomic imbalance during the second half of the 1970s is more evident from developments in the real exchange rate and wages.

As shown in Table 4, the real (effective) exchange rate of the Korean won appreciated by as much as 21 percent during 1974–79 and, despite substantial nominal depreciation in 1980, appreciated further during 1981–82. This exchange rate development seems to be the main cause for the deceleration of Korean export growth during the latter half of the 1970s. The real (effective) exchange rates for Taiwan Province of China and Singapore were much more stable. Even though the Korean real (effective) exchange rate could have been kept stable with faster nominal depreciation, that would have accelerated already-high inflation, aggravating the imbalance in other sectors of the economy.

A weakening of Korean export competitiveness was also obvious in the trend of unit labor costs. Table 5 shows that, during 1976–78, the annual increase in unit labor costs in U.S. dollars was as

Table 5. Republic of Korea and Taiwan Province of China: Wages, Labor Productivity, and Unit Labor Costs in Manufacturing
(Annual increase, in percent)

	Republic of Korea				Taiwan Province of China			
	1974–75	1976–78	1979–80	1981–84	1974–75	1976–78	1979–80	1981–84
Nominal wages	31.1	34.3	25.7	13.7	26.0	16.5	21.8	12.4
Consumer prices	24.8	13.3	23.4	8.3	24.6	5.1	14.3	5.3
Real wages	5.0	18.5	1.8	5.0	1.1	10.8	6.6	6.8
Labor productivity[1]	2.1	8.4	5.2	5.9	−3.1	9.6	1.7	3.4
Unit labor cost	28.4	23.8	19.4	7.4	30.0	6.2	19.8	8.7
Exchange rate	10.2	0.0	12.0	7.3	−1.3	−0.9	−1.3	2.6
Unit labor cost (*in U.S. dollars*)	16.5	23.8	6.6	0.1	31.7	7.2	21.5	6.0

Sources: Same as Table 3.
[1] Labor productivity is measured as value added per employee.

high as 24 percent for the Republic of Korea, against 7 percent for Taiwan Province of China. Faced with a severe profit squeeze, Korean exporters had to raise unit export values at an annual rate of 10.6 percent during this period, compared with 4.9 percent for Taiwan Province of China, which resulted in a loss of some export markets.

In addition to the effects on export profitability, an annual real wage increase of 18.5 percent for the Republic of Korea during 1976–78 was hardly consistent with an 8.4 percent growth of labor productivity in the manufacturing sector. In the absence of strong labor unions in the Republic of Korea, this wage inflation might only be explained by the overheated economy and high inflationary expectations, as well as by sectoral labor shortages.

III. Korean Adjustment Efforts in 1980s

1. Background

As mentioned above, high inflation in the Republic of Korea was mainly responsible for the dislocation of the real exchange rate and the ensuing slowdown in export growth in the later years of the 1970s. What, then, were the major factors contributing to the Korean inflation, and what other imbalances or distortions did inflation cause in the economy? As is generally the case for many high-inflation countries, rapid monetary expansion and wage-push played a major role.

In the early 1970s, the Nixon administration reduced substantially the number of U.S. troops in the Republic of Korea, and after the oil price shock, industrial countries strengthened protectionist barriers against many light manufactured goods from developing countries. These unfavorable external developments forced the Republic of Korea to make enormous investments in heavy and chemical industries, with a view to enhancing the industrial structure and developing a domestic defense industry.

In an effort to finance large-scale development projects in these industries, preferential bank loans were extended in an undisciplined manner. This effort was also responsible for the rapid monetary expansion, the credit squeeze on less-favored sectors, and the excessive and inefficient investment in heavy and chemical industries.

A sharp rise in grain import prices after the oil price shock also lent support to the argument for promoting self-sufficiency in major foodgrains. The resulting deficits in the government-run Grain Management Fund and the Fertilizer Account accounted for 37 percent of the total growth of the money supply ($M1$) during 1976–78.

On the other hand, a 20 percent devaluation of the Korean won in late 1974 and the boom in Middle Eastern construction activity resulted in a substantial improvement in the current balance of payments. The easy availability of oil money and the low cost of recycling it also contributed to heavy foreign borrowing, to which the Government failed to react in order to ensure a stable monetary expansion. As a result, the broadly defined money supply ($M2$) grew by more than 35 percent annually, leading to a 19 percent inflation rate in terms of the GDP deflator, in spite of virtually no increase in import cost during the period.

On the cost side, wage-push was the major source of inflation. With a nominal wage increase of over 34 percent a year during 1976–78, the real wage increase far surpassed labor productivity growth. The strong demand pressure of the economy, coupled with labor shortages in some fast-growing sectors, was mainly responsible for the soaring wages. The rapid growth of large business groups, usually associated with a strong investment boom in the heavy and chemical industries, brought about competitive recruiting for better college graduates and scouting of experienced workers from competing firms. The rush of many construction companies and workers to the Middle East also generated wage pressure for relatively unskilled workers.

The Korean economy during the later years of the 1970s was full of distortions and resource misallocations typical of any high-inflation country. Financial saving, which usually entailed earning a negative real interest rate, was not attractive. Instead, feverish demand for real estate and other real assets caused their prices to shoot up. Many business firms were preoccupied with borrowing as much as possible from banks, only to invest in real estate by expanding unproductive businesses, leading to an increasingly fragile corporate financial structure. The Government's attempt to repress inflation through price controls led only to inadequate investment, supply shortages, black markets, and deteriorating product quality.

Table 6. Republic of Korea: Household Income Distribution

Item	1965	1970	1976	1980	1984
Gini coefficient	0.344	0.332	0.391	0.389	0.357
One-tenth distribution ratio (lower 40 percent/ upper 20 percent)	19.3 / 41.8	19.6 / 41.6	16.9 / 45.3	16.1 / 45.4	18.9 / 42.3

Source: Korea Development Institute staff estimates.

Although the economy was still booming, it became increasingly apparent that the income/wealth distribution was worsening and that the rapid growth was undermining the long-run growth potential of the economy. Tight credit rationing in favor of larger firms in the heavy and chemical industries and various government regulations restraining competition among producers accelerated economic concentration. A still more critical factor contributing to distributive inequality was the soaring price of real estate, which more than offset the real wage gain for the poor.[5]

At the same time, it became increasingly clear that persistently high inflation was threatening sustained growth by eroding the competitiveness of Korean exports. As described in the previous section, indications were that Korean export growth, compared with nearby competitor countries, had been slowing down since 1977. Many policymakers felt that Korea—a country strongly committed to an export-oriented growth strategy—could not afford to neglect this situation for long.

2. Stabilization Policies

To correct the situation induced by high inflation, a comprehensive stabilization program was adopted in the spring of 1979. Restrictive fiscal and monetary policies, adjustment of investment in heavy industry, and special attention to stabilizing the prices of daily necessities were the major contents of the program. A 5 percent cut in current expenditures was called for; interest rates

---

[5] Between 1975 and 1978, average housing and residential land prices jumped by 180 percent and 300 percent, respectively, while consumer prices and urban household income rose by 45 percent and 123 percent, respectively.

were adjusted upward; and the investment adjustment involved the postponement, cancellation, or scaling down of some of the excessive and duplicative investment plans.

However, the significance of this stabilization program went beyond its contents. The program was an expression of consensus of the people and firm commitment of the Government. Actually, less than three months after the program was launched, the nation was hit by another oil price shock; political uncertainty caused by the sudden death of President Park, together with a poor harvest in 1980, also seriously aggravated the economic situation, and a -5.2 percent GNP growth was recorded for 1980. Noteworthy, however, was the fact that, even though the Government adopted a series of reflationary policy packages during the 1979–82 recession, it was in general very cautious not to rekindle inflation.

After experiencing negative growth in real exports in 1979 and a continuing decline in export profitability, and anticipating a substantial increase in the oil import bill, the Government devalued the exchange rate by 20 percent against the U.S. dollar and switched to a floating exchange rate system in early 1980. To offset part of the inflationary effect of the devaluation, a wide range of interest rates was also adjusted upward by 5–6 percentage points.

However, as the economic situation continued to deteriorate in the midst of social unrest, the original restrictive policy stance had to be eased gradually. Within less than two and a half years the general bank loan rate dropped, in about eight steps, from 24.5 percent to 10 percent per annum. Financial support was augmented for public construction works, small and medium-sized firms, residential construction (especially for low-income families), and export of heavy industrial products on a deferred-payment basis. Tax instruments were also actively utilized to introduce temporary investment tax credit and various tax reductions.

There was still substantial monetary expansion, and the public sector deficit rose as high as 4.6 percent of GNP in 1981. On the other hand, exchange rate management was kept somewhat rigid during 1981–82 in an effort to minimize inflationary pressure from rising import costs. Since 1981, stabilization efforts have relied heavily on an incomes policy, in the belief that relying on demand-management policy alone to stabilize prices would require too much time and an excessively large sacrifice in income growth.

In step with the economic recovery since 1983, the focus of macropolicies has shifted to both consolidating price stability and eliminating the current account deficit as soon as possible. The emphasis on improving the balance of payments has stemmed mainly from a sharp rise in the international interest rate and uncertainty surrounding the international financial market. During 1983–85, the macroeconomic policy stance was fairly restrictive, though it was relaxed slightly in response to disappointing growth performance in 1985.

On the zero-based budgeting principle, the general account budget was prepared to produce a sizable surplus to finance deficits in some of the government-run funds. Consequently, the public sector deficit was reduced to 1.4–1.6 percent of GNP during 1983–85. The expansion of the broad money supply ($M2$) also slowed down drastically during 1984–85. Bank interest rates were adjusted slightly upward to make them relatively attractive for depositors compared with nonbank rates. On the contrary, in keeping with the objective of stabilizing prices, as well as the renewed concern about the external balance, exchange rate management was flexible enough to allow a substantial depreciation of the real effective exchange rate.

a. *Fiscal Policy*

To evaluate the Republic of Korea's fiscal policy stance, the Fund's measure of fiscal impulse was estimated.[6] This is actually a crude indicator of change in fiscal stance, adjusted only for the deviation of output from its potential level.

---

[6] The Fund's measure of fiscal impulse is $\Delta \left(\dfrac{-B + t_0 Y - g_0 Y^p}{Y} \right)$ where B denotes actual budget balance for the public sector excluding provincial governments; t_0 and g_0 denote the revenue and expenditure ratios to GNP, respectively, in the base year when actual and potential GNP are judged to be the same; and Y and Y^p denote actual and potential GNP (nominal), respectively. Y^p was estimated basically by regressing peak-through interpolated GDP with capital stock. The fiscal impulse was evaluated as follows:

	1971	1972	1973	1974	1975	1976	1977	1978	1979	1980	1981	1982	1983	1984
						Percent								
Actual deficit/GNP	2.3	4.6	1.6	4.0	4.6	2.9	2.6	2.5	1.4	3.2	4.6	4.3	1.6	1.4
Fiscal impulse	0.7	1.6	−2.2	2.1	0.4	−1.0	0.1	−0.1	−1.6	−0.4	1.7	−0.3	−1.9	0.2

Note: GNP denotes gross national product.

Chart 1. Republic of Korea: Fiscal Impulse and Change in GNP Growth Rate[1]

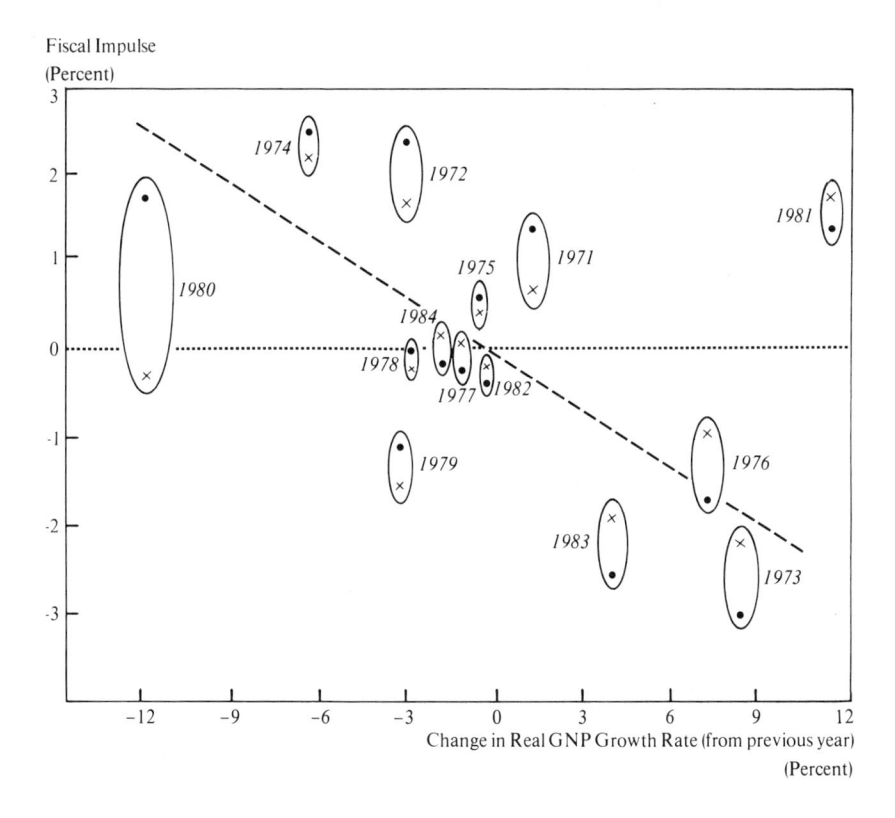

Note: The regression line was fitted for fiscal impulse excluding observations for 1980 and 1981.

$$FI = -0.162 - 0.210\, \Delta \dot{Y} \qquad R^2 = 0.496$$
$$(0.57) \quad (3.14)$$

[1] GNP denotes gross national product. An x denotes the fiscal impulse, and a dot (·) denotes the change in the actual deficit/GNP ratio.

The extent to which fiscal management was countercyclical may be evaluated by examining changes in the fiscal impulse over the business cycle. Actually, by examining Chart 1, a rather close inverse relationship between the change in the GNP growth rate and the fiscal impulse could be confirmed for the sample period of 1971–84, with notable outlying years 1979–81. These outlying years can easily be explained by the stabilization efforts which delayed (until 1981) the fiscal reaction to the sluggish economy of 1979–80.

It is noted that the fiscal impulse for a given change in the GNP growth rate was generally weaker after the launch of the stabilization program in 1979. It was particularly restrictive in 1983, in addition to the 1979–80 period. The accumulated fiscal impulse during 1971–78 was 1.6 percent of GNP, in contrast to −2.3 percent of GNP during 1979–84.

b. *Monetary Policy*

The assessment of the monetary policy stance was based on the estimation of the demand-for-money equations. Equations, run for the period 1970–78, were used to estimate the money supply anticipated in the absence of any stabilization efforts.[7] Chart 2 indicates that monetary policy was not restrictive until about the first half of 1982. The annual rate of growth for broadly defined money ($M2$) was as high as 26–28 percent during 1980–82, when a series of reflationary policy packages was adopted in the situation of delayed recovery.

From late 1982 to 1984, however, monetary expansion fell short of the demand for money, which grew much faster than nominal GNP owing to the declining inflationary expectations of the people. The average broad money supply ($M2$) grew at a rate of only 11–12 percent during 1984–85. In 1985, no indication of a restrictive

---

[7] Estimated equations (semiannual, 1970–78) are as follows:

	Constant	$\ln V^m$	$\ln\left(1+\dfrac{\dot{p}^e}{100}\right)$	$\ln\left(\dfrac{100+r}{100+\dot{p}^e}\right)$	DI	$\left(\dfrac{R^2}{\text{D-W}}\right)$
$\ln\left(\dfrac{M1}{p}\right)$	−0.77	0.965 (10.8)	−2.845 (3.83)	−1.895(r_t) (4.20)	−0.069 (2.93)	0.973 (1.18)
$\ln\left(\dfrac{M2}{p}\right)$	0.027	1.008 (22.5)	−2.687 (7.54)	−0.909(r_u) (4.79)	−0.061 (5.18)	0.992 (1.98)

where figures in parentheses are t values, and p denotes the GNP deflator; V^m the moving average of current and previous real GNP; $\dot{p}^e$ the expected inflation rate, measured as the weighted (geometrically declining) average of rates of increase in the GNP deflator over the past four years; r the interest rate (r_t denoting the one-year bank time-deposit rate, while r_u denotes the curb loan rate); and DI the dummy variable for the first half of the year.

**Chart 2. Republic of Korea:
Monetary Policy Stance,
Actual and Fitted Money Supply**

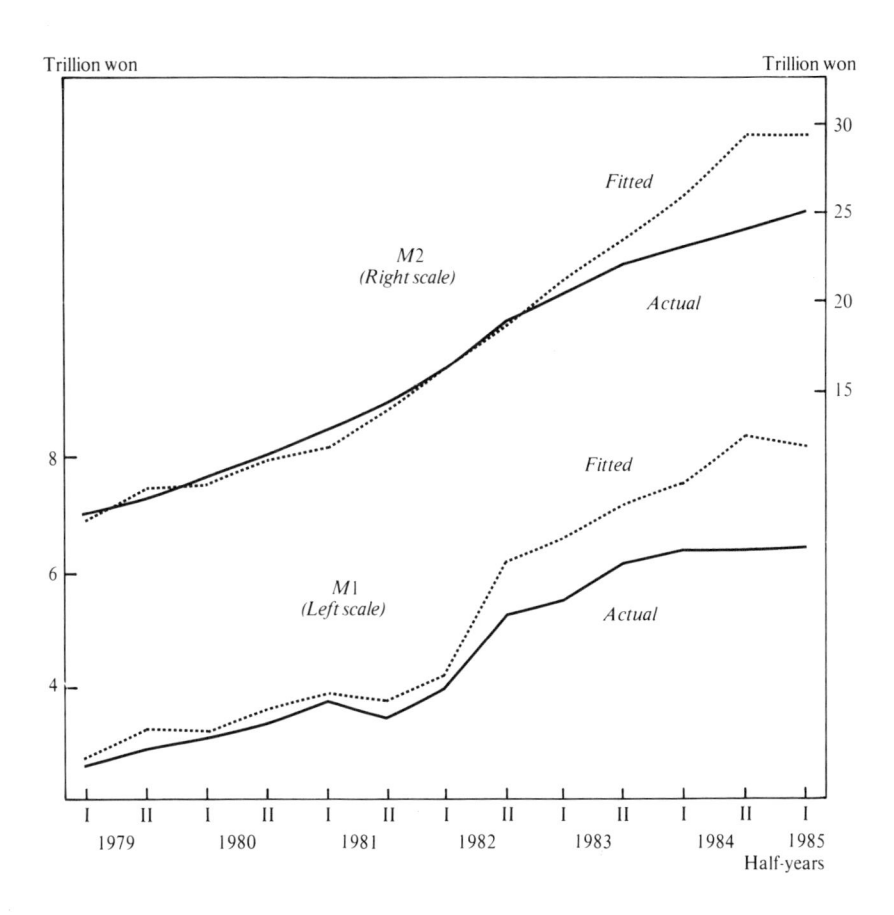

Note: For equations on which the above fitted values are based, see footnote 7 in the text.

flow of the supply of money could be found, when nominal GNP grew by only 8.9 percent and there was little additional demand for money arising from subdued inflationary expectations.

c. *Exchange Rate Management*

Owing to high inflation following the second oil price shock, the substantial devaluation of the Korean won in 1980 did not help much in correcting appreciation of the currency on a real effective basis. Actually, during 1981–82, the earlier period of the comprehensive stabilization program, there was some additional real effective appreciation, indicating that exchange rate management was somewhat biased toward curbing inflation. Moreover, the interest rate subsidy given to export financing vis-à-vis general loans was eliminated in June 1982, which is equivalent to an additional 4–5 percent appreciation for exporters in the real effective exchange rate. Thus, the exporters' competitive disadvantage was much more substantial than the real effective exchange rate indicates.

However, since 1983, by which time the deceleration of inflation was evident, exchange rate management was free of any stabilization bias and was actually tilted toward stimulating exports and growth. During the three-year period 1983–85, the Korean won showed a real effective depreciation of more than 15 percent.

d. *Incomes Policy*

The Republic of Korea's anti-inflation policy relied not only on demand management but also on incomes policy. Incomes policy was intended to keep inflationary psychology from creating a

Table 7. Republic of Korea and Taiwan Province of China: Real Effective Exchange Rates vis-à-vis the U.S. Dollar, 1970–85

(Indices, 1975 = 100)

Year	Republic of Korea Nominal	Effective	Real effective	Taiwan Province of China Real effective
1970	64.2	57.8	87.4	104.2
1973	82.3	84.4	115.3	104.8
1975	100.0	100.0	100.0	100.0
1978	100.0	111.9	94.7	114.7
1979	100.0	112.4	88.0	108.1
1980	125.5	140.7	90.7	101.0
1981	140.7	152.6	87.1	99.7
1982	151.0	153.8	86.6	103.2
1983	160.3	162.2	91.9	107.6
1984	166.5	164.1	94.4	105.7
1985	179.8	175.4	100.3	108.4

Source: Korea Development Institute, staff estimates.

bottleneck in the stabilization process. It included the imposition of informal wage guidelines, or "jawboning" efforts, to moderate wage increases, control of interest rates and dividends, and stingy adjustments to the Government's purchase price for rice.

While one may not negate the effects of these measures altogether, empirical evidence indicates that actual wage hikes in the 1980s were roughly what could be expected without any guidelines.[8] Still, the fact that the real wage increase was slightly lower than the labor productivity gain during the 1981–84 period of sharp disinflation (as shown in Table 5) is strong evidence of a flexible labor market. As can be expected, however, the incomes policy was not without side effects: it produced a wider wage gap between public servants and private employees, and some disintermediation (away from financial savings) during 1982–83.[9]

3. Structural Policies

It was argued above that, without price stability, it is difficult to maintain a realistic exchange rate, which is very critical for an exported-oriented economy, and not worsen the income/wealth distribution. Furthermore, as is evident from the Korean experience in the 1970s, high inflation is most likely to result in inefficiency in resource allocation owing to such associated phenomena as negative real interest rates, credit rationing, and shortening maturities for financial instruments.

Together with the stabilization efforts, the Republic of Korea pursued a series of structural policies designed to reduce various

---

[8] For instance, the dummy variable for the wage guidelines in the following wage equation was not statistically significant:

$$\Delta \ln W = -0.078 + 1.16 \Delta \ln CPI + 1.08 \Delta \ln PD^m + 0.39 \Delta \ln (Px/Pm)$$
$$(0.99) \quad (3.60) \quad\quad (1.67) \quad\quad (2.55)$$
$$+ 0.0045 \, (1/U) - 0.016 \, D(81-84) \quad R^2 = 0.743 \quad D\text{-}W = 1.36$$
$$(1.68) \quad\quad\quad (0.38) \quad\quad\quad\quad \text{Sample} = 1966\text{--}84 \text{ (annual)}$$

where W denotes non-agricultural wages, CPI consumer prices, PD^m non-agricultural value-added labor productivity (two-year moving average), Px/Pm the terms of trade, U the unemployment rate, and $D(81-84)$ the dummy variable for the wage-guideline period.

[9] The wide wage gap resulted because the Government used the rate of wage adjustment for public servants as a wage guideline for the private sector, whose wage increase, however, turned out to be higher than that suggested by the guideline. The phenomena of disintermediation and shortening maturities for financial assets were the result of lowering interest rates faster than the adjustment of inflationary expectations (though not faster than the deceleration of actual inflation).

inefficiencies that had become imbedded in the Korean economy. Broadly speaking, they included reducing government intervention in resource allocation, promoting competition, and restoring the functioning of the market mechanism.

Though the importance of these structural policies may be emphasized, one should note that their implementation is often constrained by the macroeconomic situation. If there is a serious balance of payments deficit, for instance, drastic import liberalization may be like a medicine that kills the patient. This is why a stabilization program usually precedes or accompanies any financial or external liberalization.

a. *External Liberalization*

The Korean current account was in equilibrium in 1977, and the Government planned to relax import controls. However, owing to the second oil price shock, it was only in early 1983 that the Government announced a time-phased schedule for import liberalization and tariff adjustments. It is interesting to note, in retrospect, that in 1982–83 there was not only a considerable improvement in the current account (owing partly to recovery of the world economy) but also a drastic deceleration of inflation as well as a turnaround in the exchange rate, which moved toward real effective depreciation. These developments strongly indicate that the successful stabilization policy facilitated realistic exchange rate management, which, in turn, was an important assurance that an import-liberalization program would be successful.

The liberalization plan has been closely implemented so far, increasing the import-liberalization ratio from 69 percent in 1981 to 91.5 percent in 1986. It is scheduled to reach above 95 percent by 1988. In liberalization, higher priorities are given to overly protected or monopolistic commodities in the domestic market, and domestic producers are given two-to-three-year advance notice of import liberalization to cushion its impact.

Though domestic producers may have been given temporary tariff protection following import liberalization, the average tariff rate has been lowered from 25 percent in 1981 to the current 21 percent, and is to reach 18 percent by 1988. The plan also calls for substantial reduction of tariff differentials to create a more uniform tariff structure.

At the same time, restrictions on technology imports and direct foreign investment have also been reduced drastically. The negative list concerning direct foreign investment is becoming shorter and shorter every year, and the ratio of foreign equity ownership is not controlled in principle.

Even though no major disruptive impact of import liberalization on business survival or the balance of payments has been noted so far, many Koreans are concerned about the speed of the opening-up of their markets when advanced nations are raising their walls against Korean export goods. Yet, the Government seems to be strongly committed to its open-door policy. This may mean that the Republic of Korea, with its large external debt, will keep the exchange rate more depreciated than it otherwise would be, which, in turn, would aggravate the adverse shift in the terms of trade and, to that extent, reduce the standard of living.

b. *Domestic Liberalization*

Other major structural policies have included lifting price controls during 1978–79, implementing the Fair Trade and Anti-Monopoly Act from 1981, adopting a more flexible and autonomous system of public enterprise management, and a series of financial reforms and realignments of the industrial-incentive system since the early 1980s.

Financial reform in the 1980s included divesting government equity shares in the major city banks, lowering entry barriers to the financial market, making institutional changes to bring about a more universal banking system, and making some progress in interest rate liberalization. Still, most interest rates in the organized financial markets are closely regulated by the monetary authorities. Moreover, the share of policy loans in deposit-money-bank credit has not declined noticeably, though the substantial interest rate subsidy attached to these loans was eliminated in 1982.

Further financial liberalization seems to have been hindered by the complications from the excessive government intervention in private resource allocation during the 1970s. Banks as well as the Government could not afford to let troubled firms whose promotion had been heavily supported go bankrupt for fear of the social and economic repercussions. In the meantime, bailout credit has snowballed, and the achievement of managerial autonomy for commercial banks still looks unlikely.

Recently, the Government attempted to improve this situation. Measures introduced included helping the banking institutions, the major victims of government intervention, by allowing attractive deposit rates, compared with those offered by nonbank institutions, and providing subsidized central bank credit, and exempting collateral supplied by the troubled firms from capital-gains taxation. In other words, the cost of imprudent government intervention is paid by consumers and taxpayers, and financial repression continues.

The other side of the problem is industrial adjustment. As early as 1981, with a view to rationalizing industrial incentives, the Government curtailed and simplified differentiated tax incentives given to selected industries, while reinforcing support for small and medium-sized firms and technological innovations. To further streamline the existing industrial incentive system and to deal with both declining industries and promising infant industries, the Industrial Development Law was passed. It is hoped that, under this law, industrial restructuring will be effectively supported by the Government with a minimum risk of failure.

IV. Lessons and Conclusions

Table 8 shows the performance of the Korean economy during the 1980s. While the balance of payments deficit and inflation declined sharply, the drop in GNP growth or the gross investment ratio was not particularly noticeable, except for the negative growth in 1980 which was influenced by a poor harvest and political instability. Although a better external environment—characterized by improved terms of trade, lower international interest rates, and the recovery of the world economy since 1983—was certainly an important factor, the Korean macroeconomic policy mix, coupled with sectoral adjustment efforts, also played a key role.[10]

The Korean stabilization efforts relied on both demand management and incomes policy. The incomes policy, though not free of

---

[10] While about one third of the $4.4 billion drop in the annual current account deficit between 1980 and 1985 was attributable to the improvement in the terms of trade, the direct contribution of the stable unit import value to the deceleration of inflation was relatively small.

Table 8. Republic of Korea: Economic Performance, 1980–85
(In percent)

	1980	1981	1982	1983	1984	1985
GNP growth[1]	−5.2	6.6	5.4	11.9	8.4	5.1
Current account balance (*percent of GNP*)	−8.8	−7.0	−3.8	−2.1	−1.7	−1.1
Inflation rate (*GDP deflator*)	24.8	15.7	7.1	2.9	4.1	3.5
Gross investment/GNP ratio	32.1	30.3	28.6	29.9	31.9	31.2
Domestic savings/GNP ratio	20.8	20.5	20.9	25.3	27.9	28.4
Real wage increase[2]	−4.2	−0.5	8.0	7.4	6.3	6.6
Real interest rate[3]	−9.2	−5.1	0.7	4.6	7.7	7.5

Source: Republic of Korea, Economic Planning Board, *Major Statistics of Korean Economy* (Seoul, 1986).
Note: GNP denotes gross national product, GDP gross domestic product.
[1] National income data for 1981–85 are based on the new system of national accounts.
[2] Real wages equal non-agricultural wages/CPI.
[3] Bank time-deposit rate (one-year maturity, year end) minus consumer price index (CPI) inflation rate (year average).

short-run side effects, was more or less successful in persuading people to revise their inflationary expectations in step with the inflation rate. Furthermore, though fiscal and monetary management was generally tight, it clearly showed an anticyclical pattern and was not significantly restrictive until 1983, when the economy picked up strongly. Conscious efforts were made to keep investment activity from shrinking so much as to weaken the medium-term growth potential of the economy. Together with augmented government investment in rural infrastructure and other construction projects, stronger investment incentives were given through tax benefits and credit availability.

Exchange rate management, however, was somewhat rigid in the initial stage of the stabilization program for fear of the inflationary impact of the depreciation. The movements of key macrovariables—the realistic real effective exchange rate, positive real interest rates, and the fairly high real wage increase still consistent with productivity growth—have been more reasonable since inflation was brought down sharply in 1983. Evidence of a restored macrobalance could also be found in the rising domestic-savings ratio, healthier corporate capital structure, and improved income distribution.

It seems impossible to quantify the impact of sectoral structural policies on the macroeconomic performance. Even though these policies were more or less simultaneously pursued with the stabilization efforts, a gradual approach was adopted to make sure that the former did not overly complicate macroeconomic management.

Finally, what lessons can be drawn from the experiences of the Southeast Asian newly industrializing countries? First, the fact that these countries weathered the two oil price shocks better than other countries suggests that the superiority of an export-oriented development strategy may well be maintained even under the current unfavorable environment of the world economy. Surely the export engine of growth will not be as powerful as it was in the 1960s and the early 1970s, and it may need more frequent tune-ups.

Still, as long as the economic structure is flexible enough and adequate incentives are given, businesses will learn to adapt to changes in the world market, generating dynamic externalities extremely valuable for the economy. A country may promote infant industries. However, the Korean experience indicates that, in order to minimize inefficiencies as well as any moral-hazard problem associated with industrial rationalization, protection should be given only to selected industries and then with a definite time limit and minimum government involvement.

Second, an export-oriented strategy may include more than an assortment of several export incentives. Exporters in the Southeast Asian NICs have been allowed to do business in a virtually free trade regime. Still important are stable and consistent macroeconomic policies. In this connection, exporters in these countries, with remarkably low inflation rates and no major second-stage import-substitution industries, seem to have been in an advantageous position compared with Latin American exporters.

They were not interrupted by frequent episodes of currency overvaluation, nor asked to use domestically produced inputs. A notable exception was the Republic of Korea in the latter half of the 1970s, when the exchange rate was overvalued under accelerating inflation, obscuring the medium-term prospect of the economy. To the extent that high and variable inflation increases uncertainty for exporters, an export-oriented strategy will have a lesser chance of success under a severely inflationary environment.

Third, its stabilization experience seems to indicate that curing chronic inflation takes time, strong leadership commitment, and a broad consensus among the people, not to mention consistent macropolicies. Incomes policy, potentially a critical element in economic stabilization, cannot be successful without the support of all parties involved, which hinges on the conviction that the stabilization effort will succeed and that, in the process, their relative income shares will not be squeezed as a result of their conforming to government guidelines.

Unfaltering presidential backing was the key ingredient in the consistency of the Korean adjustment efforts, as the program faced rough going in its initial stages as a result of the assassination of President Park and the second oil price shock, which was followed by the prolonged recession. The Government's approach in dealing with the incomes of workers, farmers, and capitalists simultaneously in a more or less balanced manner also seems to have helped secure public support for the stabilization program.

Finally, stabilization and sectoral structural policies may be pursued simultaneously as long as they do not seriously interfere with each other. This is so because they are typically mutually reinforcing. Price stability itself is limited when the allocation of scarce resources is distorted, and it is easier to adopt structural policies in a less inflationary or otherwise more favorable macroeconomic environment.

The Republic of Korea was rather cautious in pursuing financial and external liberalization for fear of their possible depressionary and adverse balance of payment effects, as well as other macroeconomic complications. Liberalization of capital transactions has been delayed until the early 1990s, in light of the recent Latin American experience. Delay in financial liberalization has been due mainly to the unhealthy asset portfolio of the banking sector accumulated during the inflationary period of the 1970s.

Bibliography

Balassa, Bela, "Exports and Economic Growth: Further Evidence," *Journal of Development Economics* (Amsterdam), Vol. 5 (June 1978), pp. 181–89.

———, "The Process of Industrial Development and Alternative Development Strategies," Essays in International Finance, No. 141 (Princeton, New Jersey: International Finance Section, Princeton University, 1980).

——— , and others, *Development Strategies in Semi-Industrial Economies*, (Washington: International Bank for Reconstruction and Development, 1982).

Corbo, Vittorio, and Jaime de Melo, "Lessons from the Southern Cone Policy Reforms" (unpublished, Washington: International Bank for Reconstruction and Development, February 1987).

Corbo, Vittorio, Anne O. Krueger, and Fernando José Ossa, eds., *Export-Oriented Development Strategies* (Boulder, Colorado: Westview Press, 1985).

Corbo, Vittorio, and Sang-Woo Nam, "The Recent Macroeconomic Evolution of the Republic of Korea: An Overview" (unpublished, Washington: International Bank for Reconstruction and Development, February 1987).

Krueger, Anne O., *Foreign Trade Regimes and Economic Development: Liberalization Attempts and Consequences* (Cambridge, Massachusetts: Ballinger, 1978).

Lau, Lawrence J., ed., *Models of Development: A Comparative Study of Economic Growth in South Korea and Taiwan*, Institute for Contemporary Studies (San Francisco: ICS Press, 1986).

McMullen, Neil, *The Newly Industrializing Countries: Adjusting to Success* (Washington: British-North American, 1982).

Michaely, M., "Exports and Growth: An Empirical Investigation," *Journal of Development Economics* (Amsterdam), Vol. 4 (March 1977), pp. 49–53.

Michalopoulos, C., and K. Jai, "Growth of Exports and Income in the Developing World: A Neoclassical View" (unpublished, Washington: U.S. Agency for International Development, 1973).

Nam, Chong-Hyun, "Trade Policy and Economic Development in Korea" (unpublished, Washington: International Bank for Reconstruction and Development, April 1986).

Nam, Sang-Woo, "Korea's Stabilization Efforts since the Late 1970s" (unpublished, Seoul: Korea Development Institute, March 1984).

Comments

*Arshad Zaman**

I must compliment Mr. Sang-Woo Nam on a most interesting paper reviewing the growth and adjustment experience of the so-called newly industrializing countries, especially of his own country, the Republic of Korea, and drawing lessons from this review for other Asian countries. Korea's remarkable postwar growth and its economic performance in the 1980s have been the envy of all similarly placed countries and have led to much speculation on the essential ingredients of its success. Mr. Nam, with his intimate knowledge of the country, has made a valuable contribution to this discourse.

The subject of the appropriate mix, timing, and efficacy of trade liberalization-cum-stabilization policies is of immense interest. In my comments, however, I would like to focus essentially on the nature and relevance of the Korean experience in this area; first, on the role of non-economic factors in its economic development; second, on just what was the early economic strategy that was pursued, how it can be said to exemplify an outward-oriented strategy, and just what is meant by this term. Finally, in the light of this experience, I will focus on the conclusions that can be drawn on appropriate future trade and industrial strategies for poor countries today.

I. The Korean Experience

Success is said to have many fathers. It is not surprising, therefore, that adherents of entirely opposed economic ideologies have seen their faith vindicated in the Korean experience: planners have seen in it the advantages of planning and government control, and liberal economists have found proof of the virtues of free trade

---

* At the time this paper was presented, Mr. Zaman was Economic Adviser and Additional Secretary, Ministry of Finance, Government of Pakistan. His participation in the seminar and his comments were in his personal capacity.

and the magic of free markets. My own views on the subject have been influenced strongly by what I consider to be one of the most balanced appraisals of the issues involved, which was presented in an article (Streeten (1982)) by the distinguished chairman of this session, Professor Paul Streeten.

For all the interest in what have come to be called the newly industrializing countries, the only careful studies of their postwar experience were carried out under the supervision of Bhagwati (1978) and Krueger (1978) for the U.S. National Bureau of Economic Research (NBER). These studies do suggest that in the countries studied, over the period examined, under carefully qualified circumstances, transitions from an import-substitution strategy to an export-promotion strategy (both carefully defined) were associated with higher growth rates.

Mr. Nam, however, believes that "although . . . the direction of the association [in terms of a significant positive correlation between openness of an economy to world trade and its growth] is ambiguous, the experiences of the Southeast Asian newly industrializing countries seem to indicate that the causality runs from openness to high growth." This in my view calls for more faith than can be supported by the evidence.

It is the prerogative of all men who are blessed with long lives to designate the secret of their longevity. Just as we do not quarrel with them, I would not take issue with Mr. Nam's views on the secrets of Korea's success. I would only say that I would favor more complex explanations of economic history over more simple, reductionist ones which identify merely one or two factors as sufficient cause for all economic developments in postwar Korea.

1. Non-Economic Factors

No one would deny that, apart from domestic policies, Korea's economic development was greatly assisted also by non-economic external factors. In assessing the relevance of the Korean miracle to countries like Pakistan and India, for example, I would raise two questions.

First, according to figures provided by the U.S. Bureau of the Census ((1984), pp. 811–12), during 1962–83 Korea received US$6.4 billion in military assistance from the United States of America; the comparable figure for Pakistan was US$469 million, and for India, US$147 million. This must have been a source of considerable strength for the Korean economy, in comparison, say, to India and Pakistan.

Mr. Nam broaches the issue when he cites, among the factors which contributed to Korea's economic problems in the late 1970s, the Nixon administration's decision in the early 1970s to reduce the number of U.S. troops in Korea. It would be useful to see a more systematic analysis of the contribution of external military assistance on this scale to Korea's growth and development.

A second consequence of Korea's close political relations with the countries of the North Atlantic Treaty Organization was the preferential access that Korea received to markets of the countries of the Organization for Economic Cooperation and Development (OECD). According to OECD figures cited by Cable (1986), in 1984 Korea accounted for 14.4 percent of total U.S. imports of textiles and clothing, 8.0 percent of Canadian imports, 12.5 percent of Japanese imports, and 2.8 percent of imports from the European Economic Community (EEC)—adding up to over US$5 billion.

Together, Hong Kong, the Republic of Korea, and Taiwan Province of China held 46.5 percent of the U.S. market share and 29.1 percent of the Canadian market share; Korea and Taiwan Province of China held 37.8 percent of the Japanese market share, and Korea and Hong Kong held 8 percent of the EEC market share. It would also be useful to evaluate the contribution of this preferential access to markets in Korea's growth and development, especially for countries with quite different political relations with the West which seek to emulate Korea.

2. Adjustment in the 1980s

Turning next to economic developments in Korea in recent years, I would suggest, first, that the appropriate comparator for evaluating the success of Korea's adjustment efforts in the 1980s would be Turkey, and not Taiwan Province of China. Apart from Turkey, which, as Hasan (1986) points out, was the most successful among those countries that pursued adjustment through greater reliance on exports, India (which did not pursue an outward-oriented strategy) and Thailand (which did) also achieved a degree of success comparable to Korea's, with all three countries relying mainly on an exceptional savings performance.

In fact, comparing the figures provided by Mr. Nam (Table 8) to those for Pakistan (which also implemented a stabilization program, without the aggressive export-promotion effort), it appears that as an average during 1979–85, economic growth in Korea was 5.2 percent, compared with 6.5 percent in Pakistan; inflation in Korea was 9.4 percent, compared with 8.7 percent in Pakistan. In the 1980s, then, Korea's economic performance was not as exceptional as in the early years.

Mr. Nam's principal lesson from Korea's recent experience, therefore, about "the superiority of an export-oriented development strategy" as being central even to successful adjustment in the 1980s, would need more proof; especially since, as Mr. Nam suggests, in the wake of U.S. troop withdrawals, Korea undertook major investments in the late 1970s and the 1980s in chemicals, heavy industries, and defense-related industries to substitute for imports, in addition to its export efforts.

This view is also supported by Hasan (1986), who identifies two phases in Korea's adjustment efforts: 1974–78, when the key factors were aggressive export promotion, success in obtaining construction contracts in the Middle East, and heavy external borrowing to increase the investment rate (including import-substitution investment), and 1980–83, when classical stabilization policies of the Fund variety were pursued to reduce inflation and restore external payments viability, with "considerable import substitution in industry," which helped to reduce import growth to only 3.5 percent a year during 1979–83.

In sum, it is difficult to support the argument that mainly outward orientation (supplemented by stabilization and "sectoral" policies secondarily) was the secret of successful adjustment in Korea in the 1980s. First, the Korean economy's performance in the 1980s was not much different from that of a number of other countries (including Turkey, India, and Thailand). Second, there is considerable evidence that during this period substantial import substitution also took place in Korea, and it remains to be established that on a net basis Korea was in fact pursuing an outward-oriented strategy.

3. Lessons for Others

Finally, in terms of the relevance of the Korean experience, both early and recent, to countries seeking higher material standards of living today, let me pick up where Mr. Sang-Woo Nam concludes his paper. Mr. Nam seeks to conclude that

(1) Export promotion is good even in the face of rising protectionism in our export markets;

(2) Export promotion is not just a matter of providing export incentives, but involves the provision of a virtually free trade environment, the pursuit of stable and consistent macroeconomic policies, the ensurance of price stability, the provision of unfaltering political support, etc.; and that

(3) Successful adjustment requires the simultaneous pursuit of stabilization and sectoral structural policies (with the latter defined as policies "designed to reduce various inefficiencies . . . in the . . . economy," which include "reducing government intervention in resource allocation, promoting competition, and restoring the functioning of the market mechanism").

In reviewing these conclusions, I shall not seek to answer whether in fact these are the right conclusions to draw about Korea's experience. Instead, I shall address the more interesting question, at least from the policy perspective, of whether it makes sense for poorer Asian countries to pursue these policies today.

In answering this question, it is important to be quite clear about some of the key words which feature in this discourse: shocks, adjustment, structural adjustment, and export promotion or outward-oriented strategy. Much of the confusion, in my view, can be accounted for by the shifting meanings of these terms. It may be fruitful, therefore, to note briefly the mainstream usage of these terms.

By shocks the literature sometimes refers to any major disruption of economic activity owing to a sudden large change in social, political, or economic conditions. In the context of the present discourse, however, it is best to define the term more narrowly, as, for example, Hasan (1986) does, to refer to a large decline in the terms of trade or, at most, in the capacity to import.

A large increase is also sometimes referred to as a shock, but this is obviously a perverse use of the term, and is best avoided. Also, to subsume wars, famines, and the like under the rubric of shocks and speak of adjustment policies may be viewed as an attempt to seek a level of generality beyond the point of diminishing returns.

If this is accepted, then adjustment policies can also be defined, once again following Hasan (1986), for example, quite precisely as policies designed to reduce aggregate expenditures and/or to switch them toward activities which either save or earn foreign exchange. (The adjective "structural," I would suggest, should be used to refer to those adjustment policies that seek parametric changes in behavioral relationships, changes which alter the structure of economic relationships—shifts of the curve rather than movements along a curve, to employ the textbook phrase.)

This is a much more restrictive view of adjustment policies than that presented in the paper. Although, to be fair to Mr. Nam, he is in good company in using the term adjustment policy interchangeably with development policy or even economic policy in general. But in doing so, Mr. Nam's discussion of Korea's adjustment efforts in the 1980s becomes somewhat diffused, and neither the magnitude of the shocks nor the precise responses and their degree of success are clear.

In examining Mr. Nam's principal conclusion that an export-oriented development strategy is superior in all circumstances, it is also useful to be clear about what is meant by this term. All too often the tendency is to pick high-growth economies, identify ex post facto the set of policies that they pursued, and label this assortment of initiatives as an export-oriented (or outward-oriented, or export-promotion) strategy. In fact, there have been cases where countries supposedly pursuing an export-oriented stategy were held later, when growth rates plummeted, to be substituting for imports during the same period.

To lend some objectivity to this discussion, I suggest we define quite clearly what is meant by an export-promotion strategy. In the mainstream usage, an "EP strategy," as Bhagwati (1986) calls it, refers to a condition in which the average effective exchange rate for exports is held at about the same level as that for imports. When the rate is higher for imports, there is a net incentive (relative to the dictates of international prices) to substitute for imports, and a country can be said to be pursuing an import-substitution strategy. (When the bias is in favor of exports, however, Bhagwati suggests that this be called an "ultra-EP" strategy.)

This definition, Bhagwati suggests, is also consistent with the conditions that were prevalent in the four Far Eastern economies (as judged by the NBER studies, which have the distinction, as mentioned earlier, of being the most extensive and careful studies of the subject) and in the Republic of Korea (according to a recent study by Chong-Hyun Nam (1986)). An export-promotion strategy, therefore, both logically and historically, consists of maintaining incentives that are neutral to exports and import substitution, rather than of providing a positive bias in favor of exports.

Once we accept this definition, a number of issues can be clarified. First, it appears to be both a rather more precise, and more useful, way of looking at export-oriented development and strategy, and a somewhat more accurate description of what happened in Korea, than that presented in the paper.

Second, it immediately makes clear that the pursuit of an export-promotion strategy is quite independent of whether there is government intervention in the economy (and Korea, Taiwan Province of China, and Singapore have intervened actively and effectively in the markets, contrary to Mr. Nam's suggestion), or whether a liberal attitude is taken toward foreign investment, as opposed to trade (where the newly industrializing countries coincidentally have been quite liberal, despite Mr. Nam's misgivings, in comparison, say, to Japan).

It also clarifies, as Bhagwati (1986) points out, some of the confusion in the theoretical literature, which in my view has served to buttress some of the most strongly held but misguided economic ideologies that have gained currency in the dialogue on economic policy. Although the literature itself is quite careful in its wording, there is a distinct effort to suggest a causal link, independent of time and space, between the pursuit of liberal trade policies and economic growth. This has often succeeded in misleading the scholars and policymakers in poor countries.

II. Relevance of the Korean Experience Today

I will conclude by making a few observations on some considerations that would be relevant to the kind of industrial and trade strategies that poor countries may pursue in the coming decade or two.

Whatever may have been the merits or demerits of the old export pessimism (to borrow Bhagwati's (1986) term once again, which could refer either to the quantities of poor countries' exports that industrial countries could absorb, which worried Nurkse (1953) and more recently Lewis (1980), or to the prices which poor countries would receive over time for their exports, which was the concern of Prebisch (1951 and 1959); see also Prebisch (1984) and Singer (1950)), there would be few today who would dismiss the very real danger which presently exists of rising protectionism in industrial countries. (See, for example, Hasan (1986).)

This rising protectionism is part of a larger historical trend in the industrial countries away from internationalism, even in the most ardent champion of this idea, the United States of America. A variety of factors, no doubt, account for this move. One aspect, however, relates to the rise of a critical realism in the industrial countries that finds the ambition to build a rational, secular, democratic industrial world, in its own image—as reflected, for example, in the language of the United Nations Charter or the Treaty of Rome—too taxing.

Another aspect relates to a degree of satisfaction with present conditions, with an unwillingness to sacrifice immediate comforts for dubious moral purpose. Yet another relates to a change in global objectives and defense strategy, which no longer require good relations around the world in order to facilitate the stationing of conventional forces.

Whatever the reasons, it is clear that the commitment to multilateralism and free trade is no longer what it used to be. The most serious victim of this development has been the credibility of the system developed under the General Agreement on Tariffs and Trade (GATT) and the Bretton Woods institutions. Trade liberalization today is simply an ideology to be forced upon the weak, while the strongest elements in the system reserve for themselves the right to pursue down-to-earth discrimination at home. Future industrial and trade policies must be based on a very clear perception of whether this new export pessimism is warranted, and the balance of caution would certainly seem to lie with some degree of contingency planning.

To put this in concrete terms, let me speak of the real problems that a country like Pakistan faces. Like all other poor countries, we suffer the misfortune of being preached at by the best and the brightest that the industrial world has to offer. Although fashions do change, the message today, among others, is that comparative advantage dictates the pursuit of liberal trade policies. (In this, through no fault of the Koreans, unfortunately, a carefully cultivated set of perceptions about the Korean experience is held up as an example.)

Now, where does our comparative advantage lie? One would think that agriculture would be a prime candidate. But here we find that in 1986 the three major trading countries or country groups (the United States, the EEC, and Japan) gave about US$200 billion in agricultural subsidies. The provisions of the U.S. Food Security Act, 1985 (under which the United States recently drove down the price of cotton) and those of the Common Agricultural Policy in Europe ensure that no poor country can remain competitive in agricultural exports. As a result, if we pursue our comparative advantage, we find ourselves in a no-win poker game with the treasuries of the industrial world.

Since the world is not perfect, we are advised to pursue the second-best course. This brings us to textiles, where most estimates show that over half the gains from trade accrue to the so-called developing countries. But, here, the fourth Multifiber Arrangement (MFA) has just been renewed until 1991, conveniently in advance of the new round of multilateral trade negotiations, and proposals to insert a clause to the effect that this would be the last MFA, or to include textiles on the agenda for the new round, were not acceptable to the major shareholders of the GATT, the Fund, and the World Bank.

In such conditions, it is difficult to take seriously the arguments for trade liberalization and the pursuit of an export-oriented strategy. The credibility of this message rests squarely on the dismantling of the MFA, the prototype for managed trade, which the richest and the most powerful industrial democracies in the world do not seem to be able or willing to put away. This, despite the fact that the cost of protection to the industrial countries is estimated to be two to eight times the annual wages of textile workers; or as the World Bank (1984) puts it, that it costs one dollar for the United States to provide seven cents of benefits to its textile workers. It also rests on the dismantling of a variety of nontariff barriers to trade, like norms, rules, and voluntary export restraints.

In practice, then, a simple adherence by all countries to outward orientation in all industries, based on a magical faith in the experience of the newly industrializing countries, is neither warranted nor desirable. Country size is obviously a major consideration. For most of the smaller countries (and most sub-Saharan African countries would be in this category), an open trade regime is a necessity, and not a matter of choice. For the larger countries (like China, Brazil, Mexico, India, and Iran—the five non-industrial countries with 12-digit U.S. dollar gross domestic products in 1984), there is considerable latitude in the choice of trade policies. For the midsize economies, like that of Pakistan, the situation is in between.

For countries that truly have a choice, the pursuit of an export-promotion strategy (that is, the provision of incentives neutral between exports and import substitution) should be based not so much on the logic of comparative advantage, nor on the postwar history of the newly industrializing countries, but on the appropriateness of lowering protection to the industry in question, in the light of a realistic assessment of their initial conditions—political, social, and economic.

As should be clear, the pursuit of an export-promotion strategy requires only that the *average* level of effective exchange rates for exports and imports be equal. Although wide dispersions should probably be avoided, there is every reason to pursue import substitution in certain industries where it seems warranted, while opening stronger industries to competition. It also seems to be desirable that a trade strategy be formulated in concert with a long-term industrial policy. Finally, the timing and sequencing of stabilization policies in relation to trade liberalization should be carefully tailored to individual circumstances; a uniformly applicable policy package probably does not exist.

References

Bhagwati, Jagdish N., *Anatomy and Consequences of Exchange Control Regimes* (Cambridge, Massachusetts: Ballinger, 1978).

———, "Export Promoting Trade Strategy: Issues and Evidence" (unpublished, Washington: Development Policy Issues Series, International Bank for Reconstruction and Development, October 1986).

Cable, Vincent, "Textiles and Clothing in a New Trade Round," paper presented at the Conference on the Role and Interests of the Developing Countries in the Multilateral Trade Negotiations, October 30–November 1, 1986 (Bangkok, 1986).

Hasan, Parvez, "Domestic Adjustment Policies and External Economic Shocks" (unpublished, Washington: International Bank for Reconstruction and Development, September 24, 1986).

International Bank for Reconstruction and Development (World Bank), *World Development Report, 1984* (Baltimore: Johns Hopkins University Press, 1984).

Krueger, Anne O., *Foreign Trade Regimes and Economic Development: Liberalization Attempts and Consequences* (Cambridge, Massachusetts: Ballinger, 1978).

Lewis, W. Arthur, "The Slowing Down of the Engine of Growth," *American Economic Review* (Nashville, Tennessee), Vol. 70 (September 1980), pp. 555–64.

Nam, Chong-Hyun, "Trade Policy and Economic Development in Korea" (unpublished, Washington: International Bank for Reconstruction and Development, April 1986).

Nurkse, Ragnar, *Problems of Capital Formation in Underdeveloped Countries* (Oxford, England: Basil Blackwell, 1953).

Prebisch, Raúl, *Theoretical and Practical Problems of Economic Growth* (Mexico City: United Nations, Economic Commission for Latin America, May 28, 1951).

———, "Commercial Policy in Underdeveloped Countries," *American Economic Review, Papers and Proceedings* (Nashville, Tennessee), Vol. 72 (May 1959), pp. 251–73.

———, "Five Stages in My Thinking on Development," in *Pioneers in Development*, ed. by Gerald Meier and Dudley Seers (New York: Oxford University Press, for the World Bank, 1984), pp. 173–91.

Singer, H. W., "The Distribution of Gains Between Investing and Borrowing Countries," *American Economic Review, Papers and Proceedings* (Nashville, Tennessee), Vol. 62 (May 1950), pp. 473–85.

Streeten, Paul, "A Cool Look at 'Outward-Looking' Strategies for Development," *World Economy* (Oxford, England), Vol. 5 (September 1982), pp. 159–69.

United States, Bureau of the Census, *Statistical Abstract of the United States* (Washington: Government Printing Office, 1984).

3
Contrasting External Debt Experience: Asia and Latin America

Azizali F. Mohammed

I. Introduction and Summary

The debt experience of countries in Asia during the past decade presents a sufficiently sharp contrast with that of the Latin American countries to raise a question whether there are systematic differences that might explain it. Fund publications classify capital-importing developing countries into those that have encountered debt-servicing problems and others that have not.[1] The former group includes countries that incurred external payments arrears during 1983–84 or rescheduled their debt during the period from the end of 1982 to mid-1985; with only a very few exceptions, countries in the Western Hemisphere are placed in this category. Again with few exceptions, Asian developing countries are placed in the group that did not encounter debt-servicing difficulties.

On the basis of a statistical examination of the debt situation in Asia (separately for East Asia[2] and South Asia[3]) and the Western Hemisphere,[4] the paper draws two broad conclusions, viz., that it is the characteristics of the debt in South Asia and the resilience of export sectors in East Asia that enabled these subregions to escape a generalized debt crisis such as affected the Western Hemisphere region.

---

[1] See pages 31–34 of the Statistical Appendix in International Monetary Fund, *World Economic Outlook: Revised Projections by the Staff of the International Monetary Fund* (Washington, October 1986) for definitions and classifications of countries.

[2] East Asia covers Hong Kong, Indonesia, the Republic of Korea, Malaysia, the Philippines, Singapore, Thailand, Viet Nam, Solomon Islands, Fiji, Vanuatu, Papua New Guinea, Western Samoa, and the People's Republic of China.

[3] South Asia covers Afghanistan, Bangladesh, Bhutan, Burma, Sri Lanka, India, Maldives, Nepal, and Pakistan.

[4] Latin America covers all developing countries included in the Western Hemisphere classification used by the Fund's *World Economic Outlook*.

II. Characteristics of External Debt

The two regions discussed constitute a very substantial part of the developing world. On a 1980 base, Asia accounts for about 31 percent of the total gross domestic product (GDP) of the developing countries and the Western Hemisphere for about 27 percent. Of total outstanding debt of capital-importing developing countries, Asia accounts for 23.5 percent and the Western Hemisphere for 40.6 percent. As the share of debt is higher, and that of GDP lower, in the Western Hemisphere relative to Asia in the global totals, Asian debt is only 25.3 percent of its GDP, whereas the percentage is 47.2 for the Western Hemisphere. More significant is the relationship of outstanding debt to exports of goods and services. Asia accounts for little over 25 percent of aggregate developing country exports of goods and services and the Western Hemisphere for only 16.6 percent. Not surprisingly, Asian debt is somewhat less than the annual value of its exports of goods and services, whereas in the Western Hemisphere, outstanding debt is almost three times its export receipts in the 1983–85 period (Table 1).

Turning to debt-service payments, the countries of the Western Hemisphere paid 43 percent of their export earnings, on average, in 1983–85. The Asian countries paid under 12 percent of their earnings. Even more interesting is the breakdown of the debt service between interest and amortization. In the case of the Asian group, the debt service is almost equally divided between the two components. In the Western Hemisphere, interest payments are more than double the amortization, and this is the case partly because of the very substantial amounts of principal ($70 billion) that were rescheduled during the period.

In understanding the differences in the servicing burden, two elements are significant: (1) the share of debt obtained from official or commercial sources, and (2) the share of debt contracted at floating interest rates. With the exception of a few island economies, all the countries in the Western Hemisphere region were "market borrowers"—that is, they obtained more than two thirds of their borrowings from commercial sources. In Asia, the two largest countries—India and China—were classified as "diversified borrowers" because their external borrowings in 1978–82 were more or less evenly divided between official and commercial creditors, and 15 of

Table 1. Western Hemisphere and Asia: Selected Indicators of External Debt Developments, 1973–85
(Period averages; in percent)

	1973–74	1975–78	1979–80	1981–82	1983–85
External debt *(as percentage of exports of goods and services)*					
Western Hemisphere	139.8	187.6	190.3	238.0	285.3
Asia	81.1	85.6	72.1	77.8	89.0
Debt-service payments *(as percentage of exports of goods and services)*					
Western Hemisphere	21.5	33.3	36.3	45.4	43.2
Interest payments ratio	...	...	17.5	28.2	30.0
Amortization ratio[1]	...	...	18.8	17.2	13.2
Asia	7.4	8.7	8.6	10.4	11.7
Interest payments ratio	...	...	4.1	5.5	5.9
Amortization ratio[1]	...	...	4.5	4.9	5.8
Share of total debt at floating interest rates					
Western Hemisphere	34.1	51.3	66.4	71.7	72.4
Asia	8.1	21.9	31.3	38.1	45.2
Share of short-term debt in total debt					
Western Hemisphere	6.3	13.1	21.3	24.4	15.3
Asia	2.9	10.8	18.4	19.5	15.4

Source: International Monetary Fund, *World Economic Outlook: A Survey by the Staff of the International Monetary Fund* (Washington, April 1986).
[1] On long-term debt only.

the remaining 21 countries were classified as "official borrowers"—that is, they obtained more than two thirds of their borrowings from official creditors. Since a substantial part of the debt contracted from commercial sources is extended at floating interest rates, over 72 percent of the total debt in the Western Hemisphere was on such terms, as against 45 percent in Asia, in the 1983–85 period.

Another major difference between the two regions is found in the currency composition of the debt. At the end of 1985, almost 82 percent of Western Hemisphere debt was denominated in U.S. dollars. In Asia, only 35 percent of debt was so denominated, while 36.4 percent was multicurrency debt, mainly from multilateral development banks, which included a certain proportion of U.S. dollars in the packages.

Before seeking to draw conclusions, one should look at South Asia and East Asia separately, as data on an all-Asia basis tend to conceal differences in debt characteristics; moreover, in each subregion, one large economy has a dominating share, and it is useful to exclude it to get a clearer picture of the remainder (Table 2).

Of the total Asian debt, only one fourth is attributable to the countries of South Asia; similarly, of the debt-service payments, as much as six sevenths of the annual payments are made by East Asia, indicating that the latter group of countries carries a predominant weight in the all-Asia averages. Measuring outstanding debt against GDP, the difference does not appear striking; as against roughly 20 percent of GDP in South Asia, the debt exposure is of the same magnitude, relative to total output, in East Asia through 1981–82 and rises to 27 percent only in 1983–85. Excluding India from South Asia roughly doubles the debt/GDP ratio for the remaining countries in that subregion. Similarly, the East Asia ratio rises to 45 percent if China is excluded, suggesting that in both subregions the exclusion of a continental-sized economy with a rather small foreign trade sector points up the much higher external debt exposure for the rest of each subregion.

A much sharper difference emerges in comparing the ratios of outstanding debt to exports of goods and services. For South Asia, outstanding debt is more than twice the annual export level for every subperiod except 1979–80 (when it is slightly lower) and reaches 2½ times annual export receipts in the latest period. If India is excluded, the ratio rises to three times export earnings, indicating that India's exposure, relative to its export receipts, is lower than that of the other countries. A startling contrast between South and East Asia is found by comparing their debt/exports ratios, which for East Asia never approach the annual level of export earnings, being 86.5 percent in the latest subperiod and even lower in earlier years. The ratios excluding China are higher but do not change this picture materially, suggesting that China's debt exposure, relative to its export earnings, is not significantly different from that of the other countries of East Asia.

Another difference between South and East Asia relates to debt servicing. While the former has a debt-service ratio of almost 18 percent of exports of goods and services (or 21.5 percent, excluding India) in the 1983–85 period, the ratio is almost one-third lower in the latter group. In South Asia, amortization payments are larger

Table 2. South Asia and East Asia: Debt Characteristics, Selected Periods
(Period averages; in percent)

	1973–74 All countries	1973–74 Excl. India	1975–78 All countries	1975–78 Excl. India	1979–80 All countries	1979–80 Excl. India	1981–82 All countries	1981–82 Excl. India	1983–85 All countries	1983–85 Excl. India
South Asia										
External debt (*as percentage of gross domestic product*)	16.9	28.1	19.1	31.7	18.3	34.1	18.9	36.7	20.9	40.5
External debt (*as percentage of exports of goods and services*)	277.5	255.8	236.6	300.0	198.0	249.1	216.1	280.1	256.3	309.8
Debt-service payments (*as percentage of exports of goods and services*)	21.4	15.1	16.8	18.5	12.2	13.6	13.1	15.1	17.8	21.5
Interest payments ratio	7.2	6.0	5.7	6.6	5.0	6.0	5.4	7.0	8.3	9.0
Amortization ratio	14.1	9.1	11.1	11.9	7.2	7.5	7.7	8.1	9.5	12.5
Share of short-term debt in total debt	—	0.1	1.1	0.3	2.9	3.6	3.5	4.5	2.0	2.5
Share of total debt at floating interest rates	0.1	0.3	1.3	0.7	4.1	4.8	6.4	6.8	12.1	7.4
	All countries	Excl. China	All countries	Excl. China	All countries	Excl. China	All countries	Excl. China	All countries	Excl. China
East Asia										
External debt (*as percentage of gross domestic product*)	10.9	23.5	14.5	27.5	16.1	29.7	20.6	35.7	27.7	45.0
External debt (*as percentage of exports of goods and services*)	58.8	62.7	68.1	71.8	63.3	65.9	70.9	78.0	86.5	92.5
Debt-service payments (*as percentage of exports of goods and services*)	6.4	6.6	8.6	9.2	9.0	9.5	11.2	11.5	12.2	13.1
Interest payments ratio	2.6	2.7	3.2	3.4	4.3	4.5	6.1	6.6	6.6	7.0
Amortization ratio	3.8	3.8	5.4	5.8	4.7	5.0	5.2	4.8	5.6	6.1
Share of short-term debt in total debt	2.2	2.4	13.3	12.1	25.7	24.6	27.0	26.7	23.5	21.6
Share of total debt at floating interest rates	10.5	11.9	29.8	30.3	41.0	41.6	47.2	49.3	53.7	56.3

Source: International Monetary Fund.

than interest payments, whereas the opposite is true in East Asia. The lower interest component in South Asia is a reflection of the official character of much of the borrowing and the smaller proportion of the debt contracted at floating interest rates. There was hardly any such debt up to 1978 in South Asia; thereafter, it rose from about 4 percent of the total debt in 1979–80 to about 12 percent in 1983–85. In East Asia, by contrast, floating-rate debt has steadily risen from about 10.5 percent of total debt in 1973–74 to 54 percent in 1983–85. Another factor in the higher interest component in East Asian debt service is the larger proportion of short-term debt (typically trade and interbank lines of credit, which are usually obtained at market rates). In South Asia no more than 2–3 percent of total debt is short term, as against almost a quarter in East Asia. A final difference of some importance is the currency denomination of the debt. For all Asia, roughly 12.5 percent of the debt is denominated in Japanese yen. However, the proportion is higher in East Asia than in South Asia, given the fact that some of the large debtors in the former region have a yen component higher than this average—for example, Malaysia (19.5 percent), Indonesia (15.9 percent), and Thailand (13.8 percent).[5]

Two inferences are suggested by the foregoing statistical survey. First, the debt exposure relative to exports is roughly equivalent in the Western Hemisphere and in South Asia. If, despite this, the latter group of countries has a debt-service ratio which is less than half that of the former, the terms on which the debt was contracted in South Asia would appear to be an important factor in explaining the differing experience. This is borne out by the low share of short-term debt; the low share of floating-interest-rate debt; and the high share of official debt, contracted on concessional terms, given the low per capita incomes of major countries in the subregion. Second, the debt/GDP ratio in East Asia (excluding China) is roughly similar to that in the Western Hemisphere The share of floating-rate debt in East Asia is more than one half of its total debt, attesting to its commercial origin, as is the case in the Western Hemisphere. Despite this similarity in the terms of debt, there is no generalized debt problem

---

[5] Institute of International Finance, "Balance-of-Payments Trends: The East Asian Economies, *IIF Overview* (Washington), Vol. 2 (August 1986), pp. 5–6.

in East Asia, and the essential difference appears to lie in the fact that its debt-service ratio is only one third of the Western Hemisphere's. A conclusion that can be drawn is that the absence of debt-servicing difficulties in East Asia must be related to the resilience of the export sector and that the Western Hemisphere's slower rate of growth of exports, relative to the rate of growth of debt and of debt service, would be a prime element in the emergence of debt problems in this region.

There are, of course, exceptions in both regions. Even in the Western Hemisphere, there is a major country, Colombia, that did not incur debt-servicing difficulties. On the other hand, there are two countries in East Asia—the Philippines and Viet Nam—that did incur difficulties despite the fact that the subregion in which they are located remained generally free of them. There were obviously special factors that allowed these exceptions to emerge despite the fact that all countries in each region were exposed to similar exogenous developments.

Comments

Sunanda Sen

The paper by Azizali Mohammed is provocative and significant, pointing out that the terms of borrowing and the export performance can both be crucial and decisive in determining the likelihood of a debt default. In particular, either one of them can be sufficient to prevent a debt collapse, such as was prevented in South Asia and East Asia, both of which were favorably situated as compared with the Western Hemisphere (Latin America), where none of these favorable factors operated. East Asia seems to have been able to borrow capital while avoiding the debt crisis because it has had a good export performance. Similarly, South Asia has been able to avoid the problem because of its practice of borrowing at concessional official terms. In the Western Hemisphere, however, the Latin American borrowing nations had access to neither concessional sources of finance nor booming export markets. Thus, commercial finance proved viable only for the regions in East Asia where export performance had been especially favorable.

Let me start my comments with a set of broad issues. I have difficulty in appreciating the use of short-term liquidity indicators (e.g., debt-service ratios or debt-exposure ratios) in judging the longer-run viability of a nation's debt program. The paper makes ample use of these two indices to judge selective performance of the borrowing countries. My own reservations in judging the dynamics of the debt process through piecemeal, short-run liquidity indicators like the ratio of debt to gross domestic product (GDP), the ratio of interest cost plus amortization to export earnings or even the ratio of reserves to imports (the last one not introduced in the paper) emanate from the following observations:

First, the use of such ratios to judge situations tends to ignore the fact that the level of *new* loans (net of amortization) to a country and their composition (e.g., direct or portfolio capital, balance of payments or project loans, etc.) often has an important bearing on the import coefficients or savings coefficients in the borrowing country. It is not an overstatement to say that the level of imports (and, hence, often the size of the trade deficit) has a tendency to adjust itself to the level of net capital inflows (via the licensing mechanism and other controls over exchange disbursement and imports). Thus, availability of external finance inevitably pushes up the import bill for the recipient nations and, hence, tends to increase the import-intensity of production and consumption. At a structural level, the phenomena can be explained by the technological changes leading to a greater import dependence on the part of the industrial units which receive borrowed funds, directly or through collaboration arrangements with foreign capitalists or governments. Simultaneously, the propensity to consume may go up, largely because of international demonstration effects, which become powerful as a result of capital inflows. Both of the above processes influence the absolute and the relative size of the foreign exchange gap (vis-à-vis GDP), which eventually is financed (ex post) by net inflows of capital. Attention also needs to be given to the *final* use of the new loans (net of amortization) in the borrowing country in order to determine whether it can meet both the payments deficit resulting from the services deficit and the ex ante merchandise deficit. If the sources of *new* loans to a country dry up, it is forced to generate a trade surplus to meet the services deficit. If this is difficult to achieve, a typical debt-default situation emerges.

The arguments can be schematized as follows. The balance of payments of a country has *three* components, viz., the balance of trade (BT), the balance of services (BS) and the balance of net lending, or new loans (BL). As long as BS (primarily interest charges) can be met by BL, the country does not have to depend on BT for finance. Beyond this point, the avoidance of a debt crisis depends on the possibility of maintaining a BT surplus. Increases in imports, which are related to availability of external finance, may create difficulties in having a net export surplus, in addition to any difficulties experienced because of an adverse international economic environment.

The above arguments make it more meaningful to look at the ratios between BS and the net finance available (BT + BL) to identify an impending debt problem. A gradual or sudden drop in BL may, owing to the structural links to imports via technology, even lead to drops in GDP growth and in export capacity. This may cause additional problems which are not indicated by the liquidity criteria. For a country struggling to find financing in order to avoid defaulting on its debt, a sudden drop in new loans may impede the growth process. Countries in the Western Hemisphere have already experienced this phenomenon.

Debt exposures, measured by debt-GDP or debt-export ratios tend to reflect judgments of the adequacy of flows (GDP or exports) on the basis of the behavior of stock variables. This is of limited value, since the stock of outstanding debt may have a qualitative dimension, depending on the history or background of the debt contracts. Thus the 139 percent ratio between debt and GDP in Latin America during 1973–74 did *not* prevent U.S. multinational corporations from adding to fresh capital inflows. This does not tally with the more recent skepticism, in the context of Latin America, concerning new lending or direct investment, which, in my judgment, could have been proved risky even earlier. The debt-exposure ratios cannot identify the critical turning point beyond which debt collapse would be imminent.

Ratios between interest charges and export value do not reveal the real cost of the interest burden. The use of the real interest rate (deflated by export unit value) may be extended to develop a new criterion, viz., real value of interest charges, deflated by the unit value of the debtor country's exports. It should not go unnoticed that the Western Hemisphere went through the severest price declines for exports—a phenomenon which explains a part of the aggravated problem in the region. (This also occurred in sub-Saharan Africa, which includes nations that had borrowed largely from official sources.)

My comments continue by drawing attention to the global tendencies in the terms of capital flows. According to Bank for International Settlements estimates relating to aggregate capital flows across nations, about 40 percent is channeled through the Eurobond market, where the debtor nations in the developing world have little access. Again, official development assistance has been tapering off in recent years, with such financing (on a net basis) providing not more than about 22.3 percent of the total current account deficit of developing countries in 1983. Bank credit, which financed about 70 percent of the current account deficit of developing countries in 1981, financed only about 20 percent in 1983. The sources of direct finance have been rather steady, meeting around 12 percent of the current account deficit during 1980–83. Given the above trends, it is unlikely that developing countries and, in particular, those in the Western

Hemisphere would have gotten access to concessional sources of credit in the 1980s, even if they had not been in debt crisis. This description of capital flows to the developing world tallies with the huge current account deficit of the United States, which was about 3.5 times the total deficit of all developing countries put together during 1985. Thus, the simple macroeconomic balance of international capital flows has led to a global restructuring of investment, in much the same way investment was redirected away from its old empire by the United Kingdom in the late nineteenth century. Discussions of issues relating to the dire necessity of recycling the Japanese current account surplus in the 1980s highlight additional dimensions of the contradiction.

Finally, I would like to draw attention to the situation in sub-Saharan Africa, where the debt-exposure and debt-service ratios have been high. Although these African countries had not borrowed much at market rates, they could not, unlike the countries of South Asia, avoid a debt crisis. Thus, the generalizations arrived at in the paper to the effect that borrowing at market rates was the main source of the debt problem and that export performance was the major alleviating factor are not supported by Africa's experience.

Use of liquidity indicators to judge the creditworthiness of debtor nations does not permit one to identify actual or potential debt-default situations. As a rule of thumb, the ratio between interest-income payments (net), BS, and the sum of the lending balance, BL, and the trade balance, BT, may prove more useful in identifying turning points.

The debt-servicing capacity of a borrowing nation is influenced, in the long run, by the structural changes relating to savings and imports, both of which are subject to the influence of capital inflows from abroad. Net inflows of capital from abroad may bring about increases in imports, as well as in domestic consumption. These changes may, in turn, eventually lead to sharp increases in the liquidity indicators of the borrowing country if it cannot generate exports and GDP growth. Outcomes such as the above are related to the actual quantum, as well as the composition, of the foreign capital inflows, on the one hand, and to the functioning of the borrowing economy, on the other. Placing an uncritical reliance on short-term liquidity indicators as measures of debtor capacity may lead one to overlook additional dimensions of the issue which are equally important.

4

Trade Regimes and Export Strategies with Reference to South Asia

*Ehtisham Ahmad**

I. Introduction

The issue of structural adjustment and growth in developing countries essentially involves changes in domestic production possibilities relative to trade opportunities. This paper is concerned mainly with which sectors a country ought to encourage, whether there should be recourse to foreign trade, and what policy instruments should be chosen. There are two strands in the literature dealing with these issues. *Trade theory* has traditionally been concerned with the choice between domestic production and exports or imports. And the central questions in the *public economics* literature concern what to produce, what instruments to choose, and the consequences of policy for households and government revenue. There is thus an overlap between the two approaches, and Subsection II.1 juxtaposes the main findings of each with respect to the selection of trade regime—including the arguments for free trade and the case for protection—and the choice of instruments.

Policymakers and economists in developing countries have been much concerned with building up "appropriate" domestic productive capability to ensure growth (defined in terms of gross national product (GNP), GNP per capita, living standards, and so on). And the "development literature" has also addressed the problem of trade versus domestic production—given the vagaries of the international economic environment—and problems of adjustment to movements in the terms of trade. Subsection II.2 refers to some

---

* The author wishes to thank seminar participants, especially the discussants of this paper—as well as Shahid Husain, Stephen Lewis, and Nicholas Stern—for helpful comments. Responsibility for the views expressed and any errors or omissions rests with the author.

of the debates in this strand of literature, including the discussion of the possibility of export-led growth.

Trade policy in the Indian subcontinent during this century has illustrated many of the policy options debated, from laissez faire to autarky, as well as some of the problems with policy instruments, such as quotas and import licensing. Section III deals with the choice of tariffs or quotas for protection and possibilities for export promotion with reference to the experience of countries in South Asia, with illustrations mainly from India, but also from Pakistan and Bangladesh. It is not intended to provide a comprehensive survey of the empirical literature relating to these three countries.

Section IV draws on work done on India in the late 1970s that uses a system of economy-wide shadow prices to show which sectors might be encouraged to permit adjustment with growth in output, given a concern for the welfare of the poor. Section V contains some concluding remarks.

II. Growth, Trade, and Theory

The relationship between growth and trade has been the subject of some controversy in the development literature, and this has been extensively surveyed in recent papers by Bliss (forthcoming), Krueger (1984), and Findlay (1984). Section II.1 contains a brief review of the case for free trade and arguments for restrictions from the theoretical literature of international trade and public economics. The gains-from-trade proposition is put in the context of developing countries. Section II.2 examines arguments put forth in the development literature for restricting trade, including early import-substitution theories; export pessimism, which has been a recurrent theme; and infant-industry arguments. A synthesis of the trade and development literatures suggests that the gains from trade need not be synonymous with free trade and that, in general, some trade is better than no trade.

1. The Gains from Trade

The central proposition from normative trade theory is that there are gains from trade and that free trade is Pareto superior to autarky under certain assumptions and is also superior to various forms of trade restriction. (The developments in the normative trade literature are reviewed in Corden (1984).)

The gains-from-trade proposition rests on very simple arguments. Under autarky, a country's consumption possibilities are limited by its production-possibility frontier. These consumption possibilities are increased by net trade with the rest of the world. Thus, with trade, the consumption-possibility frontier lies outside the country's production-possibility frontier and touches the latter only where the marginal rates of transformation (MRT) in domestic production equal those attainable with trade. For the small-country case, the marginal rates of transformation are given by world prices. The gains-from-trade result could be extended to the large-country case—where a country has monopoly power in trade and the marginal rates of transformation no longer equal the price ratios—by applying the optimal tariff at the chosen point. Consequently, feasible consumption in autarky can be dominated by combinations of trade and domestic production.

Although the early proofs for the potential gains from trade were based on a number of restrictive assumptions—absence of increasing returns, no distorting domestic taxes, no externalities, the feasibility of lump-sum transfers, and flexible factor prices that ensure full employment of factors—recent work has relaxed some of these assumptions. Dixit and Norman (1980) show that lump-sum transfers are not necessary for the gains-from-trade result and that factor taxes, including the income tax, will suffice. Ohyama (1972) examined the gains from trade in the presence of tariffs and subsidies, and the condition for a welfare improvement from a move to such a distorted situation is that net revenue be positive. Thus, trade under self-financing subsidies is preferable to autarky. The introduction of uncertainty has been shown by Helpman and Razin (1978) to be like an adverse movement in the terms of trade, although gains from trade exist. And in the intertemporal case, it has been shown by Smith (1979) that gains from trade exist, as in the static case, subject to similar qualifications: that balanced trade in goods at each date is preferable to autarky and, further, that when international borrowing and lending are permissible, a small country will gain further if trade is balanced over time in terms of present discounted values.

The literature concerning trade and imperfect competition is surveyed in Dixit (1984). For a pure domestic monopolist or price leader in an import-competing industry, trade serves to limit monopoly power, and protection is harmful. Where an exporting firm has monopoly power in the home market, it is likely to have less monopoly power in export markets. While the firm would wish to charge higher prices at home than abroad, the home country's interests are in having marginal-cost pricing at home and monopoly pricing in the export market. When a foreign firm has monopoly power in the home market, protection provided either by imposing import tariffs or increasing domestic firms' profits would appropriate some of the pure profits earned by the foreign firm, although loss of the home-country consumer surplus would have to be considered also. The case of cartels and the producing country's export tax policy are considered by Dixit and Stern (1982). Monopolistic competition has also been considered in the literature. It makes a distinction between intra-industry trade (based on product diversity and scale economies) and interindustry trade (based on factor endowments). The result that intra-industry trade should occur in countries that are similar, leading to a greater product variety, is what has been observed empirically. Dixit (1984) shows that policies under oligopolistic conditions vary from those under competitive conditions and that trade restrictions might be desirable, since prices are set above marginal cost. However, this is an area of active research, and it is still to be established whether other policies might achieve the same result more efficiently. Moreover,

> vested interests want protection, and relaxation of anti-trust activity, for their own selfish reasons. They will be eager to seize upon any theoretical arguments that advance such policies in the general interest. Distortion and misuse of the arguments is likely, and may result in the emergence of policies that cause aggregate welfare loss while providing private gains to powerful special groups.[1]

Newbery and Stiglitz (1981, 1984) compare autarky and free trade between two competitive, but risky economies with no insurance markets and show that free trade may be inferior to no trade. However, some trade is shown to be preferable to no trade. The policy choice of trade restrictions, tariffs, or quotas is examined in Section III.

---

[1] Dixit (1984), p. 15.

The case of "immiserizing" growth was brought back into the discussion by Bhagwati (1958). (It had been considered, in a less general setting, in 1894 by Edgeworth, who referred to it as "damnifying.") Thus, national welfare declines with growth in national income, provided that the decline in the terms of trade exceeds the favorable effects of the expansion at constant relative product prices. However, a country that could affect its terms of trade would levy an optimal tariff, and immiserizing growth would not occur.

Another type of "immiserizing" growth was considered by Johnson (1967). With fixed terms of trade, in a two-sector, two-factor open economy, a tariff or trade distortion that results in the output of the import-competing good being too large, and the output of the exportable good being too small, may lead to the immiserization. This occurs because factor endowments change so as to expand the inefficient protected sector at the expense of the efficient export sector. This result also applies to the trade in factors. In the model of Brecher and Bhagwati (1981), where some of the factors of production in the home country are owned by foreigners, the optimum tariff vector must be worked out simultaneously for goods trade and foreign factor income, since otherwise immiserizing trade can result. See Bhagwati and Srinivasan (1983), chapters 16–25, for a discussion of growth, comparative statics, and many kinds of distortions.

Dixit (1985) surveyed the modern public finance approach to the open economy. International trade—which represents a new set of transactions, possible externalities, and distortions—enlarges the consumption-possibility set. Government objectives may still be characterized as raising revenues, increasing household welfare, and facilitating production; and there may also be other, non-economic objectives or constraints. The policy instruments are the set of taxes and subsidies on domestic or foreign transactions and activity, subject to administrative feasibility. And central features of the public finance approach are that tariffs affect domestic-resource allocations and income distribution and that domestic taxes affect trade, given the interdependence of the economic system. (See also Stephen Lewis (1984).)

A major result from the public finance literature has a bearing on trade policy. This is the application of the Diamond-Mirrlees

(1971) aggregate-production-efficiency theorem, which implies that marginal rates of transformation between domestic production activities and foreign trade should be equalized. In the case of foreign trade, these equal world prices, except in those cases in which there is monopoly power, where the optimum tariff will yield the necessary equality. For domestic production, marginal rates of transformation equal producer prices. A consequence of the efficiency theorem is that there should be no taxation of (or subsidy on) producer or intermediate goods. This paper will return to this result in discussing tariffs and protection in Section III.

There are two results from international trade theory that carry over to the public finance analysis of trade. First is the Bhagwati-Johnson principle of targeting, according to which, if there is a distortion, it should be countered directly; or if a distortion is to be introduced in an effort to achieve a non-economic objective, then a tax instrument should be used that acts directly on the relevant margin. And if there is an external economy in production, the first-best policy is to use an appropriate Pigovian subsidy. "It is only if this is impossible that the indirect effect of a tariff to stimulate domestic production can be useful as a second-best (or worse) policy."[2] This has a direct bearing on the choice of instruments once it can be established that a particular industry or sector should be encouraged domestically. The second result is that if particular groups are affected adversely through trade, then domestic goods or factor taxes or subsidies, rather than tariffs, should be used to compensate them.

The gains from trade have been established in principle. However, these are only potential and may not be realizable per se. It is possible, however, for laissez faire to lead to Pareto-inefficient equilibria in the face of market distortions or policy failures. In such cases, adding another distortion or restriction, such as prohibition or taxation of trade, may prove beneficial in accordance with the general theory of the second best.

2. Development and Trade

Although the burden of the theoretical literature surveyed above suggests that some trade is better than no trade, and that free trade

---

[2] Dixit (1985), p. 314.

might Pareto dominate both under given circumstances, development economists have remained divided over the issue of trade, and there is considerable skepticism concerning feee trade. In this subsection, two sets of arguments used for justifying departures from free trade are examined: these may be broadly classified as the "export-pessimism" and "infant-industry" cases. Shadow prices, which provide a guide as to which industries should be encouraged, are also discussed briefly.

a. *Export Pessimism*

Pessimism concerning developing country exports to developed countries underlies some of the demands for import substitution that have been made since the 1950s. At the extreme there is a claim, associated with Prebisch and Singer, that the terms of trade must inevitably move against primary products in favor of manufactures. And Nurkse, in considering the balance between the global demand and supply for primary products, concluded that developing countries generally cannot expand primary product production without suffering terms-of-trade losses. This is because a "rational" strategy by a poor, small country to expand production of the (primary) good(s) in which it has a comparative advantage might lead to global overproduction of such good(s) or to immiserization of a group of such countries. While a solution to the problem of overproduction of primary commodities may lie in collaborative behavior, the problems encountered in reaching agreement on policy recently faced by the Organization of Petroleum Exporting Countries (OPEC) (which has been the most successful such experiment) do not bode well for other commodity-producing cartels.

Developing countries are often characterized as primary producing countries of the South that are dependent on their trade with an industrialized North. Terms of trade "play a key role . . . as the regulator that makes the growth rate of the South conform to the exogenously given long run growth rate of the North. Trade is the 'engine of growth' for the South, but the pace of the engine is set by the growth rate of the North."[3] A number of North-South models are reviewed in Findlay (1984), as are variants of "unequal-

---

[3] Findlay (1984), p. 225.

exchange" models that may be seen as special cases of such North-South models. However, the proposition that there has been a secular decline in the terms of trade for developing countries has been challenged by Krueger (1984), among others. This is because it is difficult to establish which commodities are exported by poor countries and which by richer countries; and, indeed, a classification of countries as poor and rich is problematical. Also distinguishing between cyclical and secular trends is particularly difficult, since the results obtained are strongly affected by the choice of initial and terminal periods, and the data are often of poor quality. Krueger ((1984), p. 560) discusses unpublished work by Michaely which showed that for the years 1952, 1955, 1960, 1965, 1970, and 1973,

> the price of exports of the poor countries rose more than that of the rich; the price of imports of the rich countries rose more than that of the price of the poor; and the ratio of the two moved in favor of the poor countries. Hence, the terms of trade had necessarily moved in favor of the poor countries over the period covered by his data. He then proceeded to show that using the conventional measure of manufactured goods prices relative to primary commodity prices provided the "orthodox" Prebisch-Singer result.

No doubt critics could apply the Krueger strictures to the Michaely analysis and argue about choice of period, countries, and commodities. However, the point remains that it is simplistic to equate developing countries with primary producers and vice versa.

In his Nobel lecture, W. Arthur Lewis (1980) also argued that over the past century, the "rate of growth of output in the developing world has depended on the rate of growth of output in the developed world"[4] and that the principal link between the two growth rates is trade. On the assumption that growth rates in developed countries would be lower in the future than in the immediate postwar era, and that the prospects for developing country manufacturing exports would be further limited by Organization for Economic Cooperation and Development (OECD) tariff and nontariff barriers, the future of developing country growth rates would depend on those diverse countries, such as India, that have the capacity for self-sustaining growth and trade with other developing countries. Thus growth rates in leading developing

---

[4] W. Arthur Lewis (1980), p. 555.

countries would substitute for growth in the developed countries and provide a demand for the exports of other developing countries.

The empirical evidence examined by Reidel (1984) suggested that many developing countries (and particularly those in East Asia) diversified into manufacturing exports to developed countries and that only a few countries, mainly in Africa, were exporting a single primary product. The share of manufacturing exports (in total developing countries exports) had increased from 7 percent in the mid-1950s to over 20 percent by the late 1970s, and the proportion of developing country manufactured exports going to the developed countries increased from 45 percent in 1955 to over 60 percent in 1978. However, it should be borne in mind that 60 percent of developing country manufactures exported in 1978 were from the Republic of Korea, Taiwan Province of China, Hong Kong, or Singapore. And as Fields (1983, 1984) points out, these countries are characterized by competition in the labor market, which clears through wage adjustment. Thus, relatively low unit-wage costs (in terms of levels of productivity and the nominal exchange rate) and an efficient functioning of the labor market facilitate an export-led growth strategy. Fields contends that the Jamaicas, Mexicos, and Indonesias of the Third World have wages in the exporting sectors that are two or three times the market-clearing levels and that these "countries start out at an enormous disadvantage in trying to compete successfully in world markets with the U.S., the European Economic Community, Japan, and the East Asian NICs [newly industrializing countries]. . . . Not to be able to export profitably is bad. To export unprofitably is worse."[5] Thus, the overall picture indicates that for individual countries there are possibilities of exploiting trading opportunities, and that there may be scope for extending exports to other developing countries if OECD policies are too restrictive. However, this conclusion assumes "appropriate" domestic policies and does not suggest that developing countries export solely for the sake of exporting.

b. *The Infant-Industry Argument*

One of the oldest arguments for an exception to the free-trade proposition is the case for infant-industry protection. Corden (1984)

---

[5] Fields (1983), p. 17.

equates this with an argument for temporary protection to account for some market imperfection or externality. A tariff to correct for the distortion, in comparison with a production subsidy, would create a consumption distortion, and a production subsidy would be preferable if only these two instruments were available. However, more direct methods might be preferable to the production subsidy, as the following examples indicate.

Where there are dynamic internal economies, as in a firm or an industry going through a period of investment in human capital, the learning benefits stay within the firm or industry, and it may not be possible to finance investment in such an industry, given capital-market distortions. The first-best policy is to improve the capital market and then subsidize the factor or input that gave rise to the internal economy. A general output subsidy may fail to correct the capital-market distortion or to encourage the dynamic factor sufficiently. A tariff would create further distortions, and an export subsidy would be the least preferred policy option.

In the case of dynamic external economies, given mobility and market imperfections, such as capital-market imperfections or wage rigidities, the effects of labor training would not be internalized by the firms at the infant stage or any other, since trained workers would move to better-paid jobs quickly. The preferable policy options would be to improve the capital markets, and to finance or subsidize the labor training. Less attractive would be the subsidizing of the employment of labor in those sectors that provided more trained manpower than others. Least favorable would be an output subsidy.

A third argument that has been discussed extensively concerns knowledge diffusion, also an example of a dynamic external economy. This diffusion is rapid in the infancy stage, although it is in the private interests of firms to restrict the diffusion.

There is little direct evidence about the behavior of specific infant industries in developing countries: estimates of the pattern of cost reductions and benefits over time and the duration of infancy. Krueger and Tuncer (1982), however, found that in the Turkish case, more protected industries did not have greater reductions in costs than less protected industries. And there is a strong presumption that because high levels of protection have continued in developing countries for long periods, "protection in developing countries generally has not been justified on infant-industry grounds" (Krueger (1984), p. 525). Despite the presumption that the period of infancy should not exceed five to eight years (Balassa (1975)), fragmentary historical evidence suggests that the Japanese cotton textile industry took two to three decades to mature, the Japanese automobile industry three to six decades, and the Korean textile industry about four decades. However, the period of maturation for some Korean industries has been as short as a couple of years, as in the shipbuilding industry. And the rapid industrialization and diversified exports of countries such as the Republic of Korea and Brazil show that the period of maturity can come about reasonably quickly, although the differences between the Korean textile and shipbuilding industries tend to suggest that there may be significant differences across sectors. (See Bell, Ross-Larson, and Westphal (1984) for further references.)

c. *Shadow Prices*

The question of which industries or sectors ought to be encouraged involves issues of the intertemporal social costs and benefits of the proposed policy change. This essentially involves the use of shadow prices, defined as the increase in social welfare resulting when an extra unit of public supplies becomes available. There has been a voluminous literature on the concept of shadow prices, and a recent integration of the theory has been provided by Drèze and Stern (1985). A natural application is to the theory of reform in which the planner inherits an environment—including distortions, warts, and all—and pursues policy objectives within a given area of control. (For a statement of the theory of reform in a simple context, see Ahmad and Stern (1986 b) and Drèze and Stern (1985); for an application, see Ahmad, Coady, and Stern (1986)).

Although shadow prices have been calculated for many economies, since they are extensively used in project appraisal, care should be taken to ensure that these are consistent with the models used for the reform discussion, for "when the social value of projects depends upon the 'reforms' accompanying them, projects can no longer be evaluated in isolation."[6]

The shadow prices essentially capture the full general-equilibrium effects of a policy change on welfare. And, in principle, they should be derived from a fully articulated general-equilibrium model of

---

[6] Drèze and Stern (1985), p. 18.

the economy. However, the shadow prices provide summary statistics for policy from the full model and are often more flexible and more easily understood than the full model. Thus, consistent with a plausible set of shadow prices, it should be possible to construct a general-equilibrium model and to make appropriate welfare judgments. For example, if certain policies are known to affect the shadow wage, then one can examine the consequences for trade and tax policy fairly quickly, although it may prove difficult to modify the general-equilibrium model to incorporate the changed circumstances.

The use of world prices as shadow prices goes back to the Little-Mirrlees 1969 OECD Manual (revised version provided in Little and Mirrlees (1974)) and has been the subject of much discussion. (See Bliss (forthcoming) and Corden (1984) for reviews of the recent literature.) The use of marginal border prices as shadow prices for tradables is fairly robust and extends to the case where world prices are affected by domestic policy, given optimum tariffs. And the presence of nontradables does not affect the rules for shadow prices for tradables. (See Dixit (1984).) Price wedges, such as tariffs, do not affect the classification of tradables, although quantitative restrictions, such as binding quotas, imply that at the margin, a commodity is not traded and should be treated correspondingly. In the absence of distortions, the shadow prices of nontradables would equal their domestic market prices. With distortions, the two can differ and may be negative, as shown by Bhagwati, Srinivasan, and Wan (1978). The Ahmad, Coady, and Stern (1984, 1986) estimates of shadow prices for Pakistan and India use world prices for tradables and take into account the distorting effects of trade restrictions on prices that producers face, imperfections in factor markets, and premiums on savings. Different sets of shadow prices were calculated, using input-output techniques in large part, that corresponded to different assumptions governing the classification of goods as traded and nontraded and to different valuations of factors. Some of the results are discussed below.

III. Tariffs, Quotas, and Trade Policy in South Asia

The laissez-faire approach of the British authorities to economic policy during the colonial period has been blamed for turning India into a market for British manufactures and a source of supply of cheap raw materials. "For many years, Indian tariffs were kept low, and the overall tariff structure afforded minimal protection for Indian industries, thus strengthening the complementary position of the Britsh and the Indian economies."[7] However, the case for tariff protection was conceded after the First World War. The ensuing pattern of industrialization is documented in Bhagwati and Desai (1970). Direct import controls, however, were introduced during the Second World War to regulate foreign exchange and shipping space for the war effort and for essential civilian supplies. These controls continued in various forms until India achieved independence, and these have been a feature of policymaking in both India and Pakistan since. (For India, see the Ministry of Finance's *Report of the Committee on Controls and Subsidies* (or Dagli Committee) (1979)) and Lal (1980); and for Pakistan, for the period up to 1970, see Islam (1981).)

The experience of wartime controls, as well as colonial laissez-faire, led Indian policymakers to adopt an import-substitution strategy after independence that allowed for imports of raw materials and intermediate goods while tightening control of other imports. With the analytical planning framework of the Mahalanobis model, the Second Five-Year Plan continued the import-substitution policies. The imports of capital goods and raw materials increased until they were checked by a foreign exchange crisis in 1958, which led to a drastic reduction in imports through extensive controls. A tight import policy continued into the mid-1970s.

With the pursuit of the import-substitution policy, it soon became apparent that an overvalued exchange rate and import controls discriminated against exports. Thus, explicit policies for export promotion were introduced in the early 1960s, although these were related to the system of import controls. The extant export subsidies in the late 1970s were described by the Dagli Committee as having been based on "'hit or miss' methods, with an eye to securing a 7 to 8 per cent rate of growth of overall exports, without reference to either the costs or the long term benefits."[8] More recently, the Indian Ministry of Commerce's *Report of the Committee on Trade Policies* (Hussain Committee) (1984) has

---

[7] Birnberg and Resnick (1975), p. 17.
[8] India, Ministry of Finance (1979), p. 87.

argued that while a country like India cannot have export-led growth, there should be a "quantum jump" in exports, and that the emphasis of import policy "should move from import substitution per se to efficient import substitution." While agreeing that Indian import substitution in some sectors has been too costly and that there is a need to improve export performance, Chakravarty (1984) expressed reservations about export-led growth, on the East Asian pattern, in the Indian context. This was because of (i) the relative size of the nontraded goods sector; (ii) the limit to which efficiency wages could be reduced to ensure competitiveness; and (iii) the uncertainty concerning the changing international division of labor (an example of the export pessimism that was discussed in Section II) meant that the prospects for greatly increasing exports were limited.

With the switch to an import-substitution policy after independence, the Indian Government, for example, had a limited number of policy instruments in hand with which to implement these policies. In this connection, both tariffs and quotas have been used, along with investment licensing and price and output controls. Subsequently, measures to counterbalance the bias against exports arising from the instruments used to encourage import substitution came into being in the early 1960s. The standard equivalence theorems in the trade literature concerning tariffs and quotas are discussed in Subsection III.1.

While tariffs are an instrument of commercial policy that guide the pattern of domestic investment allocation, it is known (Tanzi (1987)) that customs duties are convenient "tax handles" and that revenues from international trade are easier to collect than general sales taxes or taxes on income. Thus, in India, customs duties averaged more than 40 percent of the tax revenue of the central and state governments until the mid-1950s. However, with the growth of the domestic production base, and the introduction of quotas and direct controls on trade, customs duties had declined in importance relative to excises on domestic production by the early 1960s (with the latter providing 45 percent of total tax revenue in 1959/60, as compared with 20 percent from customs duties). By the 1980s, customs still accounted for around 20 percent of total tax revenue—a not unsubstantial amount of revenue, given that tax revenues in India by the late 1970s were of the magnitude of 19 percent of gross domestic product (GDP). (This proportion had also been projected in the 1986/87 budget estimates. See the Indian Ministry of Finance's *Economic Survey,* 1985/86.) Since revenues are of obvious importance to countries like India and Pakistan, the prevalence of quantitative restrictions and quotas in the subcontinent needs to be examined in this context. Moreover, the major tax tools, customs duties, and excises in both countries bear quite heavily on intermediate goods and raw materials, causing problems of possibly unintentional taxation of final goods and exports.

After brief discussions of the trade control instruments, tariffs, and quotas in Subsection III.1, and of protection in Subsection III.2, the paper proceeds to an assessment of export policy in India in Subsection III.3.

1. Tariffs and Quotas

A decision by, say, the Bangladesh Government to protect the domestic steel industry—for example, the Chittagong Steel Mill—either by tariffs or quotas on imports, has an immediate impact on domestic users of steel through its increased price, and if some of these firms are exporting establishments, then the import tariff on steel is like an export tax. In this section, some of the important "equivalence results" from the trade literature are discussed.

Of policy importance is Lerner's symmetry proposition, which in a two-good real model postulates that since both an import tariff and export tax lower the domestic price of the exportable relative to the importable, they have the same impact on production and consumption. This result has been extended to the case of several goods, where relative prices matter, and the treatment of nontradables introduces particular exchange rates. (See, for example, Corden (1984) or Stephen Lewis (1984), Part IV.) This equivalence result has important implications for countries that rely heavily on import duties for revenues, since these duties have the same effect as export duties.

Within the Walrasian general-equilibrium context, each quota or nontariff barrier has its shadow price, which could be replaced by an equivalent tariff and, abstracting from income effects, if this were done, the equilibrium would not be affected. The main difference, even in this context, would be in possible differential distributional effects if quota rents were to go to nongovernment agents, whereas it is presumed that tariff revenue accrues to the government. Thus, in cases where the quotas were not auctioned domestically, there would be a revenue loss to the government. Further if the quotas are allocated inefficiently by the bureaucracy, and if there is no resale, further deadweight losses may occur that would have been avoided by the imposition of a tariff. There is evidence that in both India and Pakistan, there has been a differential access to quotas and that the inefficiency referred to above is quite common. Thus, even in the general-equilibrium sense, a tariff may be preferable to quotas or quantitative restrictions.

Non-equivalences between tariffs and quotas in the case of monopoly have been extensively discussed in the literature, following Bhagwati (1965). This occurs when there is either actual or potential monopoly on the part of domestic import-license holders, domestic import-competing producers, or foreign suppliers. Thus, a quota that has the same effect as a tariff on the amount of imports may differ with respect to the effects on domestic prices and production. A case in point is when a quota, while raising the domestic price, provides a degree of monopoly power to the domestic producer, who thus might reduce output. A tariff, while also raising the domestic price and reducing imports, would encourage domestic production and the non-equivalance results.

This discussion has assumed that it is possible to choose tariffs or quotas for identifiable commodities. In practice, tariffs or quotas are levied on relatively broad commodity groups. Dixit (1985) illustrates the problem with the choice of policy instruments for a group of commodities like "automobiles," which is, in fact, composed of different types of vehicles that are less than perfectly substitutable for each other. Ideally, the choice of policy would involve a separate tariff or quota for each type, though the policymaker may be constrained to a choice between a uniform tariff or quota. Since such groups usually involve goods that are reasonable substitutes, the public economics literature suggests, they should be taxed at roughly similar ad valorem rates. If this were not the case, relative prices would differ and would result in large substitutions and quantity changes, with attendant deadweight losses. Thus, uniform ad valorem tariffs for such groups would result in the closest approximation to the best policy. A uniform quota would act as a uniform specific tariff, implying a too-low tariff on commodities with high world prices and a too-high tariff for commodities with low world prices, and would cause a shift in the world supply of goods toward those whose tariffs were too low.

The choice between tariffs and quotas has also been discussed in the context of uncertainty. It is not generally possible to rank tariffs as equivalent or preferable to quotas, and the answers would depend, inter alia, on the nature of the uncertainty and on the slopes of the demand and supply curves (Newbery and Stiglitz (1981)).

Quotas and tariffs also differ in terms of their costs of implementation. The administrative costs of collecting tariffs would vary, depending on the nature of the commodity, the efficiency of the customs officials, and whether there were opportunities to evade payment of duties. These administrative arguments are often proposed in favor of quotas when there is a multiplicity of high tariff rates. The incentives to smuggle would exist with quotas and high tariff rates. The real resource cost of smuggling has been examined by Sheikh (1974).

Krueger (1974) discusses the "rent-seeking" costs involved in the imposition of tariffs and quotas. On the one hand, real resources will be expended to capture the monopoly rents conferred by the quotas. This may be done through competition between potential licensees or bribery of the license-giving agencies. On the other hand, tariffs also generate protection for domestic producers, and there are powerful pressure groups which lobby for the continuation or extension of this protection. Bhagwati and Srinivasan (1980) extended the concept of rent-seeking to the case of "revenue-seeking," arguing that since tariffs are a fruitful source of revenue, this would generate a lobby for the perpetuation of the benefits obtained in the same way that individuals indulge in rent-seeking activities. Such profit-seeking activities do not generate commodities for consumption, but rather lead to income transfers.

2. Protection

The concepts of effective tariffs and effective protection have come to be widely used. Where intermediate goods are involved, the extent to which an industry is protected is taken to depend not only on the protection accorded to the output but also on that accorded to the inputs, since output tariffs increase the domestic price above world levels and make production more profitable, and input tariffs make production of output more costly, and hence less profitable. A common definition of effective protection is the difference between value added at domestic prices and value added at world prices as a proportion of value added at world prices. This is a positive concept that involves an attempt to measure the resource pulls resulting from trade restrictions. However, it is not, in general, true that resources will flow toward a sector if its effective protection increases. (See Jones and Neary (1984).) Attempts have been made to salvage the "effective protection" idea by imposing strong restrictions on the technology (fixed coefficients or separability between intermediate goods and factors of production), or to suggest formulas which might predict gross output changes. If technical coefficients are not fixed, it is not clear whether the relevant coefficients to be used in the effective-protection calculations should be based on world or domestic prices; they are functions of relative prices of all inputs and also involve nominal tariffs in the calculation of domestic prices. Moreover, gross output levels in conventional welfare analysis "are of no concern. What matters is the net production that is available to consumers,"[9] and the nominal tariff rate is the appropriate measure for this. These difficulties render the concept far from useful as a normative measure, although effective protection as a descriptive tool describes ex post the difference between foreign exchange earned and factor payments made in terms of border prices or trade opportunity costs.

Effective protection calculations do not, in fact, guide policy toward sectors that should be protected or indicate which activities should be contracted. The analysis of sectoral policy essentially involves information on the opportunity costs of nontraded goods and factors. "In this regard, the domestic resource cost measure will appropriately reflect the opportunity cost of tradable-goods production. The effective tariff measure, by ignoring the indirect cost of home goods, does not."[10] Apart from its treatment of income distribution and factors, the domestic-resource-cost method is like that used in the Little-Mirrlees shadow-pricing calculations. (See

---

[9] Dixit (1985), p. 361.
[10] Krueger (1972), p. 57

Section IV.) Note that effective protection measures, domestic resource costs, and shadow prices all adjust domestic market prices to reflect trade opportunity costs; however, shadow prices provide the most general guide to policy formulation.

It may be argued that from the normative point of view, protection of any kind is irrelevant. Using the principle of targeting, the best way is to institute subsidies to factors that do not cause by-product distortions and to not use protection at all. Dixit (1985) dismisses the criticism by laymen that

> import tariffs raise revenue, while production subsidies cost money and put additional strain on other uses of the government's budget. We see this argument to be fallacious. The size of the government's budget has no *direct* welfare relevance. The optimality conditions show that, on considering the overall effects, it is desirable to provide these production subsidies and adjust other taxes appropriately.[11]

This may be seen intuitively if one considers the fact that a tariff is equivalent to a production subsidy and consumption tax, and thus is just one "way of financing (in fact overfinancing) the subsidy."[12] Thus, the arguments for using tariffs to provide protection are largely political or administrative—suggesting that it might be easier to levy a tariff than to provide a production subsidy—though both methods would be open to rent-seeking activities.

3. Export Promotion

A number of export-promotion measures were extant in India in the late 1970s, and not all of them could be described as subsidies, since they were designed to compensate for some of the biases against exports introduced elsewhere. These measures included, inter alia, (i) a duty-drawback scheme; (ii) cash compensatory support and rebates for market development; and (iii) an import-replenishment scheme. Similar instruments have been used in the other countries of the subcontinent. This paper will, however, concentrate on the Indian case.

The duty-drawback scheme refunds duties paid on inputs used to produce exported goods. Import duties are generally refunded

---

[11] Dixit (1985), p. 338.
[12] Ibid.

in full, although this does not apply to capital goods. Excise duties are also refunded to the extent these can be related to identifiable inputs. In 1975/76, 62 percent of duty-drawback rates were less than 10 percent of the f.o.b. value of the exported goods, and 89 percent of drawbacks were less than 20 percent of the f.o.b. price. The commodities affected covered 97 percent of the cumulative f.o.b. value of exports.[13]

It is clear that the duty-drawback scheme only partially corrects for the taxation of intermediate goods in the economy, since only some of the directly identifiable taxation of inputs is rebated. The cash-compensatory-support scheme provided assistance in the export of nontraditional products to compensate for unrefunded taxes and levies paid on exported goods and their inputs through the production process. The percentage of cash compensatory support with respect to the f.o.b. value of exports is shown in Table 1 for much of the 1970s, and Table 2 shows that most of the exports receiving cash compensatory support did so in the 10–15 percent range. An interest subsidy is paid out of the market development assistance fund, which also covers the cash-compensatory-support scheme. In 1976/77, this amounted to Rs 100 million out of the market development assistance fund of Rs 2,400 million.

The import-entitlement scheme, which was of considerable importance before the devaluation of the rupee in 1966, allowed exporters to retain a part of the foreign exchange they earned, which entitled them to import twice their input content. These licenses carried a substantial market premium. (See Bhagwati and Desai (1970).) The import-replenishment scheme, which replaced the entitlement scheme, licensed the full import content of the exports of specified goods for import replenishment. The changes made in this scheme through the late 1970s are described in Bagchi (1981). In 1977/78, the value of import licenses issued against exports was Rs 7,410 million, as against Rs 4,670 million on account of the duty-drawback and market-development schemes (including cash compensatory support).

In Table 2, the cash compensatory support (CCS) for the export of some of the goods shown in Table 1 may be compared with estimates of the tax element in the price of final goods that arises

---

[13]India, Ministry of Commerce (1978).

Table 1. India: Cash Compensatory Support Relative to Exports (f.o.b.)
(In percent)

Products	1970/71	1974/75	1975/76	1976/77	Simple Average for Period to 1976/77	Difference Between Minimum and Maximum for 1970/71–1976/77
(1) (2)	(3)	(4)	(5)	(6)	(7)	(8)
1. Engineering products	14.5	16.1	14.8	15.3	15.6	2.20
2. Chemical and allied products; paper products	13.7	14.4	13.3	12.7	14.16	2.60
3. Plastic goods	9.4	9.2	9.7	10.1	9.76	2.10
4. Sports goods	14.5	19.4	16.2	14.9	17.64	5.40
5. Woollen carpets; rugs and druggets	10.5	5.7	11.0	15.1	10.27	9.40
6. Processed food items	8.5	8.0	13.8	12.8	9.91	6.40
7. Woollen blended knitwear	—	—	15.0	12.1	13.55	2.90
8. Fish and fish preparations	—	—	6.1	4.9	5.5	1.20
9. Instant teas; packet teas and tea bags	—	—	10.0	9.9	9.95	0.10
10. Jute manufactures	—	—	9.8	9.2	9.5	0.6
11. Rayon and synthetics	—	—	14.9	13.9	14.4	1.0
12. Finished leather and leather manufactures	—	5.06	5.2	6.1	6.5	3.30
13. Natural silk fabrics, garments, and made-ups	—	7.06	9.6	10.9	9.5	3.30
14. Instant coffee extracts and essence	—	—	—	10.0	—	—
15. Walnut kernels and walnuts in shell	—	5.01	8.7	12.1	8.63	7.0
16. Iron and steel scrap (ferrous scrap)	5.00	3.08	19.9	—	7.2	16.10
17. Decorticated cottonseed cakes	12.06	10.08	10.0	18.6	14.15	8.60
18. Groundnut cake extractions	3.02	—	—	—	4.53	7.20
19. Prime iron and steel	14.02	—	5.9	4.9	12.18	13.00
20. Iron ore and manganese ore	0.05	—	—	—	4.77	6.70
21. Machine-twisted curled coir fiber and carpets	14.03	4.07	5.1	6.3	9.44	9.40
22. Rice bran (extractions)	—	1.00	—	7.3	7.33	12.70

Source: India, Ministry of Commerce (1978).

Table 2. India: Classification of Exported Items Subject to Cash Compensatory Support at Different Rates, 1976/77[1]

Products	<10 percent	≥10 percent and <15 percent	≥15 percent and <20 percent	≥20 percent	Total Number
Engineering products	6	133	70	37	246
Chemicals and allied products	2	179	25	5	211
Plastics	—	31	—	—	31
Leather	1	4	2	—	7
Sports goods	—	—	1	—	1
Fish products	1	1	1	1	3
Fresh and processed foods	2	27	11	9	49
Carpets and handicrafts	1	1	1	1	4
Woollen fabrics and made-ups	3	—	—	—	3
Natural silk fabrics and garments	—	2	4	—	6
Synthetic fabrics and garments	2	21	23	—	46
Coir products	3	—	—	—	3
Decorticated cottonseed extractions	—	—	4	4	8
Decorticated cottonseed expeller cake	—	4	4	—	8
Cotton bagging	—	—	3	—	3
Miscellaneous group	—	5	—	1	6
Total	21	408	148	58	635

Source: India, Ministry of Commerce (1978).

[1] This table refers to the number of different items, which may be subject to different rates of cash compensatory support, within a broad sectoral classification.

from the taxation of intermediate goods and raw materials. The effective tax, t^e, defined as the total tax component of the price of final goods, is calculated using actual revenue collections for India for 1979/80. (For details, see Ahmad and Stern (1983, 1987).) This takes into account the taxation of inputs, of inputs into inputs, and so on using a transaction-flow table based on the assumption of full forward shifting of taxes. At the sectoral level of classification of the input-output table, this is not an unreasonable assumption, although for individual commodities whose prices are fixed by the world market, say, changes in input taxes affect payments to factors rather than the final price. The taxation of a good through the taxation of inputs, t^{diff}, is the difference between t^e and the nominal tax. Table 3 presents estimates from Ahmad and Stern (1987) for 89 input-output sectors for 1979/80.

Although the element of taxation arising through capital goods is not included in the Ahmad and Stern estimates, t^{diff} is of the order of 10–15 percent of the producer price of most of the exportable-goods categories, and is as high as 24 percent for "plastics and synthetic rubber goods," 32 percent for "woollen and silk textiles," and 44 percent for artificial "silk textiles." Compare these figures with the cash-compensatory-support estimates for immediately preceding years (Table 1). Although the commodity classifications are not quite identical, a number of commodities appear to have CCS levels considerably lower than t^{diff}: plastic goods, knitwear, rayon and synthetics; and commodities such as engineering goods, chemicals, and iron and steel products have CCS levels roughly in line with the taxation of intermediate goods. In a number of cases, however, the CCS level exceeds both the effective tax and the tax element arising from the taxation of intermediate goods: these include carpets, leather products (though not footwear), and processed food items. In other cases, the CCS level lies between t^e and t^{diff}.

While export incentives have been used to correct for distortions created by policy for protection and for revenue, export subsidies have also been given, as was done under the Pakistan Bonus Voucher Scheme (see Islam (1981)) prior to the 1972 devaluation, to correct for an overvaluation of the currency. In this case, the right policy, which was followed by both the Indian and Pakistan Governments in the recent past, is not to maintain extremely overvalued exchange rates.

Table 3. India: Taxation of Inputs

Commodity	i^e	t^{diff}	t^{diffc}	t^{diffs}	Proportion of Gross Domestic Output
1. Rice and products	−0.035	−0.009	−0.014	0.006	0.0445
2. Wheat and products	0.069	−0.018	−0.027	0.008	0.0226
3. Jowar and products	0.012	0.002	0.001	0.002	0.0075
4. Bajra and products	0.003	0.004	0.002	0.005	0.0025
5. Other cereals	0.009	0.013	0.002	0.011	0.0066
6. Pulses	0.048	0.038	0.022	0.016	0.0108
7. Sugarcane	0.003	−0.010	−0.015	0.005	0.0135
8. Jute	−0.001	−0.003	−0.004	0.001	0.0010
9. Cotton	−0.005	0.005	0.000	0.005	0.0077
10. Plantations	−0.014	−0.016	−0.043	0.027	0.0060
11. Other crops	0.005	−0.001	−0.003	0.002	0.0617
12. Milk and products	0.009	0.008	−0.003	0.011	0.0308
13. Other animal husbandry products	0.014	0.014	−0.004	0.018	0.0157
14. Forestry and logging	0.051	0.012	0.007	0.005	0.0070
15. Fishing	0.012	0.012	0.007	0.005	0.0042
16. Coal and lignite	0.065	0.018	0.009	0.008	0.0060
17. Petroleum and natural gas	0.201	0.036	0.027	0.009	0.0023
18. Iron ore	0.233	0.134	0.104	0.030	0.0006
19. Other minerals	0.058	0.073	0.056	0.017	0.0020
20. Miscellaneous food products	0.067	0.047	0.021	0.026	0.0178
21. Sugar	0.202	0.038	0.016	0.022	0.0088
22. Gur and khandsari	0.059	0.042	0.004	0.038	0.0107
23. Vanaspati	0.191	0.075	0.039	0.036	0.0064
24. Other edible oils	0.074	0.015	−0.008	0.024	0.0062
25. Tea and coffee	0.221	0.050	0.020	0.030	0.0044

26. Other beverages	3.590	0.074	0.049	0.025	0.0012
27. Tobacco manufactures	0.939	0.115	0.097	0.015	0.0047
28. Cotton textiles excluding handloom and khadi	0.108	0.051	0.034	0.017	0.0248
29. Cotton textiles, handloom and khadi	0.070	0.082	0.056	0.026	0.0122
30. Woollen and silk textiles	0.411	0.325	0.297	0.028	0.0026
31. Artificial silk fabrics	0.598	0.442	0.432	0.010	0.0035
32. Jute textiles	0.142	0.069	0.053	0.016	0.0045
33. Readymade garments	0.093	0.081	0.067	0.013	0.0084
34. Miscellaneous textile products	0.132	0.114	0.091	0.023	0.0065
35. Carpet weaving	0.052	0.048	0.038	0.011	0.0015
36. Wood products	0.093	0.078	0.057	0.021	0.0066
37. Paper, products and newsprint	0.275	0.106	0.075	0.031	0.0061
38. Printing and publishing	0.090	0.090	0.068	0.022	0.0046
39. Leather and products	0.053	0.054	0.027	0.027	0.0033
40. Leather footwear	0.183	0.122	0.101	0.021	0.0023
41. Rubber products	0.408	0.161	0.124	0.037	0.0065
42. Plastics and synthetic rubber	0.480	0.248	0.216	0.032	0.0036
43. Petroleum products	0.548	0.013	0.009	0.004	0.0153
44. Miscellaneous coal and petroleum products	0.518	0.087	0.065	0.022	0.0029
45. Inorganic heavy chemicals	0.262	0.079	0.060	0.019	0.0039
46. Organic heavy chemicals	0.362	0.127	0.103	0.024	0.0010
47. Chemical fertilizers	−0.235	0.042	0.017	0.025	0.0102
48. Insecticides, fungicides, etc.	0.241	0.173	0.119	0.053	0.0010
49. Drugs and pharmaceuticals	0.300	0.166	0.116	0.050	0.0096
50. Soaps and glycerines	0.267	0.119	0.072	0.047	0.0024
51. Cosmetics	0.260	0.086	0.050	0.036	0.0020
52. Synthetic rubber and fibers	1.029	0.131	0.099	0.031	0.0029
53. Other chemicals	0.388	0.174	0.143	0.031	0.0047
54. Refractories	0.102	0.049	0.035	0.013	0.0037
55. Cement	0.457	0.079	0.058	0.022	0.0024
56. Other nonmetallic products	0.148	0.096	0.074	0.022	0.0101
57. Iron and steel, ferroalloys	0.134	0.113	0.093	0.020	0.0157
58. Castings and forgings	0.110	0.110	0.093	0.017	0.0013

Table 3 (concluded). India: Taxation of Inputs

Commodity	t^e	t^{diff}	t^{diffC}	t^{diffS}	Proportion of Gross Domestic Output
59. Iron and steel structures	0.557	0.141	0.123	0.018	0.0035
60. Nonferrous metals, alloys	0.171	0.101	0.084	0.017	0.0106
61. Metal products	0.170	0.114	0.098	0.017	0.0147
62. Tractors and agricultural implements	0.220	0.089	0.056	0.034	0.0024
63. Machine tools	0.228	0.125	0.099	0.026	0.0015
64. Office, domestic, and commercial equipment	0.228	0.073	0.055	0.018	0.0007
65. Other non-electrical machinery	0.163	0.134	0.120	0.014	0.0151
66. Electric motors	0.267	0.125	0.100	0.025	0.0024
67. Electrical cables and wires	0.331	0.151	0.129	0.022	0.0033
68. Batteries	0.337	0.087	0.072	0.015	0.0010
69. Household electrical goods	0.357	0.112	0.091	0.021	0.0011
70. Communications and electronic equipment	0.239	0.137	0.115	0.022	0.0022
71. Other electrical machinery	0.219	0.129	0.106	0.023	0.0065
72. Ships and boats	0.070	0.070	0.054	0.016	0.0008
73. Rail equipment	0.107	0.107	0.079	0.028	0.0046
74. Motor vehicles	0.376	0.118	0.089	0.029	0.0088
75. Motorcycles and bicycles	0.157	0.114	0.093	0.021	0.0035

		t^e	t^{diff}	t^{diffC}	t^{diffS}
76.	Other transport equipment	0.130	0.086	0.062	0.024	0.0005
77.	Watches and clocks	0.358	0.151	0.115	0.036	0.0004
78.	Miscellaneous manufacturing industries	0.360	0.111	0.094	0.017	0.0121
79.	Construction	0.065	0.065	0.043	0.022	0.0695
80.	Electricity, gas, and water supply	0.113	0.073	0.055	0.018	0.0202
81.	Railways	0.052	0.052	0.037	0.015	0.0127
82.	Other transport	0.150	0.115	0.081	0.034	0.0438
83.	Communications	0.011	0.011	0.007	0.004	0.0048
84.	Trade, storage, warehouses	0.010	0.018	0.010	0.004	0.0907
85.	Banking and insurance	0.004	0.006	0.003	0.002	0.0184
86.	Real estate, owner dwellings	0.007	0.008	0.005	0.003	0.0216
87.	Education	0.092	0.093	0.066	0.027	0.0451
88.	Medical health	0.210	0.210	0.117	0.093	0.0186
89.	Other services	0.046	0.040	0.026	0.014	0.0593

Source: Ahmad and Stern (1987).

Note: t^e = effective taxes from all sources as a proportion of the producer price

t^{diff} = $t^e - t$, where $t^e - t$ denotes the overall effective tax vector and t denotes the nominal vector of commodity taxes

t^{diffC} = $t^{eC} - t^C$, where t^{eC} denotes the effective tax from union taxes: excises, import duties, and subsidies, with t the corresponding nominal tax vector

t^{diffS} = $t^{eS} - t^S$, where t^{eS} denotes the effective state tax vector, comprising sales tax, state excises, and other taxes, and t^S denotes the equivalent nominal tax vector.

The proportion of sectoral gross value of output in total domestic output is shown in the column on the far right.

Whether export subsidies through CCS and the duty drawbacks are sufficient to provide a substantial impetus to exports cannot be determined, except on a case-by-case basis which examines not only the determinants of domestic supply but also the relationship between the ex-factory and world prices, and the foreign sources of demand. If there are costs of entry into established markets, including explicit quotas and import barriers imposed by third countries, these would be subsumed under the latter. The Dagli Committee (India, Ministry of Finance (1979)) argued that although there had been a significant increase in India's exports since 1972/73 (shown in Table 4),

> assisted exports showed a really significant increase only in the last two years, namely, 1975–76 and 1976–77, when the simple average of yearly growth rates of such exports was as much as 54 per cent, against only 16 per cent for non-assisted exports.[14]

Bagchi (1981) has questioned this view, and that of the Alexander Committee (India, Ministry of Commerce (1978)), on the grounds that the subsidies were, in fact, larger than was assumed; that a breakdown of the commodities covered under the CCS suggested that only 6 out of 22 groups had export growth rates higher than the average growth of exports of commodities not covered; and that a comparison of growth rates per se cannot lead to any firm conclusions. The Dagli Committee (India, Ministry of Finance (1979)) also correctly cautions against the duty drawbacks and export subsidies in the case of commodities in which India enjoys monopoly power, since these would only serve to turn the terms of trade against the country. In general, however, the small-country assumption is valid for most goods, and rebating the taxation of inputs merely removes the domestic bias against exports and does not necessarily imply that all commodities could, or should, be exported.

Although most taxes are liable to be evaded to some extent, the rebating of a complex structure of excises and import duties is not simple. These rebates are liable to much abuse and rent-seeking activity, and there is much anecdotal evidence that this has been the case in both India and Pakistan. In Western Europe, in particular, the principle of "border tax adjustment" permits the

---

[14]India, Ministry of Finance (1979), p. 91.

Table 4. Cash Compensatory Support (CCS) and Duty Drawback (DD) on Exports from India over 1970–71 to 1976–77

Year	f.o.b. Value of Total Exports from India	f.o.b. Value of Exports on Which CCS Exists	f.o.b. Value of Exports of Items Not Having CCS	Value of CCS Paid to Exporters	Value of DD Allowed to Exporters	Total Value of CCS and DD Received by Exporters	(3)/(2)	(5)/(3)	(7)/(3)	Yearly Growth Rate of Total Exports	Yearly Growth Rate of Assisted Exports	Yearly Growth Rate of Non-Assisted Exports
(1)	(2)	(3)	(4)	(5)	(6)	(7)	(8)	(9)	(10)	(11)	(12)	(13)
			million rupees							percent		
1970–71	15,350	3,380	11,980	410	330	740	22.0	12.1	21.9	—	—	—
1971–72	16,080	3,550	12,540	540	360	900	22.1	16.1	25.7	4.8	5.0	4.7
1972–73	19,710	4,380	15,330	620	470	1,090	22.2	14.1	25.0	22.6	23.4	22.3
1973–74	24,830	5,680	19,150	620	430	1,050	22.9	10.9	18.5	26.0	29.8	24.9
1974–75	33,290	6,500	26,790	740	600	1,340	19.5	11.7	20.6	34.0	14.4	39.9
1975–76	40,430	10,620	29,810	1,480	820	2,300	26.3	13.9	21.7	21.4	63.4	11.3
1976–77	51,340	15,270	36,070	2,400	1,000	3,400	29.7	15.7	22.3	27.0	43.8	21.0

Source: India, Ministry of Finance (1979).

refund of all indirect taxes involved in the production of export goods through the zero-rating of exports under the value-added tax (VAT). A partial VAT on manufacturing (MANVAT) was suggested for India by the Indirect Taxation Reforms Committee (the Jha Committee (India, Ministry of Finance (1978))), and a modified version has recently been introduced. A major constraint on the adoption of a full-scale VAT in India is the constitutional division of taxation powers between the federal government and the states, with the former responsible for sales taxes and the latter for customs and excises. Authorities in other countries are not so constrained, and more than 20 developing countries have now adopted variants of the VAT (Tanzi (1987)). A recent report on tax reform in Pakistan has also recommended a VAT to overcome the problems of the taxation of inputs, the unintended protection of some sectors, and the bias against exports and the rent-seeking activities associated with ad hoc tax rebates. (See Ahmad and Stern (1986 b).)

Whether there should be subsidies additional to the rebate of taxes depends on arguments which parallel the discussions relating to infant industries and which are subject to similar objections. These could also be analyzed in a game-theoretic context of retaliatory policies by trading partners and several "beggar-thy-neighbor" results can obtain. Some subsidies run afoul of General Agreement on Tariffs and Trade (GATT) rules, and accusations of dumping reinforce protectionism around the world, even among the richer OECD nations. In any case, if the social costs of export promotion exceed the social benefits, perhaps the country would be better advised to follow alternative policies.

IV. Shadow Prices and Policy

The use of shadow prices as a guide to policy and reform has been discussed briefly in Section II. Empirical estimates for India based on the Planning Commission 1979–80 inter-industry flows matrix were presented in Ahmad, Coady, and Stern (1986). Shadow prices of tradables are determined with reference to border prices. The shadow price for nontradables, in terms of the Little-Mirrlees method, is the marginal cost valued at shadow prices of an extra unit of production (discussed in Drèze and Stern (1985)), and this involves knowing the input requirements and the shadow prices of these inputs. These inputs include traded goods, nontraded goods, and factors of production; and input-output methods are used in the estimation. Table 6 in the Appendix sets out schematically the determination of endogenous shadow prices for nontradables and exportables. (The latter are endogenous in this case, since the input-output table is formulated in terms of producer prices, and nontraded margins are involved in getting the goods to the border.) The shadow prices for importables and factors are exogenously determined. (For details concerning method and limitations, see Ahmad, Coady, and Stern (1986).)

For India, different sets of shadow prices were calculated, corresponding to various assumptions concerning the classification of goods into tradables and nontradables and the valuation of factors. This corresponds to different policy options concerning trade, labor markets, and the treatment of capital goods and factors, and encompasses a range of plausible scenarios for the Indian economy. (For applications to the Pakistan economy, see Ahmad, Coady, and Stern (1984).) Table 7 in the Appendix sets out the classification of sectors into importable, exportable, and nontraded. In Case 1, 32 sectors are treated as importable at the margin, 39 as exportable, and 18 as nontradable. Case 2 treats some of the agricultural and service sectors taken as tradable in Case 1 as nontradable, and there are 36 exportable, 27 importable, and 26 nontradable sectors. In Case 3, additional manufacturing sectors are treated as nontradable, and there are 47 nontradable, 27 exportable, and 15 importable sectors. The different classifications are influenced partly by the possibility that there may be a policy change, since a relaxation of an import quota might change a good's status from nontradable to tradable, and partly by the heterogeneity of some of the sectors, which could include, for example, commodities which are importable as well as those produced domestically on the margin. Thus, a movement from Case 3 toward Case 1 could be seen as an adjustment from a restrictive to a more traded environment.

A further degree of sensitivity is introduced in the treatment of the shadow prices of factors, which represent the opportunity cost in terms of social welfare of the employment of, and the payment to, each factor. The market price of the factor can be converted to a shadow price for the type of good the factor might produce, using a standard conversion factor (SCF). Given that the numeraire is foreign exchange, the SCF may be seen as the reciprocal of the "shadow exchange rate." Alternative values have been chosen for the conversion factors for assets and labor. These are 0.75, 0.50, and 0.25 for assets; and 0.90, 0.75, and 0.50 for labor. This provides a "plausible" range for a sensitivity to alternative models of the Indian economy relating to capital and labor markets. The value of 0.75 could represent, for instance, an average value for the extent to which domestic prices exceed world prices for tradable goods and could crudely represent the SCF. In this case, using 0.75 for wages and assets would represent the assumption that wages and assumed capital costs (an 8 percent real rate of interest and given sectoral incremental capital-output ratios (ICORs)) reflect opportunity costs at market prices. With unemployed factors, opportunity costs may be lower than market prices, as is true for labor. The different combinations of conversion factors could also reflect changes in the exchange rate, and thus a wide range of policy options could be covered.

The social profitability of the 89 sectors, defined as the shadow profit divided by the shadow value of output, for a conversion factor of 0.75 for assets and the three alternatives for labor (0.90, 0.75, and 0.50) for Case 1 (the more traded option) is shown in Table 5. Nontraded sectors break even by definition. (The other sets of calculations are described in Ahmad, Coady, and Stern (1986).) Despite the sensitivity analysis involved in the widely varying valuations for factors and the alternative classification of sectors from the most restrictive set of trade policies to gradual liberalization, the results from Ahmad, Coady, and Stern (1986) suggest that a number of sectors that appeared to make a commercial loss were socially profitable across some assumptions. These include cotton textiles, jute textiles, leather footwear, metal products, and household electrical goods. On the other hand, some sectors which made a commercial profit were socially unprofitable, including plastics and synthetic rubber, petroleum products, inorganic heavy chemicals, and drugs and pharmaceuticals.

In general, agricultural and natural-resource sectors were socially profitable, as was the light-engineering sector, reflecting India's relative resource endowments. And these might be industries that would qualify for further expansion in either domestic or export

Table 5. Social Returns and Their Sensitivity to the Accounting Ratio (AR) for Labor with the AR for Assets at 0.75 (Case 1)

	Labor 0.9	Labor 0.75	Labor 0.5
1. Rice and products	0.1594	0.2233	0.3281
2. Wheat and products	0.1556	0.2125	0.3058
3. Jowar and products	0.0000	0.0000	0.0000
4. Bajra and products	0.0000	0.0000	0.0000
5. Other cereals	0.0000	0.0000	0.0000
6. Pulses	0.0000	0.0000	0.0000
7. Sugarcane	0.0000	0.0000	0.0000
8. Jute	0.1682	0.2438	0.3675
9. Cotton	0.2030	0.2689	0.3774
10. Plantations	0.1710	0.2030	0.2564
11. Other crops	0.2211	0.2899	0.4028
12. Milk and products	0.0840	0.1320	0.2119
13. Other animal husbandry products	0.0000	0.0000	0.0000
14. Forestry and logging	0.3159	0.3913	0.5127
15. Fishing	0.1967	0.2411	0.3137
16. Coal and lignite	0.1865	0.2443	0.3406
17. Petroleum and natural gas	0.2256	0.2835	0.3800
18. Iron ore	0.4551	0.4854	0.5339
19. Other minerals	0.2170	0.2713	0.3619
20. Miscellaneous food products	0.1094	0.1414	0.1929
21. Sugar	0.1635	0.2306	0.3397
22. Gur and khandsari	0.0000	0.0000	0.0000
23. Vanaspati	0.0000	0.0000	0.0000
24. Other edible oils	0.0801	0.0894	0.1051
25. Tea and coffee	0.2531	0.2743	0.3087
26. Other beverages	0.0000	0.0000	0.0000
27. Tobacco manufactures	0.1467	0.2005	0.2852
28. Cotton textiles excluding handloom and khadi	0.0859	0.1267	0.1930
29. Cotton textiles, handloom and khadi	0.1353	0.1750	0.2399
30. Woollen and silk textiles	0.3327	0.3555	0.3930
31. Artificial silk fabrics	0.5373	0.5668	0.6148
32. Jute textiles	0.0676	0.1128	0.1861
33. Readymade garments	0.1884	0.2432	0.3333
34. Miscellaneous textile products	0.2358	0.2651	0.3128
35. Carpet weaving	0.1595	0.2231	0.3250
36. Wood products	0.2687	0.3192	0.4007
37. Paper, products and newsprint	0.0640	0.1053	0.1741
38. Printing and publishing	0.1702	0.2287	0.3264
39. Leather and products	0.2239	0.2591	0.3161
40. Leather footwear	0.1153	0.1712	0.2609

Table 5. (*continued*) Social Returns and Their Sensitivity to the Accounting Ratio (AR) for Labor with the AR for Assets at 0.75 (Case 1)

		Labor	
	0.9	0.75	0.5
41. Rubber products	0.2441	0.2788	0.3346
42. Plastic and synthetic rubber	−0.1641	−0.1228	−0.0540
43. Petroleum products	−0.1187	−0.1160	−0.1116
44. Miscellaneous coal and petroleum products	0.1882	0.2180	0.2659
45. Inorganic heavy chemicals	−0.5450	−0.4784	−0.3674
46. Organic heavy chemicals	−0.3502	−0.2965	−0.2070
47. Chemical fertilizers	0.1242	0.1568	0.2112
48. Insecticides, fungicides, etc.	0.0957	0.1218	0.1654
49. Drugs and pharmaceuticals	−0.1356	−0.0972	−0.0330
50. Soaps and glycerines	0.2010	0.2302	0.2778
51. Cosmetics	0.1502	0.1706	0.2039
52. Synthetic rubber and fibers	−0.9619	−0.8775	−0.7368
53. Other chemicals	−0.0111	0.0246	0.0842
54. Refractories	0.1535	0.1969	0.2691
55. Cement	0.1418	0.1689	0.2140
56. Other nonmetallic products	0.1947	0.2460	0.3281
57. Iron and steel, ferroalloys	−0.2098	−0.1473	−0.0432
58. Castings and forgings	0.3607	0.3878	0.4316
59. Iron and steel structures	0.3208	0.3478	0.3929
60. Nonferrous metals, alloys	−0.1864	−0.1386	−0.0590
61. Metal products	0.2579	0.3063	0.3845
62. Tractors and agricultural implements	−0.4144	−0.3327	−0.1965
63. Machine tools	−0.1283	−0.0811	−0.0024
64. Office, domestic, and commercial equipment	−0.2781	−0.1820	−0.0220
65. Other non-electrical machinery	−0.3189	−0.2654	−0.1761
66. Electric motors	−0.3015	−0.2569	−0.1827
67. Electrical cables and wires	0.3439	0.3789	0.4348
68. Batteries	0.2727	0.3155	0.3844
69. Household electrical goods	0.2149	0.2657	0.3479
70. Communications and electronic equipment	−0.4373	−0.3614	−0.2350
71. Other electrical machinery	−0.6996	−0.5886	−0.4036
72. Ships and boats	−0.3514	−0.2570	−0.0997
73. Rail equipment	0.1518	0.1951	0.2651
74. Motor vehicles	0.1982	0.2376	0.3009
75. Motorcycles and bicycles	0.2132	0.2595	0.3338
76. Other transport equipment	0.1064	0.1465	0.2132
77. *Watches and clocks	−0.2563	−0.1825	−0.0596
78. Miscellaneous manufacturing industries	0.2245	0.2912	0.3974
79. Construction	0.0000	0.0000	0.0000
80. Electricity, gas, and water supply	0.0000	0.0000	0.0000

Table 5. (concluded) Social Returns and Their Sensitivity to the Accounting Ratio (AR) for Labor with the AR for Assets at 0.75 (Case 1)

	Labor		
	0.9	0.75	0.5
81. Railways	0.0000	0.0000	0.0000
82. Other transport	0.0000	0.0000	0.0000
83. Communications	0.0000	0.0000	0.0000
84. Trade, storage, warehouses	0.0000	0.0000	0.0000
85. Banking and insurance	0.2474	0.3516	0.5251
86. Real estate, owner dwellings	0.0000	0.0000	0.0000
87. Education	0.0000	0.0000	0.0000
88. Medical health	0.0000	0.0000	0.0000
89. Other services	0.1671	0.2490	0.3854

Source: Ahmad, Coady, and Stern (1986).
Notes: (i) The social returns are defined as the shadow profit divided by the shadow value of output.
(ii) Nontraded sectors break even.
(iii) The classification of sectors is given in Table 2.

markets. However, some of the heavier, mainly capital-intensive sectors displayed negative commercial and social returns, including tractors and agricultural implements, machine tools, electric motors, other non-electrical machinery, and communications equipment. This might indicate either that during the period of infancy, some of these sectors had not succeeded in reducing unit costs of production, or that quotas and licensing resulted in poor capacity utilization, reflecting the fact that "the framework of economic policies governing industrialization does not induce or permit systematic attention to costs."[15] If a case could be made that the heavy manufacturing activities were operating well below their potential levels of efficiency, then policies should be directed toward ameliorating constraints on the efficient use of existing resources. Otherwise, additional investment should be directed toward more socially profitable sectors. And the shadow prices could be used to guide import and licensing policies toward these sectors, rather than operating on a first-come, first-served or an indigenous availability basis.

---

[15] Bhagwati and Srinivasan (1975), p. 177.

Thus, the use of shadow prices is helpful in identifying the areas in which adjustments in the economy might proceed with respect to exchange rates, to policy changes reflecting changes from quotas to tariffs, or to other policy measures affecting capital or labor markets. These shadow-price calculations indicate sectors that might be encouraged, but a more detailed analysis at the commodity level would be needed to make the recommendations operational. And the previous sections of this paper have indicated which instruments might be used to carry out the adjustments.

V. Concluding Remarks

This paper has examined the approaches to trade regimes in view of the discussion relating to structural adjustment in South Asia. The literature review of Section II suggests that while there are likely to be gains from trade, neither laissez faire nor autarky emerge as desirable policy options. Section IV illustrates that under a variety of assumptions, there are several sectors in India that should be encouraged. The choice of instruments is seen, in Section III, to be particularly important, since some methods of protection are open to abuse and may have unintended consequences for other sectors of the economy. In particular, the Indian system of input taxation, which was designed to generate revenue and provide protection, has had the effect of "excessively" taxing exportables. This paper also stresses the interrelationship between different aspects of public policy, and it is only when these linkages are recognized that serious policy errors can be avoided.

Appendix

Table 6. Shadow Prices for Nontraded Goods and Exportables

		(I) Endogenous		(II) Exogenous	
		Nontradables	Exportables	Importables	Factors	f.o.b.

Nontradables margins:
$$p_1^n = p_1^n a_{11} + \ldots + p_r^n a_{r1} + \ldots + p_n^n a_{n1} + p_{n+1}^a a_{n+1,1} + \ldots + p_k^a a_{k1} + p_{k+1}^a a_{k+1,1} + \ldots + p_m^a a_{m1} + p_{m+1}^a a_{m+1,1} + \ldots + p_\ell^a a_{\ell 1} \quad 0 \ldots 0$$

$$p_r^n = p_1^n a_{1r} + \ldots + p_r^n a_{rr} + \ldots + p_n^n a_{nr} + p_{n+1}^a a_{n+1,r} + \ldots + p_k^a a_{kr} + p_{k+1}^a a_{k+1,r} + \ldots + p_m^a a_{mr} + p_{m+1}^a a_{m+1,r} + \ldots + p_\ell^a a_{\ell r}$$

$$p_n^n = p_1^n a_{1n} + \ldots + p_r^n a_{rn} + \ldots + p_n^n a_{nn} + p_{n+1}^a a_{n+1,n} + \ldots + p_k^a a_{kn} + p_{k+1}^a a_{k+1,n} + \ldots + p_m^a a_{mn} + p_{m+1}^a a_{m+1,n} + \ldots + p_\ell^a a_{\ell n} \quad 0 \ldots 0$$

Exportables:
$$p_j^a = \quad -p^t a_{rj} + \quad \ldots 0 \quad \ldots 0 \quad + p_i^{fob}$$

$p_i^n \ (i = 1, \ldots, n)$ = shadow prices of nontradables
$p_i^a \ (i = n+1, \ldots, k)$ = shadow prices of exportables (endogenously determined)
$p_i^a \ (i = k+1, \ldots, m)$ = shadow prices of importables (exogenously determined)
$p_i^a \ (i = m+1, \ldots, \ell)$ = shadow prices of factors
$p_i^{fob} \ (i = n+1, \ldots, k)$ = f.o.b. price of the ith exported good
a_{ij} = requirement of ith good per unit production of the jth good
a_{rj} = trade and transport margin for jth good

Table 7. India: Classification of Sectors[1]

Sector	Case 1	Case 2	Case 3
1. Rice and products	X	X	X
2. Wheat and products	X	N	N
3. Jowar and products	N	N	N
4. Bajra and products	N	N	N
5. Other cereals	N	N	N
6. Pulses	N	N	N
7. Sugarcane	N	N	N
8. Jute	X	N	N
9. Cotton	X	X	X
10. Plantations	M	X	N
11. Other crops	X	N	N
12. Milk and products	M	X	N
13. Other animal husbandry products	N	N	N
14. Forestry and logging	X	N	N
15. Fishing	X	N	N
16. Coal and lignite	M	M	M
17. Petroleum and natural gas	M	M	M
18. Iron ore	X	X	X
19. Other minerals	M	X	M
20. Miscellaneous food products	X	X	X
21. Sugar	X	X	X
22. Gur and khandsari	N	N	N
23. Vanaspati	N	N	N
24. Other edible oils	M	M	N
25. Tea and coffee	X	X	X
26. Other beverages	N	N	N
27. Tobacco manufactures	X	X	X
28. Cotton textiles excluding handloom and khadi	X	X	X
29. Cotton textiles, handloom and khadi	X	X	X
30. Woollen and silk textiles	X	X	X
31. Artificial silk fabrics	X	M	X
32. Jute textiles	X	X	X
33. Readymade garments	X	X	X
34. Miscellaneous textile products	X	X	X
35. Carpet weaving	X	X	X
36. Wood products	X	X	X
37. Paper, products and newsprint	M	M	M
38. Printing and publishing	M	N	N
39. Leather and products	X	X	X
40. Leather footwear	X	X	X
41. Rubber products	X	X	X
42. Plastic and synthetic rubber	M	M	M
43. Petroleum products	M	M	M
44. Miscellaneous coal and petroleum products	X	X	X
45. Inorganic heavy chemicals	M	M	M

Table 7 (concluded).   India: Classification of Sectors[1]

Sector	Case 1	Case 2	Case 3
46. Organic heavy chemicals	M	M	M
47. Chemical fertilizers	M	M	N
48. Insecticides, fungicides, etc.	M	M	M
49. Drugs and pharmaceuticals	M	X	N
50. Soaps and glycerines	X	X	X
51. Cosmetics	X	M	N
52. Synthetic rubber and fibers	M	M	M
53. Other chemicals	M	M	M
54. Refractories	M	M	N
55. Cement	M	M	N
56. Other nonmetallic products	X	X	X
57. Iron and steel, ferroalloys	M	M	M
58. Castings and forgings	X	X	X
59. Iron and steel structures	M	X	N
60. Nonferrous metals, alloys	M	X	N
61. Metal products	X	M	N
62. Tractors and agricultural implements	M	M	N
63. Machine tools	M	M	N
64. Office, domestic, and commercial equipment	M	X	N
65. Other non-electrical machinery	M	X	N
66. Electric motors	M	M	N
67. Electrical cables and wires	X	X	N
68. Batteries	X	X	X
69. Household electrical goods	X	X	X
70. Communications and electronic equipment	M	M	N
71. Other electrical machinery	M	X	M
72. Ships and boats	M	M	M
73. Rail equipment	X	X	X
74. Motor vehicles	X	M	N
75. Motorcycles and bicycles	X	X	X
76. Other transport equipment	M	M	N
77. Watches and clocks	M	M	N
78. Miscellaneous manufacturing industries	X	M	N
79. Construction	N	N	N
80. Electricity, gas, and water supply	N	N	N
81. Railways	N	N	N
82. Other transport	N	N	N
83. Communications	N	N	N
84. Trade, storage, warehouses	N	N	N
85. Banking and insurance	X	N	N
86. Real estate, owner dwellings	N	N	N
87. Education	N	N	N
88. Medical health	N	N	N
89. Other services	X	N	N

Source: Ahmad, Coady, and Stern (1986).

[1] X denotes an exported good, M an imported good, and N a nontraded good. For a discussion of Cases 1, 2, and 3, see the second paragraph of Section IV.

References

Ahmad, Ehtisham, David Coady, and Nicholas Stern, "Tax Reform, Shadow Prices, and Effective Taxes: Illustrations for Pakistan for 1975–76" (unpublished, Development Economics Research Center, University of Warwick, England, July 1984).

———, "Shadow Prices and Commercial Policy for India 1979/80" (unpublished, Development Economics Research Center, University of Warwick, England, June 1986).

Ahmad, Ehtisham, and Nicholas Stern, "Effective Taxes and Tax Reform in India" (unpublished, Development Economics Research Center, University of Warwick, England, January 1983).

———, "Theory of Reform and Indian Indirect Taxes," *Journal of Public Economics* (Amsterdam), Vol. 25 (December 1984), pp. 259–98.

——— (1986 a), "Tax Reform of Pakistan: Overview and Effective Taxes for 1975–76," *Pakistan Development Review* (Islamabad), Vol. 25 (Spring 1986), pp. 43–72.

——— (1986 b), "Analysis of Tax Reform for Developing Countries: Lessons from Research on Pakistan and India" (unpublished, Development Research Program, London School of Economics, December 1986).

———, "Alternative Sources of Government Revenue, Examples from India, 1979–80," in *The Theory of Taxation for Developing Countries*, ed. by David M.G. Newbery and Nicholas H. Stern (New York: Oxford University Press, 1987), pp. 281–332.

Bagchi, Amaresh, "Export Incentives in India: A Review," in *Change and Choice in Indian Industry*, ed. by Amiya K. Bagchi and Nirmala Banerjee (Calcutta: K.P. Bagchi, 1981), pp. 297–327.

Balassa, Bela, "Reforming the System of Incentives in Developing Countries," *World Development* (Oxford, England), Vol. 3 (June 1975), pp. 365–82.

Bell, Martin, Bruce Ross-Larson, and Larry E. Westphal, "Assessing the Performance of Infant Industries," *Journal of Development Economics* (Amsterdam), Vol. 16 (October 1984), pp. 101–28.

Bhagwati, Jagdish N., "Immiserizing Growth: A Geometrical Note," *Review of Economic Studies* (Edinburgh), Vol. 25 (June 1958), pp. 201–205.

———, "On the Equivalence of Tariffs and Quotas," in *Trade, Growth, and the Balance of Payments: Essays in Honor of Gottfried Haberler*, ed. by Robert E. Baldwin and others (Chicago: Rand McNally, 1965), pp. 53–67.

———, and Padma Desai, *India: Planning for Industrialization: Industrialization and Trade Policies Since 1951* (London: Oxford University Press, 1970).

Bhagwati, Jagdish N., and T. N. Srinivasan, *India, Foreign Trade Regimes and Economic Development*, Vol. 6 (New York: National Bureau of Economic Research, 1975).

———, "Revenue Seeking: A Generalization of the Theory of Tariffs," *Journal of Political Economy* (Chicago), Vol. 88 (December 1980), pp. 1069–87.

———, *Lectures on International Trade* (Cambridge, Massachusetts: MIT Press, 1983).

———, and Henry Wan, Jr., "Value Subtracted, Negative Shadow Prices of Factors in Project Evaluation, and Immiserizing Growth: Three Paradoxes in the Presence of Trade Distortions," *Economic Journal* (London), Vol. 88 (March 1978), pp. 121–25.

Birnberg, Thomas B., and Stephen A. Resnick, *Colonial Development: An Econometric Study* (New Haven, Connecticut: Yale University Press, 1975).

Bliss, C., "Trade and Development: Theoretical Issues and Policy Implications," in *Handbook of Development Economics*, ed. by Hollis Chenery and T.N. Srinivasan (Amsterdam: North-Holland, forthcoming).

Brecher, Richard A., and Jagdish N. Bhagwati, "Foreign Ownership and the Theory of Trade and Welfare," *Journal of Political Economy* (Chicago), Vol. 89 (June 1981), pp. 497–511.

Chakravarty, Sukhamoy, "Aspects of India's Development Strategy for the 1980s," *Economic and Political Weekly* (Bombay), Vol. 19 (May 19, 1984), pp. 845–52.

Corden, W. Max, "The Normative Theory of International Trade," in *Handbook of International Economics*, Vol. 1, ed. by Ronald W. Jones and Peter B. Kenen (Amsterdam: North-Holland, 1984), pp. 63–130.

Diamond, Peter A., and James A. Mirrlees, "Optimal Taxation and Public Production I: Production Efficiency," *American Economic Review* (Nashville), Vol. 61 (March 1971), pp. 8–27.

———, "Optimal Taxation and Public Production II: Tax Rules," *American Economic Review* (Nashville), Vol. 61 (June 1971), pp. 261–78.

Dixit, Avinash K., "International Trade Policy for Oligopolistic Industries," *Economic Journal* (London), Vol. 94 (Supplement, 1984), pp. 1–16.

———, "Tax Policy in Open Economies," in *Handbook of Public Economics*, Vol. I, ed. by Alan J. Auerbach and Martin S. Feldstein (Amsterdam: North-Holland, 1985), pp. 313–74.

———, and Victor D. Norman, *Theory of International Trade: A Dual, General Equilibrium Approach* (Welwyn, England: J. Nisbet, 1980).

Dixit, Avinash K., and Nicholas Stern, "Oligopoly and Welfare: A Unified Presentation with Applications to Trade and Development," *European Economic Review* (Amsterdam), Vol. 19 (September 1982), pp. 123–43.

Drèze, Jean, and Nicholas Stern, "The Theory of Cost-Benefit Analysis" (unpublished, Development Economics Research Center, University of Warwick, England, March 1985). This article is to be published in *Handbook of Public Economics*, Vol. II, ed. by Alan J. Auerbach and Martin S. Feldstein (Amsterdam: North-Holland, forthcoming).

Fields, Gary S., "Export-Led Growth and Labor Markets" (unpublished, Development Economics Research Center, University of Warwick, England, June 1983).

———, "Employment, Income Distribution and Economic Growth in Seven Small Open Economies," *Economic Journal* (London), Vol. 94 (March 1984), pp. 74–83.

Findlay, Ronald, "Growth and Development in Trade Models," in *Handbook of International Economics*, Vol. I, ed. by Ronald W. Jones and Peter B. Kenen (Amsterdam: North-Holland, 1984), pp. 185–236.

Helpman, Elhanan, and Assaf Razin, *A Theory of International Trade Under Uncertainty* (New York: Academic Press, 1978).

India, Ministry of Commerce, *Report of the Committee on Import-Export Policies and Procedures* (New Delhi, 1978).

———, Ministry of Commerce, *Report of the Committee on Trade Policies* (New Delhi, 1984).

———, Ministry of Finance, *Report of the Indirect Taxation Enquiry Committee* (Delhi: Controller of Publications, 1978).

———, Ministry of Finance, *Report of the Committee on Controls and Subsidies* (New Delhi, 1979).

———, Ministry of Finance, *Economic Survey 1985–86*, (New Delhi, 1986).

Islam, Nurul, *Foreign Trade and Economic Controls in Development: The Case of United Pakistan* (New Haven, Connecticut: Yale University Press, 1981).

Johnson, Harry G., "The Possibility of Income Losses from Increased Efficiency or Factor Accumulation in the Presence of Tariffs," *Economic Journal* (London), Vol. 77 (March 1967), pp. 151–54.

Jones, Ronald W., and J. Peter Neary, "The Positive Theory of International Trade," in *Handbook of International Economics*, Vol. I, ed. by Ronald W. Jones and Peter B. Kenen (Amsterdam: North-Holland, 1984), pp. 1–62.

Krueger, Anne O., "Evaluating Restrictionist Trade Regimes: Theory and Measurement," *Journal of Political Economy* (Chicago), Vol. 80 (January/February 1972), pp. 48–62.

———, "The Political Economy of the Rent-Seeking Society," *American Economic Review* (Nashville), Vol. 64 (June 1974), pp. 291–303.

———, "Trade Policies in Developing Countries," in *Handbook of International Economics*, Vol. I, ed. by Ronald W. Jones and Peter B. Kenen (Amsterdam: North-Holland, 1984), pp. 519–69.

———, and Baran Tuncer, "An Empirical Test of the Infant Industry Argument," *American Economic Review* (Nashville), Vol. 72 (December 1982), pp. 1142–52.

Lal, Deepak, *Prices for Planning: Towards the Reform of Indian Planning* (London: Heinemann, 1980).

Lewis, Stephen R., *Taxation for Development: Principles and Applications* (New York: Oxford University Press, 1984).

Lewis, W. Arthur, "The Slowing Down of the Engine of Growth," *American Economic Review* (Nashville), Vol. 70 (September 1980), pp. 555–64.

Little, I.M.D., and J.A. Mirrlees, *Project Appraisal and Planning for Developing Countries* (London: Heinemann, 1974).

Newbery, David M.G., and Joseph E. Stiglitz, *The Theory of Commodity Price Stabilization: A Study in the Economics of Risk* (Oxford, England: Clarendon Press, 1981).

Comments

Wilhelm G. Ortaliz

Through no fault of the organizers, a copy of Mr. Ahmad's paper failed to reach me before my departure. This little misfortune has, however, turned into an advantage, because it forced me to prepare my paper after sharing in yesterday's discussion, as well as this morning's very stimulating exchange. I must warn you, however, that my views are very personal and may not reflect those of my government—even my ministry—and that for the most part they are really the views of a chemist rather than an economist. Therefore, they must be treated with a lot of caution.

Import liberalization, I believe, must not be discussed as a matter of religion. High tariffs and controls on imports are instituted by governments in response to the perceived needs of certain sectors at certain points in time. Therefore, reduction of excessive and redundant protection should be neither done nor discussed without first reviewing the specifics of the products involved, the history of protection of the domestic industry, and the relevance and consistency of continued protection to the development needs of the country. The perceived need should be regularly re-examined to determine whether it is a real national need or simply a need of a specific minority group. Moreover, the cost of continued protection, particularly the cost to consumers, must also be evaluated.

The case for protection of infant industries is seemingly simple. However, in actual application, very serious economic problems are often encountered owing to the failure of governments to do the following: first, objectively scrutinize the specific nature of the alleged infancy; second, quantify the length of time for which the infancy will be tolerated; third, provide for the phasing out of the protective measures to be extended to the activity or sector during the period of infancy; and, finally, identify specific measures which should be used to directly address the factors of inputs critically responsible for such infancy.

In the Philippines, even though we started the industrialization program right after the end of World War II, there are people

REFERENCES

———, "Pareto Inferior Trade," *Review of Econom[ic Studies],* Vol. 51 (January 1984), pp. 1–12.

Ohyama, Michihiro, "Trade and Welfare in General Equ[ilibrium,] *Studies* (Tokyo), Vol. 9 (1972), pp. 37–73.

Reidel, James, "Trade as the Engine of Growth in [Developing Countries] Revisited," *Economic Journal* (London), Vol. 94 (M[arch 1984)]

Sheikh, Munir A., "Smuggling, Production and Welfare, [Journal of International] *Economics* (Amsterdam), Vol. 4 (November 1974),

Smith, M.A.M., "Intertemporal Gains from Trade," *[Journal of International] Economics* (Amsterdam), Vol. 9 (May 1979), pp. 2[39–48.]

Tanzi, Vito, "Quantitative Characteristics of the Tax S[ystems of Developing] Countries," in *The Theory of Taxation for Developing [Countries,]* ed. by M.G. Newbery and Nicholas H. Stern (New Yo[rk: Oxford University] Press, 1987), pp. 205–41.

to phase them out over time, could not be eliminated immediately. The fact that the Government's restructuring program was addressing existing market distortions and would lead eventually to a phasing out of incentives was not considered at all. The tariff reform program and the lifting of import controls and a very substantial number of other measures undertaken unilaterally by the Government of the Philippines did not count for anything. Subsequently, another U.S. case filed by the U.S. Department of Commerce against Philippine textile exports forced us to accede to the GATT code on subsidies, which led to our making very painful commitments concerning the phasing out of export incentives over a very short period. While I do not blame the U.S. Department of Commerce for anything, this painful experience has convinced me of the need to appeal to international institutions to do something to shield the restructuring efforts of developing countries from harassment, even though the international institutions are not having much success in convincing the developed countries to abolish their export subsidies and to lift their trade barriers. It is difficult enough for governments in developing countries to manage the politics of import liberalization in their own territories and to convince domestic industries that freer trade is good for the nation in the long run. These efforts should not be made even more difficult by allowing protectionist pressures in developed countries to add to the burden of governments in developing countries that are making honest efforts to reorient their economies.

In closing, allow me to apologize to Mr. Ahmad for straying very far from the topic that he covered in his paper.

Charan D. Wadhva

Dr. Ehtisham Ahmad has presented an analytical paper. It is an interesting paper which graduate students should be reading in the universities. It is technically impressive. Personally, it was enjoyable reading for me and it helped me to update my knowledge on the subject. May I begin by congratulating Professor Ahmad for giving us a very useful survey for updating our knowledge in the area of trade and development policies.

The empirical work reported in this paper is quite elaborate. It, in fact, demonstrates the usefulness of the tools of economic theory in analyzing the problems at hand.

Let us look at the main contributions of Professor Ahmad's paper.

First, in the section on the theoretical survey of the literature, the author has been able to present a reasonable overview of the major contributions on the subject. He has succeeded in juxtaposing the modern theory of international trade, particularly of tariffs and quantitative restrictions, with the modern theory of public finance. I think that in the standard literature on international trade, very little is found that integrates the two theories. He has referred to the work of Dixit and others, as well as his own and that of a number of his colleagues, in this context. Our understanding of the interface between public finance and international economics has certainly been improved by this masterly survey.

Although Professor Ahmad has concentrated on the cases of India and Pakistan, I am sure his paper has a bearing on other South Asian countries, as the paper's title indicates. We have heard from Mr. Ortaliz on the Philippine situation, which has provided new inputs on the subject. Professor Streeten has already stated that Mr. Ortaliz has brought in the central issues in the theory and practice of protection in the Philippine case. I am sure we will also have the benefit of further discussions on the experiences of other developing countries which are represented at this seminar.

I would like to make a comment on the title of Mr. Ahmad's paper. It is entitled "Trade Regimes and Export Strategies with Reference to South Asia." It should be noted that the term "strategies" can be interpreted in several ways. The only consistent strategy followed in India, for example, has been that of import substitution. Now, professors of business management—I can see Professor Muzaffer Ahmad and Professor Javed Hamid, and there must be other business economists and representatives from various industries present here—interpret the word strategy to mean something different than what Professor Ahmad implies in his academic economist's version. In this context, a basic question can be asked: Do most of the developing countries of South Asia have an export strategy at all? We often read that the governments in South Asian countries have merely undertaken certain ad hoc measures for export promotion, tinkered with certain policies, and tried to improve procedures. However, there has been no integrated comprehensive export policy at the national level in these countries. Without such a policy, an export strategy—as business economists and management experts understand the term—cannot be formulated. In fact, the economists have usually shied away from the "strategic" policy approach based on questions related to the "ins and outs": For example, what products should we be exporting? And what markets should we be in? Which export markets should we get out of? And what products should be taken out of the thrust areas of our exports? Professor Ahmad might want to get into certain interdisciplinary issues, bringing in the jargon of management, and to try to refine the concept of strategy within the framework of the choice of appropriate product-market portfolios.

Professor Ahmad has tried to remove certain fallacies. Of these, I find two quite fascinating. The first one relates to so-called export pessimism. Export pessimism, as those of us who read the literature several years ago will recall, was essentially the pessimism generated by low price elasticity of demand and low income elasticity of demand associated with the export of primary commodities. All that has changed, substantially, in recent years. Professor Ahmad might do well to bring in the new elasticity pessimism which is beginning to be felt. The concept of new elasticity pessimism should be modified to show that it arises essentially from the recognition of the interdependence of the economies of developing countries and the developed countries. The current international economic situation, however, is, as we all know, leading us to a slow-growth scenario for the developed countries. Although world trade registered an 8 percent volume gain in 1984, because of the economic growth in the United States, trade volume has since fallen flat again. The World Bank people may be recalling that they characterized the recent economic recovery in the developed countries as a hesitant recovery (or anemic recovery). There is a school of thought which holds that developed countries will now not be able to have the same kind of golden age of growth they experienced in the 1950s and 1960s. The reason for this does not lie in elasticity pessimism, but rather in the kind of structural shifts which have occurred after the second oil crisis and been manifested in the asymmetric response to oil price decreases. The fall in oil prices since 1983 is not leading to the kind of recovery that would have occurred had the response been symmetric, in the way that the response to increases in oil prices—widespread stagflation—was.

On the dynamic concept of infant-industry protection, Ahmad has put an important question to all of us: Would it be fair to say, *à la* Balassa, that a period of five to eight years is enough for infant-industry protection? I would like to suggest that it is not. This is because in the case of the developing countries, the transition to international competitiveness takes a much longer time—perhaps decades. It should also be remembered that the developing countries no longer enjoy the kind of environment that facilitated the development of competitive industries in the presently developed countries.

On one of the basic issues, I agree with Professor Ahmad that the degree of impetus given to import substitution—what we call the degree of effective protection—has been, by any economic calculation, higher in most South Asian countries than the effective degree of export subsidization. This is clear to the managers of business firms, which uniformly find it much more profitable to sell anything at home than abroad, excepting the traditional exports. Taking the case of India, we find that in certain thrust areas of nontraditional goods and in other areas where the old elasticity pessimism does not prevail, it is still much more profitable for Indian producers and units to sell at home than abroad. As long as that remains true, the current export strategy is not going to yield dividends. How to increase the relative profitability of exports is a question which Indian policymakers are still debating.

Professor Ahmad has cited several reports of expert committees. The work of these committees has been an exercise in soul-searching. It appears that we Indians excel in setting up committees and producing reports and examining each issue again and again. In addition to the excellent reports that the author has cited, there are two others that are relevant to his work. One is the Narasimhan Committee report. It deals with shifting over from physical controls to price-based (market-based) controls; and, in particular, from quotas to tariffs, about which Mr. Ortaliz has spoken in the Phillippine context. The Narasimhan Committee's main recommendation is clear: the Indian economy must move away from quantitative restrictions and toward greater use of the price mechanism. The second relevant report is called the *Report of the Technical Group on Central Excise Tariff*, which was published in 1986. I was a member of this technical group. When working with bureaucrats, I found that it was important to discover how, having fully understood economics, they were able to say that economics would not work. It was fascinating, personally, for me to learn why the bureaucrats preferred *specific* rates to *ad valorem* rates, although the public finance literature has, from the beginning, made it clear that, from an economic angle, ad valorem rates are better than specific rates. The reasons given are not just administrative—ease of collection of taxes. I did find that, in practice, it was easier to curb evasion and nonreporting when rates were specific. Specific tax rates are effectively applied in the case of several commodities in India.

To bring this system nearer to economic logic, we need periodically to revise the rates to take care of both inflation and value accounting. This procedure can be adopted in case of specific duties on the import side, too. The Technical Group examined only the excise side. The manufacturing value-added tax (MANVAT) has now been given the new name of modified value-added tax (MODVAT), to which Professor Ahmad has made a reference. This meets his principal criterion that duties on raw materials and semiprocessed goods should be nearly zero, with as many of the duties as possible put on manufactured goods. The Government of India has also simplified the excise structure into six or seven categories. Once these changes are implemented, we will no longer have too many rates and the resulting mess.

Let me turn to the main findings the paper includes, particularly those in the preview of the work by Ahmad and Stern that is to be published next year.[1] I regard it as a classic work on this subject. The authors of that work have drawn some major policy inferences for the consideration of Indian policymakers. I would like to know from Mr. Ahmad how much selling of these findings has been

---

[1] "Alternative Sources of Government Revenue, Examples from India, 1979–80," in *The Theory of Taxation for Developing Countries*, ed. by David M. G. Newbery and Nicholas H. Stern (New York: Oxford University Press), pp. 281–332. This book was (subsequently) published in 1987.

undertaken and how much buying has taken place in dealings with the concerned policymakers. Particularly on the matter of buying, it would be useful to know what aspects of the authors' suggestions were not acceptable. I see that Shankar Acharya from the Ministry of Finance has already left but K.L. Deshpande of the Reserve Bank of India is here. I expect that the Finance Ministry would be glad to see the calculations produced by Mr. Ahmad (and his colleagues). In the first instance, all of us have been saying in international forums that we do not oversubsidize our exports. We try to take shelter under our messy taxation structure, for which even Indian researchers cannot calculate the effective rate of subsidy. Professor Ahmad's findings are revealing: there is no oversubsidization, and the level of cash compensatory support, which was earlier damned as a cash subsidy or cash support, turns out in many cases to be lower than the tax rates he has worked out through the input-output mechanism. Of course, the input-output mechanism he used was the 1979–80 framework, which was then the latest available to researchers. Professor Ahmad may be aware that S.P. Gupta of the Planning Commission has recently constructed even capital-goods matrices for the Indian economy. You [Professor Ahmad] also have. One can now compare them. These developments are not taken into account in the calculations presented by you. [Professor Ahmad (in reply): We have constructed capital matrices, but we did not want to present these calculations.]

Professor Ahmad has given us a preview of 1986's publication, but not one of 1987's.

Furthermore, in terms of the results generated, it is quite amazing to find that there are three classes: one, for which commercial and social returns justify our thrust into various kinds of protection, and two others, for which they do not. You have a number of products and sectors that appear to make losses yet are considered socially profitable. You also have identified certain sectors which are commercially profitable and yet are considered socially unprofitable. These kinds of calculation are bound to produce considerable food for thought.

Let us understand some of the limitations of the findings of Professor Ahmad and associates under the circumstances. First is the reliability of the data base which any researcher, including Professor Ahmad, has to use. The researcher must use what is produced by the Central Statistical Office, the Planning Commission, or whatever authority. The second limitation is the reliability of results after time has passed and the economy has undergone several changes. In fact, this is a major problem, and Professor Ahmad has always said as much. The third limitation is, of course, the attitude of the government: whether its policymakers will take decisions based solely on economic criteria while facing several pressure groups—a point Professor Ahmad has brought out extremely well. His discussions of rent seeking versus revenue seeking and of different sources of perpetuation of interest groups are very illuminating. The Government of India itself has become a determined revenue seeker, in order to meet development needs. In fact, the usual mandate given to the study groups appointed by the Government on tax reforms is to ensure that revenues do not go down as a result of the proposed reforms. This indicates the attachment of the Government to the objective of revenue seeking. In any case, more and more revenues will always be needed for development finance.

Professor Ahmad's paper makes a visibly excellent contribution in the areas of tax policy on internationally traded goods. The question really is whether policy planners would, in fact, wait for results from such studies before taking decisions. Even if such studies cannot be updated as frequently as would be desirable, the basic findings of the study by Ahmad and associates are unlikely to be changed dramatically in the short run. At least the direction indicated by the paper for reforms is very clear, and deserves fullest consideration by the policymakers.

To conclude, let us ask ourselves: Where does Mr. Ahmad lead us? What I found from his study was essentially a reconfirmation of the view that India's comparative advantage lies in agricultural products rather than capital-intensive products. In fact, this is not necessarily the case. Mr. Zaman and others have discussed the Korean example. How many people have made decisions concerning economic development based on their country's so-called comparative advantage in terms of historical facts or in terms of existing factor endowments? Comparative advantage is no longer just cost-of-production advantage. We have now learned about comparative marketing advantage and the role of nonprice factors, which obviously will, to a considerable extent, be kept outside the framework of studies such as the one under discussion. I would therefore like to see some work done by economists on these non-price aspects of comparative advantage. Professor Ahmad has made a plea for the undertaking of disaggregated studies, because aggregates essentially hide reality. I fully agree. In response, we would like to ensure that Professor Ahmad's methodology and approach can be usefully applied in research work at the Indian Council for Research on International Economic Relations (ICRIER). We at ICRIER are undertaking a comparative study of the potential international competitiveness of six Indian industries. Four of them are engineering, machine tools, bicycles, and four-wheeled (commercial) vehicles; and the other two are non-engineering products: soaps, cosmetics, and detergents; and drugs and pharmaceuticals. The issues involved in these studies are precisely of the kind that Professor Ahmad has posed, and we would very much like to learn something from his work. ICRIER may seek his help on these disaggregated studies.

The work of Professor Ahmad and his colleagues is of great relevance to the current trade-policy debates in India on both export promotion and import substitution. The basic issue of trade-policy liberalization, which will be discussed in several forums, is essentially as follows: On what items shall we cut tariffs, and to what level? On what items shall we reintroduce tariffs? I think we can learn something about the optimal-tariff argument from Professor Ahmad's work. I hope that, following the example of the setting-up of the Technical Group on Central Excise Tariff, one day very soon a Technical Group on Customs will be set up to recommend appropriate changes in the structure of tariffs.

The Government of India has been thinking of identifying selected thrust areas in our export promotion strategy at the disaggregated level. In marketing jargon, this exercise relates to identifying an optimal product portfolio and market portfolio for our exports. Here again, the social costs and social benefits of such an exercise must be explicitly calculated. It will not suffice to say that we will stop subsidizing as soon as the incremental social costs of export promotion equal the incremental social benefits. Obviously, such an exercise has to be undertaken at a disaggregated level, and here the expertise of Professor Ahmad and his colleagues would be worth drawing upon.

Finally, we want to learn more from the Asian setting. That is what this seminar is all about. While there are dissimilarities between the economy of India and other Asian economies, there are also many similarities. I hope these deliberations will generate enough material to give us some idea of what these similarities are and thus enable us to learn more from each other's experiences in the area of trade policy.

5
Structural Adaptation and Public Enterprise Performance
V. V. Bhatt

The most important change that has occurred in the developed as well as the developing countries since the Second World War is that in the role of the state. Previously, the state had played an active role in facilitating economic development in the various developed countries (Bhatt (1960)), but development had not been the overriding objective of economic and social policy. Now, the state has assumed direct responsibility for full employment and growth in the developed countries and for initiating and sustaining the process of rapid development in the developing countries.

Since the developing countries are faced with structural imbalances, the state has been engaged in the process of structural change or adaptation (which is what development, in contrast to growth, implies) and has been using, apart from other policy instruments, public enterprises as an instrument for that purpose. The role of public enterprises (engaged in the production and distribution of goods and services), hence, is obviously greater, from the point of view of their share in national as well as public investment, than it is in the developed countries.

However, except for the socialist countries, the pattern of public enterprises does not differ very much between the developed and the developing countries, and even among the developing countries. They operate largely in infrastructure, such as transport, communications, power, and financial institutions; these are the sectors that have external economies. They also operate in strategic industries like telecommunications, steel, fertilizers, mining, motor vehicles, petrochemicals, and electronics; these industries have long gestation lags, are capital-intensive, use sophisticated technology, and are significant from the development point of view (Ayub and Hegstad (1986)). In these sectors, in some countries, there were already some private enterprises, and one of the reasons for the establishment of public enterprises was to create a competitive environment for the private sector monopolies. The differences in the actual public enterprise pattern in different countries arise largely as a result of differences in the size of the country, its stage of development, its initial situation, and its resource endowments. Thus, the public enterprise pattern in India, with a "socialistic pattern," for example, is *not* basically different from that of the Republic of Korea with a private enterprise ideology (Jones and Mason (1982)).

Of course, the lack of an entrepreneurial-managerial tradition and skills has also induced the state to have public enterprises in such fields as cement and textiles, which could have been cultivated by the private sector, if it had had the required tradition and experience. Further, nationalization of foreign enterprises or sick enterprises in the private sector has also been instrumental in the growth of the public enterprise system. And finally, purely ideological and political factors have been operative in some countries.

The initial rationale for public enterprises in developing countries was not only to create a favorable environment for rapid development through the provision of key inputs and services to the public sector as well as the nongovernmental enterprises but also to generate investable surpluses; private profits would be used partly for conspicuous consumption, while the entire public enterprise profits could be mobilized for financing public sector investment.

The actual performance of public enterprises, however, has not been good, not only from the purely financial point of view but also from the point of view of the effective and efficient supply of key inputs and services to the economy. The governments of the developing countries did not realize, in the initial stages, the urgency for an appropriate institutional and policy framework for decision making relating to public enterprises. There was a lack of recognition of the problems relating to management, technology choice and development, and the financing pattern; there was a sort of feeling that these problems would not be serious, and that civil servants could manage the enterprises as efficiently as private entrepreneurs. There was not much appreciation of the role of the entrepreneurial-managerial function in the process of economic development.

In spite of this relatively poor overall performance, it must be recognized that the public enterprise did play a vital role in initiating the process of development in general and of industrial development in particular. Hence, the unsatisfactory performance of the public enterprise system as a whole was not seen by policymakers as a significant constraint in the initial two decades of the 1950s and 1960s. Until 1973, the developing countries experienced fairly high growth rates, and the international environment was quite favorable for the expansion of trade and for net resource inflow from abroad.

However, since 1973, the development pace has stagnated in all countries, developing as well as developed, because of several exogenous shocks, as well as inadequate policy response to what Peter Drucker (1986) calls a changed world economy. The resource constraint, as a result, became very severe. The net resource inflow from abroad has been diminishing, the payments problems have become acute, and the governments have been faced with a critical shortage of financial resources in their requirements for sustaining the pace of public sector development.

To regain the development momentum, it is thus essential for the developing countries to restructure their policies with a view to overcoming this resource constraint and adapting creatively to the increased uncertainty in the international economic environment.

In this context, the instrument of the public enterprise system needs to be sharpened for promoting and accelerating the process of viable and effective import substitution, export promotion, technological self-reliance, and the generation of investable surpluses. For this purpose, it is essential to develop a partnership—instead of the current adversary relationship—between public enterprises and private, cooperative, and family enterprises; between controlling ministries and top management of public enterprises; and between top management of public enterprises and professional, technical, and other employees of public enterprises. The top management of a public enterprise needs to assume the role of a leader of a team with the vision to create an identity of purpose and convergence of expectations among the team members to facilitate the processes of participative decision making, creative adaption to the changing environment, and continuous improvement in the capabilities of the team members. The successful public enterprises have been those in which the top management has performed such a leadership function. Thus, the institutional and policy framework for decision structures and processes relating to public enterprises needs to be restructured. The need for such restructuring is realized even in socialist countries like China and Hungary (Balassa (1986) and Kornai (1985)). This paper seeks to indicate in general terms the institutional and policy framework essential for the effective and efficient functioning of the public enterprise system.

Section I deals with the size and performance of the public enterprises and indicates how their poor financial performance has created a resource problem for the governments. This resource constraint has been accentuated since 1973 because of developments in the world economy, which are the theme of Section II. Some detailed studies of successful public enterprises are mentioned in Section III. Based on these studies, tentative generalizations—conjectures—relating to the strategic factors and in particular the decision structures and processes that account for good public enterprise performance are presented in the subsequent sections. Section IV deals with the decision framework, while Section V deals with the motivational and inducement mechanisms. The impact of distributional pressures on decision making is discussed in Section VI, and the role of ideology in Section VII. Some concluding observations are provided in Section VIII.

I. Size and Performance

The size of the public enterprise sector appears to be directly related to the degree of relative economic backwardness of a country or a region.[1] The share of the public enterprise sector in gross fixed capital formation, industrial investment, and industrial gross domestic product (GDP) is much higher in developing countries than it is in the developed countries (Table 1). Among the developing

---

[1] The role of public enterprises is indicated by some authors by relating nonfinancial state-owned enterprise shares in gross domestic product (GDP) at factor cost. This index is misleading, since the share of agriculture in GDP is quite high in the developing countries. The generalization based on this index about the relative roles of the public enterprise sector in the developing and the developed countries is, hence, not valid.

Table 1. Size of Public Enterprise Sector[1]

Regions/Countries	Share in GDP at Factor Cost	Share in Gross Fixed Capital Formation	Share in Industrial GDP	Share in Industrial Investment
		Percent		
World (*average*)	9.5	13.4	35.6	53.0
Industrial countries (*average*)	9.6	11.1	22.5	27.2
Developing countries (*average*)	8.6	27.0	42.1	65.9
Africa	17.5	32.4	—	—
Asia	8.0	27.7	—	—
Western Hemisphere	6.6	22.5	—	—
Asian developing countries				
India (1978)	10.3	33.7	35.0	75.0
Pakistan (1974–75)	6.0	33.3	26.0	50.0
Republic of Korea (1974–77)	6.4	25.1	—	—
Philippines (1974–77)	1.7	9.5	—	—
Sri Lanka (1974)	9.9	15.7	—	—
Thailand (1970–73)	3.6	8.5	—	—

Sources: For columns 1 and 2: Robert H. Floyd, Clive S. Gray, and R. P. Short, *Public Enterprise in Mixed Economies: Some Macroeconomic Aspects* (Washington: International Monetary Fund, 1984), pp. 116–22.

For columns 3 and 4: International Bank for Reconstruction and Development staff estimates; International Bank for Reconstruction and Development, *World Development Report, 1985* (Washington, 1985); United Nations Industrial Development Organization, papers presented at the Expert Group Meeting on the Changing Role and Function of the Public Industrial Sector in Development, Vienna, October 5–9, 1981; and Ayub and Hegstad (1986), Table SA-2, p. 77.

Note: Data are incomplete and not strictly comparable. For inadequacies of data, see the sources quoted above.
[1] GDP denotes gross domestic product.

Table 2. Overall Balance of Public Enterprises[1]

Region/Country	Operating Surplus/ Deficit Before Depreciation and Subsidies	Overall Surplus/ Deficit	Budgetary Burden of Public Enterprises
	Percentage of GDP at market prices		
World (*average*)	1.0	−2.0	2.2
Industrial countries (*average*)	0.5	−1.7	1.6
Developing countries (*average*)	3.8	−3.9	3.3
Africa	2.8	−3.1	3.8
Asia	3.5	−5.6	3.6
Western Hemisphere	3.3	−2.5	1.7
Asian developing countries			
India (1978)	3.6	−6.2	5.5
Republic of Korea (1978–80)	—	−5.2	0.5
Thailand (1978–79)	—	−2.0	0.2
Pakistan (1978–81)	—	—	3.2
Sri Lanka (1978–80)	—	—	11.3

Source: Robert H. Floyd, Clive S. Gray, and R.P. Short, *Public Enterprise in Mixed Economies: Some Macroeconomic Aspects* (Washington: International Monetary Fund, 1984).

Note: Data are incomplete and not strictly comparable. For inadequacies of data, see the source quoted above.

[1] Minus signs indicate deficit figures. GDP denotes gross domestic product.

countries, the share of the public enterprise sector in gross fixed capital formation is highest in Africa and is higher in Asia than in the Western Hemisphere; among the Asian countries, this share is higher in India and Pakistan than in the Republic of Korea, Thailand, and the Philippines. This pattern supports Gerschenkron's (1962) thesis about the relationship between the role of the state and the relative backwardness of a country.

Partly because of its poor financial performance, the public enterprise sector has an overall deficit; it does not generate adequate revenues to finance its capital expenditures. These deficits are financed through the government budget, and the bugetary burden of the public enterprise sector is almost twice as high in the developing countries as in the developed countries (Table 2). This budgetary burden is highest in Africa and is higher in Asia than in the Western Hemisphere; among the Asian countries, it is much higher in India and Pakistan than in the Republic of Korea or Thailand (Tables 2 and 3). This again illustrates the inverse

Table 3. Share of Public Enterprise Savings in Public Enterprise Capital Formation
(percentage)

Country	1980–83
India	5.6[1]
Republic of Korea	25.4[2]
Sri Lanka	26.4
Thailand	5.6

Source: United Nations, Economic and Social Commission for Asia and the Pacific, *Economic and Social Survey of Asia and the Pacific, 1984* (Bangkok, 1985).
[1] 1980 only.
[2] Average for 1980–81 only.

Table 4. Profitability of Industrial Enterprises by Subsector, 1984[1]
(In percent)

Subsector	Public Enterprises	Private Enterprises
Mining	7.4	15.5
Petroleum	3.8	4.4
Tobacco	1.8	8.5
Chemicals	1.6	3.5
Aerospace	0.9	2.9
Electronics	0.4	3.6
Steel and metal manufacturing	−3.8	0.7
Motor vehicles	−5.7	3.3
Weighted average for all of above	1.7	4.0

Source: "The 500 Largest Corporations Outside the U.S.," *Fortune* (New York), Vol. 112 (August 19, 1985), pp. 182–211.
[1] Relating to the 500 largest non-U.S. companies on the *Fortune* list for 1985.

relationship between the stage of relative development of a country and the intensity of its resource constraint.

Public enterprises in both the developed and the developing countries generally have good financial performance in the mining and petroleum sectors; their worst performance is in steel and metal manufacturing and the motor vehicle sectors (Table 4). Their performance is not as good as that of the private enterprises in comparable sectors.

Of course, the performance criteria of public enterprises, particularly in the developing countries, cannot be the same as those for private enterprises for several reasons. First, unlike private enterprises, they have an *instrumental* role. Second, quite often there are no comparable private enterprises in terms of size, structure, technology, and product mix in the domestic private sector. Third, the rationale for having these enterprises in the public sector is partly the lack of experience in the country with regard to the management of new complex enterprises based on sophisticated technology; thus, they represent, in part at least, investment in learning. Nonetheless, it is true that the failure of the public enterprise sector to generate investable surpluses is adversely affecting the pace and pattern of socioeconomic development in the developing countries; as a result, these countries are facing a severe resource constraint, and the governments are unable to cope with the large budget deficits.

II. Resource Constraint in Context of Recent Global Trends

Since 1973, resource constraint has become more severe. The annual average rate of growth of GDP of all developing countries was 4.5 percent during 1951–60, 5.6 percent during 1961–70, and 6.3 percent during 1971–73. These growth rates were attained largely through domestic saving performance; the saving rate as a proportion of GDP rose from 12.8 percent during 1951–60 to more than 17 percent during 1961–73. External resources did not finance more than 11–12 percent of gross investment and amounted to only 2–3 percent of GDP during 1961–73 (Table 5).

For historical perspective, it is interesting to observe that, even during a relatively more advanced stage of development and with higher per capita incomes, during 1861–90 the present-day developed countries had an average saving rate (12–13 percent) which was significantly lower than that of all developing countries during 1961–70 and was more or less equal to the saving rate of the low-income developing countries during 1961–70; further, the GDP growth rate of these developed countries (1861–90) was roughly

Table 5. Saving, Investment, and Growth Rates, 1951–73[1]
(In percent)

	1951–60	1961–70	1971–73
All developing countries			
Growth rate of GDP (*annual average*)	4.5	5.6	6.3
Gross investment/GNP	14.9	19.2	20.8
Investment financing			
National saving/GNP	12.8	18.4	19.3
Net resource inflow/GNP	2.1	1.4	1.7
Middle-income developing countries			
Growth rate of GDP (*annual average*)	—	5.8	5.9
Gross investment/GDP	—	20.05	21.60
Investment financing			
Domestic saving/GDP	—	18.78	19.86
Net resource inflow/GDP	—	1.28	1.76
Low-income developing countries			
Growth rate of GDP (*annual average*)	—	5.0	1.9
Gross investment/GDP	—	16.98	15.69
Investment financing			
Domestic saving/GDP	—	14.69	13.84
Net resource inflow/GDP	—	2.29	1.85

Sources: For 1951–60, United Nations, *Statistical Yearbook* (New York), various issues; for 1961–73, all developing countries, International Bank for Reconstruction and Development (World Bank), *Annual Report, 1975* (Washington, 1975); and for 1961–74, middle- and low-income developing countries, World Bank Data System.

[1] GDP denotes gross domestic product, GNP gross national product.

half the growth rate of even the low-income developing countries (1961–70) (Kuznets (1966), Goldsmith (1969)).

However, the development pace of the developing countries slackened after 1973 because of a conjunction of several exogenous factors: (a) a violent boom breaking into an equally violent recession in the developed countries, accompanied by a breakdown of the old international monetary system during the early 1970s; (b) the simultaneous occurrence of crop failures in many parts of the world, causing a world food crisis during 1972–75; (c) a sudden and sharp rise in oil prices in 1973 and again in 1979–80; (d) sudden and sharp declines in food output owing to severe drought in sub-Saharan Africa in the early 1980s; and (e) a prolonged recession in the developed countries in 1981–83. As a result of the combined impact of all these factors and the inadequacies in their domestic policies, the pace of development faltered in all developing countries during 1973–80 and slackened considerably after 1980; the growth rate was 5.4 percent during 1973–80 and only 3–4 percent thereafter. The impact on sub-Saharan Africa was much more severe; there was hardly any increase in per capita income during 1973–80, and there was an actual decline in living standards after that period. The decline in per capita income in Latin America and the Caribbean after 1980 was even greater. In Asia, the impact was much less severe than in the other regions (Table 6).

In spite of such slackening in the pace of development, the developing countries were able to maintain fairly high saving and investment rates up to 1980; thereafter, the rates declined. In the low-income African countries, the saving rate declined significantly after 1973.

The investment rates were more or less maintained at fairly high levels up to 1981 with increased external borrowing; the net resource inflow into the developing countries increased from about 1 percent of GDP in 1973 to 2.3 percent in 1980 and 3.2 percent in 1981. Since then, the net resource inflow has been declining and was negative in 1984. In the low-income countries of Asia, the net resource inflow declined from 3 percent of GDP to 2.2 percent in 1984.

Because of the heavy burden of external debt, the external debt-service ratio increased to about 20 percent in 1984 for the developing countries as a whole. In the low-income Asian countries, the external debt-service ratio increased only moderately—from 8 percent in 1980 to 8.4 percent in 1984 (Table 7).

For the next several years, it is unlikely that there will be any net resource inflow into the developing countries; in all likelihood, there will be a reverse flow because of interest payments and debt repayments. In Asian countries, too, the net resource inflow as a proportion of GDP is likely to decline (Bhatt (1986)).

The resumption and acceleration of the pre-1973 momentum of development, thus, would critically depend on the development in the world economy and improvement in the saving, import-substitution, and export performance of the developing countries generally and of the Asian countries in particular. In this context, it is essential to improve the performance of the public enterprise sector; this is the sector that has a large share in gross domestic capital formation, industrial investment, and industrial output. It

Table 6. Growth of GDP and GNP per Capita, 1965–85[1]
(Annual percentage change)

	1965–73	1973–80 (Average)	1981	1982	1983	1984 (Estimated)	1985 (Projected)
All developing countries							
Growth rate of GDP	6.6	5.4	3.5	2.0	2.0	5.4	4.3
Growth rate of GNP per capita	4.1	3.2	1.0	−0.7	0.0	3.3	2.4
Low-income countries							
Growth rate of GDP	5.6	4.7	5.0	5.3	7.8	9.4	7.8
Growth rate of GNP per capita	3.0	2.7	3.0	3.2	6.1	7.4	6.1
Low-income countries, Asia							
Growth rate of GDP	5.9	5.0	5.4	5.7	8.6	10.2	8.3
Growth rate of GNP per capita	3.3	3.0	3.5	3.7	6.9	8.3	6.6
Low-income countries, East Asia and Pacific							
Growth rate of GDP	8.6	8.1	6.5	3.9	6.4	6.4	2.7
Growth rate of GNP per capita	5.7	5.7	3.9	1.8	4.7	4.7	1.0
Low-income countries, Africa							
Growth rate of GDP	3.9	2.7	1.6	0.8	0.3	0.7	2.1
Growth rate of GNP per capita	1.2	0.1	−1.3	−2.4	−2.7	−2.8	−0.4
Middle-income oil importers							
Growth rate of GDP	7.0	5.6	2.0	0.8	0.7	3.3	—
Growth rate of GNP per capita	4.6	3.1	−0.8	−2.0	−1.6	1.1	—
Middle-income countries, Latin America and Caribbean							
Growth rate of GDP	7.1	5.4	−1.0	−1.5	−1.7	3.7	4.1
Growth rate of GNP per capita	4.5	2.9	−4.2	−4.9	−4.5	1.2	2.1

Source: International Bank for Reconstruction and Development, *World Development Report, 1986* (Washington, 1986).
[1] GDP denotes gross domestic product, GNP gross national product.

Table 7. Savings, Investment, Resource Inflows, and Debt Indicators, 1980–84

(Percentage of GNP [1] unless otherwise indicated)

	1980	1981	1982	1983	1984
All developing countries					
Investment	26.7	26.0	24.6	22.9	22.3
Saving	24.4	22.8	21.9	22.0	23.1
Net resource inflow	2.3	3.2	2.7	0.9	−0.8
External debt/exports *(percent)*	89.8	96.8	115.0	130.8	135.4
External debt-service ratio *(percent)*	16.0	17.6	20.5	19.0	19.7
Low-income countries, Asia					
Investment	27.2	25.4	25.7	26.1	26.5
Saving	24.2	23.2	24.2	24.5	24.3
Net resources inflow	3.0	2.2	1.5	1.6	2.2
External debt/exports *(percent)*	96.7	89.5	95.1	98.9	100.0
External debt-service ratio *(percent)*	8.0	9.3	10.9	8.3	8.4
Low-income countries, Africa					
Investment	19.2	18.5	16.9	15.3	11.8
Saving	9.0	8.4	6.9	7.2	4.3
Net resource inflow	10.2	10.1	10.0	8.1	7.5
External debt/exports *(percent)*	175.8	216.5	260.6	279.5	278.1
Debt service/exports *(percent)*	12.5	13.8	15.7	16.5	19.9

Source: International Bank for Reconstruction and Development, *World Development Report, 1985* and *1986* (Washington, 1985 and 1986).

[1] GNP denotes gross national product.

is this sector, therefore, that has to contribute to viable import substitution, export promotion, technological development, and generation of investable surpluses. The development of the nongovernmental sectors depends critically on the effectiveness and efficiency of the public enterprise sector. Hence, it is essential to *restructure* the institutional and policy framework for decision making relating to the public enterprise sector as a whole, with a view to making it an effective engine for socioeconomic development.

III. Case Studies of Successful Public Enterprises

In what directions the institutional and policy framework needs to be restructured can be inferred from the experience of successful public enterprises. Though the overall financial performance of the public enterprise sector as a whole is not that good, there are some enterprises in almost all the countries, developed and developing, that have been very effective and efficient in the attainment of their objectives. However, there have not been many in-depth studies of such enterprises linking the decision structures and processes relating the public enterprises to their performance (Bhatt (1984)). Whatever studies are available show that

(a) public enterprises can be quite successful, and sometimes their performance can be more or less similar to that of the private enterprises *functioning in a similar context*;

(b) they can be innovative in technology as well as product improvement; and

(c) with regard to price and quality, they can be competitive in international markets.

These studies relate to the following enterprises in Asian countries: Hindustan Machine Tools Ltd., India (Ramachandra (1985)); Swaraj Tractor, India (Bhatt (1978)); and Pohang Iron and Steel Co. Ltd., Republic of Korea (Kim (1986)). In addition, there are the following detailed studies of quick turnarounds of sick public enterprises: The Pakistan Industrial Development Corporation (Mufti (1982)); Bharat Pumps and Compressors, India (Khandwalla (1981)); Bharat Heavy Plate and Vessels, India (Khandwalla (1981)); Richardson and Cruddas, India (Khandwalla (1981)); Burn Standard, India (Khandwalla (1985)); and Travancor Cochin Chemicals, India (Khandwalla (1985)).

Similarly, there have been a few detailed studies of enterprises in Latin American countries. There is a comparative study of Corporación Venezolana de Guayana, Venezuela, and Companhía Vale do Rio Doce, Brazil (Escobar (1982)). There are some less detailed studies of public enterprises in Africa. For example, there are studies of Tanzanian Electric Supply Company Ltd., Kenya Tea Development Authority, and Ethiopian Telecommunication Authority (International Bank for Reconstruction and Development (1983)).

On the basis of these studies of successful public enterprises, it is possible to make some tentative generalizations—conjectures—concerning the strategic factors and in particular the decision structures and processes that account for good public enterprise performance. These studies show that there is no inherent reason why the performance of public enterprises—which is often impaired by ineffectiveness and inefficiency—in attaining their major goals has to be poor, provided certain key decision mechanisms are institutionalized.

IV. Decision Framework and Performance

The distinguishing characteristics of a public enterprise are (a) the sharing of top management functions between the government and the enterprise and (b) the lack of intensity of pressure or compulsion exerted by market forces for efficient and effective performance as a result of the possibility of covering losses through the government budget. It is, however, possible to provide substitute mechanisms—"substitutes for missing prerequisites," to use the expressive phrase of Gerschenkron (1962)—for effective decision making in public enterprises, as shown by the case studies of successful enterprises. What, then, are these substitute mechanisms that need to be institutionalized?

1. Top Management and Enterprise Performance

The crucial determinant of enterprise performance is the nature, quality, and style of top management. The survival and growth of an enterprise depends critically on how its functioning is adapted to the changing task, and the regulatory and general environment. An effective top management can turn constraints into opportunities and thus, while adapting to a changing environment, can also make the environment adapt to its goals and objectives. It regards constraints, including those that originate in the government regulatory framework, as variables and not as parameters. The process of selecting top management (including the Board of Directors) thus assumes strategic significance.

It is thus essential to institutionalize the selection process so that purely political and bureaucratic influences are minimized; the process needs to be *depoliticized* and *debureaucratized*. India, for example, has set up a Public Enterprises Selection Board for this purpose.

At the same time, the existing top management team should deliberately groom its successors to ensure continuity and stability of enterprise functioning. In fact, one of the yardsticks to evaluate top management performance should be its ability and willingness to groom its successors. Except in a crisis-like situation, the top management team should be selected from within the enterprise.

Such grooming is not possible without a well-planned strategy of training managers at all levels—in the enterprise as well as in good management training centers. The management training centers cannot be effective in their training function unless they also undertake management consultancy and research. Further, they would not be effective without the active support and cooperation of public enterprise managers. Very few management institutes in the developing countries have specialized in public enterprise management; one of them is the Indian Institute of Management in Ahmedabad. The Economic Development Institute of the World Bank added this theme to its agenda in 1982, and it has collaborated so far in organizing two-week seminars on public enterprise management with the Industrial Development Bank of India, the Indian Institute of Management, the International Center for Public Enterprises in Developing Countries (Ljubljana, Yugoslavia), and the Eastern and Southern African Management Institute.

2. Sharing Top Management Functions: Government-Enterprise Relationship

The effectiveness of top management is enhanced if the regulatory framework provides mechanisms for a creative dialogue between the government and the enterprise management on the top management tasks that they share. These tasks or functions relate to (a) translation of high-level goals into operative goals that are attainable and in terms of which performance can be measured; (b) monitoring performance in terms of the operative goals; and (c) altering the operative goal mix and the strategy, and even the top management structure, in the light of the feedback received from such monitoring.

Such a dialogue should be initiated by the enterprise, since it has much better information and a feel for the enterprise's functioning. The enterprise management should be able to formulate the operative goals as well as a corporate strategy and plan in terms of which its performance can be measured. The administrative ministry or a sectoral holding company in that case would have a sound basis for suggesting alterations in the enterprise plan in the light of the government development objectives and strategy. As a result of such a creative dialogue between the enterprise and the government (administrative ministry or holding company), it would be possible for them to agree on the operative goals, strategy, and performance criteria, as well as mutual obligations and commitments. Of course, the government should have adequate professional competence for that purpose. Pakistan, for example, created, in 1981, an Expert Advisory Cell in the Ministry of Production.

The administrative or sectoral ministry, however, would not be able to enter into such a dialogue from the point of view of the public enterprise system as a whole and in the light of the overall national development objectives and strategy, unless there were a central coordinating body or a focal point to provide clear guidelines and criteria to the ministry. Thus, there is a need for such a central body that has the expertise and competence to view the public enterprise system as a whole in the context of the national development objectives and strategy. Such a focal point needs to be located in the office of the head of the state—prime minister or president—to invest it with the authority it requires.

India, for example, set up the Bureau of Public Enterprises (Trivedi (1985)) in 1965 within the Ministry of Finance. (The location has been changed since 1985.) Malaysia has set up the Implementation Coordination Unit in the Prime Minister's office (Haron (1982)). The Republic of Korea established in 1983 the Government Invested Enterprises Evaluation Committee, chaired by the Deputy Prime Minister, at the Economic Planning Board and also a Management Evaluation Task Force (Republic of Korea, Economic Planning Board (1984)). (For details, please see Hyung-Ki Kim, "Institutional Framework for Decision Making in Korean Public Enterprises: Some Implications for Developing Countries," which is Chapter 6 in this volume.)

With such institutionalized mechanisms, an operative goal mix would be determined with the full knowledge of the relative cost of each goal, and it would be feasible, as a result, to assign relative weights to the various goals. With such weights, it may be possible to devise a single yardstick of enterprise performance. Of course, it is not possible to evolve meaningful performance criteria without a rational price system, based on relative scarcities of goods and services.

If such an institutionalized decision framework exists, it also has several implications for a government-enterprise relationship. In that case, it is possible for the government or regulating agency to consider rationally several courses of action for the attainment of its operative goals, such as

(a) entering into a management contract, of the type experimented with in France, with the enterprise management (International Bank for Reconstruction and Development (1983));

(b) privatization of management[2] with government ownership as and when entrepreneurial-managerial skills develop in the private sector or with viable contractual arrangements with foreign firms;

(c) sharing partially even the ownership with the private sector in enterprises that are financially viable;

(d) privatizing both ownership and management in enterprises that are financially viable and have no strategic development objectives—an experiment that is being tried in the United Kingdom and was indeed a great success in Japan during the late nineteenth century (Lockwood (1954); Okawa and Rosovsky (1973)) and;

(e) privatizing in some way or liquidating enterprises that are a complete failure and that cannot be made viable with government ownership as well as management.

It is essential that there be a creative dialogue between the government and the enterprise; their relationship should be one of partnership in a joint venture and not adversarial. The government

---

[2] In this connection, the innovation of the managing agency system in India is quite relevant. This system divorced management from ownership and was in the nature of a management contract. See Parekh (1971).

perspective should not be that of control; it must be positive. Similarly, the government and the public enterprises should establish a partnership with the nongovernmental sectors; each should reinforce the other. Only then is it possible to make rational decisions relating to development strategies and policies.

Creative dialogue and a partnership between the government and public enterprises would be greatly facilitated if there were an association of public enterprise managers. Such an association can highlight issues and problems associated with administrative processes and general government policies that affect the public enterprise sector as a whole. This would help the government in adapting its administrative processes and policies to the requirements of efficient performance of the public enterprises and the changing environment. Such an association, for example, has been formed in India.

3. Technology Choice, Project Evaluation, and Financing

The mechanisms for sharing the top management functions also relate to the formulation and evaluation of initial investment projects. Unless the enterprise management is associated with the formulation and evaluation of the project it has to manage later on, its effectiveness and efficiency would be impaired. Top management of the proposed enterprise should be selected immediately after the project idea is identified and should be actively associated with its formulation and evaluation. Obviously, the public sector should have institutionalized machinery for project identification and formulation, as well as for project appraisal, evaluation, and selection for financing. India, for example, has set up a Project Evaluation Division in the Planning Commission.

Projects quite often are not well formulated and are not evaluated in terms of social cost-benefit criteria; the failure of many public enterprises to perform well is due largely to this poor formulation and evaluation of projects. Hence, there is an urgency to set up institutionalized mechanisms for project evaluation.

Related to the task of project formulation is the choice of technology. This choice quite often is not made rationally and in the light of adequate information and criteria. It is not realized that the public enterprises have to be one of the major instruments for attaining the objective of technological self-reliance. This is another major reason for the poor performance of public enterprises.

It is essential to choose technology that is suited to the resource endowments and environment of a country. Further, when technology is acquired from abroad, adequate technological competence should be developed for its absorption, adaptation, diffusion, and improvement. It is only then that technological self-reliance can be generated. For this purpose, the public enterprise sector needs to develop design-engineering competence and consultancy organizations. The project evaluation criteria should thus have a clear, explicitly stated technological dimension.[3]

The tasks of project evaluation, selection, and financing are performed more effectively and efficiently when they are entrusted to a development bank (Bhatt (1980)) rather than to government ministries or departments. A development bank, because of its history and expertise, is better suited to accumulating experience and improving its competence in the fields of project evaluation, selection, financing, and monitoring, provided it has competent management and has the degree of operational autonomy required for effective and efficient functioning.

V. Motivational and Inducement Mechanisms

1. Top Management Motivation and Functional Needs

It is essential that the top management of the enterprise be highly motivated and be in a position to motivate the enterprise personnel to make it a successful venture. But motivation by itself is not enough. There has to be recognition of performance and adequate remuneration—whether monetary or nonmonetary—that is essential for effective functioning. To quote Schumpeter ((1952), pp. 207–10):

> We had better recognize from the start that exclusive reliance on a purely altruistic sense of duty is as unrealistic as would be a wholesale denial of its importance and possibilities. Even if full

---

[3] For a discussion of the critical significance of technical consultancy service centers and the financial system for attaining the objective of technological self-reliance, see Bhatt (1980).

allowance be made for the various elements that are cognate to sense of duty, such as the satisfaction derived from working and directing, some system of rewards at least in the form of social recognition and prestige would presumably prove advantageous. On the one hand, common experience teaches that it is difficult to find a man or a woman, however high-minded, whose altruism or sense of duty functions in complete independence of at least that kind of self-interest or, if you prefer, of his or her vanity or desire for self-assertion. On the other hand, it is clear that the attitude which underlies this often pathetically obvious fact is more deeply rooted . . . and belongs to the logic of life within any social group. . . .

As regards preferential treatment in terms of real income it should be observed first of all that to a certain extent it is a matter of rational behavior toward the existing stock of social resources quite independently of the stimulus aspect. Just as race horses and prize bulls are the grateful recipients of attentions which it would be neither rational nor possible to bestow on every horse and bull, so the supernormal human performer has to be accorded preferential treatment if the rules of economic rationality are to prevail. . . . Many incomes high enough to evoke adverse comment do not give their receivers more than the conditions of life and work—distance and freedom from minor worries included—that are sufficient to keep them fit for the kind of thing they are doing.

. . . These devices have emerged in the capitalist world but have been greatly developed in Russia. Essentially, they amount to a combination of payments in kind with a liberal provision in money for what are supposed to be expenses of the proper discharging of certain duties. In most countries the higher ranks of the civil service are no doubt very modestly paid, often irrationally so, and the great political offices mostly carry decorously small money salaries. But as least in many cases this is partly, in some cases very amply, compensated not only by honors but also by official residences staffed at public expense, allowances for "official" hospitality, the use of admiralty and other yachts, special provisions for service on international commissions or in the headquarters of an army and so on.

2. Initial Size and Performance

It is likely that there would be a progressive improvement over time in an enterprise's performance if its initial size in relation to the market for its products were small, leaving considerable scope for expansion and diversification. Initial small size has several advantages: it makes it possible for the enterprise management to (a) absorb, assimilate, and improve technology/product; (b) acquire managerial and technical skills; (c) create a climate of confidence and commitment within the enterprise; and (d) generate resources for further expansion and diversification, thus ensuring to some extent the operational autonomy of the enterprise.

3. Profits and Performance

Since a public enterprise quite often has an instrumental role, it cannot, obviously, concentrate exclusively on its financial performance. However, whatever the other operative goals, a satisfactory financial performance of the enterprise creates a climate of confidence and trust between the government and the enterprise, makes it possible for enterprise management to obtain and ensure operational autonomy, and even permits the firm to have a strong voice concerning the choice of new investment projects. With good financial performance, the government's role vis-à-vis the enterprise tends to become supportive and facilitative, thus providing adequate scope for effective strategic management. Further, some public enterprises, at least, should have the function of mobilizing resources in order to attain the major national development goals.

4. Competitive Environment and Its Surrogates

A competitive environment seems to provide a stimulus to top management to improve enterprise performance. However, even when such an environment does not exist, it is possible for the regulatory framework to provide substitute mechanisms that can generate pressures and compulsions for improving the effectiveness and efficiency of enterprises, and that can facilitate management tasks in a variety of ways.

It is possible to generate a competitive environment for enterprises that produce tradable goods and services by adopting trade policies that compel domestic enterprises to compete with foreign enterprises in domestic, as well as foreign, markets. For large countries, such an environment can be generated even within the public sector. Further, an external agency fully qualified to evaluate performance, a development bank with expertise and experience in monitoring projects, strong pressures from consumers/clients, and political commitment to growth and efficiency can all serve as powerful substitutes for a competitive environment.

VI. Distribution Pressures and Government Interference

The policy implication of this analysis is that mechanisms for decision making regarding top management tasks that are shared between the government and the enterprise need to be institutionalized in a manner that stimulates the learning process and avoids ad hoc, unprincipled government intervention in decision making relating to operational and technical matters.

1. Rationale for Government Reluctance to Institutionalize

Why is it, then, that there is a general reluctance on the part of the governments in many countries to institutionalize the mechanisms relating to decision structure and processes? Even in a mature democracy like the United Kingdom (Redwood and Hatch (1982)), where public enterprise performance is rather poor in the manufacturing sector, or in a nondemocratic regime like the Republic of Korea (Jones and SaKong (1980)), with fairly satisfactory public enterprise performance, these mechanisms are not adequately institutionalized to delimit the effective range of purely political decisions.

There seems to be a conflict between development imperatives and distributional pressures. The distributional pressures have to be distinguished from the development objective of attaining equitable distribution of income and wealth. In fact, these pressures quite often tend to increase the degree of inequality in the distribution of income and wealth. In any society, the interests of various socioeconomic groups that are politically articulate do diverge, and the nature and intensity of this divergence changes with time and the pace and pattern of development. The changing pattern of distributional conflicts impinges on the different organs of the government, and hence on public enterprises, in different ways and gives rise to the phenomenon Aharoni (1982) calls "an agent without a principal," or what Hurvicz (quoted in Jones (1982), p. 5) calls "plural principals" with different functions and objectives. This phenomenon exists not only in countries with mixed economies but also in socialist countries like Hungary. The Hungarian situation is well described by Nyers and Tardos ((1980), p. 173):

> . . . the participation of the state or the centre is described in
> the discussions in an idealised form. It is dealt with as if it were
> the manifestation of a single, central will. In practice—at least in
> Hungary—interference by the centre in the problems of development
> takes the form of pressures from many institutions, frequently in
> sharp debate with one another. The supervising Ministry, the
> National Bank, the Development Bank, the Ministry of Finance,
> the National Board of Technological Development, and frequently
> even different departments of these institutions represent particular
> opinions, rational in themselves, until a decision on development is
> finally reached in the Council of Ministers, which, often, none of
> the state organs considers as its own. Such participation of the
> central agencies in development decisions is not only extremely
> complicated and slow but, for lack of proper harmonisation of
> interests, it is frequently not suited even to represent the internal
> rationality of a central decision.

Such a situation is common in all the countries, and distributional pressures are exerted through all the different organs of the government. For the stability of the government and the development process, the ruling groups are likely to use whatever instruments they have for the quasi-resolution of conflicts as and when they emerge. The intensity of such conflicts is likely to be greater in countries with what Schumpeter ((1952), p. 198) calls the "conflict of structural principles." Since public enterprise is also one of the policy instruments, governments generally do not like any institutionalized mechanisms that may restrict their freedom of maneuver for conflict resolution.

2. Operational Relevance of Decision Framework

However, these decision-making mechanisms do operate in practice when developmental imperatives dominate or are consistent with the distributional objectives, as in the Republic of Korea (Jones and SaKong (1980)) or Austria (Kaldor (1980)), resulting in satisfactory public enterprise performance. They also operate in some sectors like mining and manufacturing at times when the developmental objective is dominant for these sectors, as in Italy during 1953–65 (Marsan (1980)), in France during the postwar period (Dreyfus (1980)), or in Brazil during 1965–80 (Trebat (1983)).

Enterprises in these sectors generally are export oriented or have some links with the domestic or foreign private enterprises and thus operate in competitive or semicompetitive environments; even when they do not operate in such an environment, they are subject to effective pressures from consumer groups, which are homogeneous, organized, and politically articulate. When there is a lack of consensus regarding the structural principles of social fabric, the distributional pressures dominate, resulting in poor enterprise performance, as in the United Kingdom (Redwood and Hatch (1982)) or Turkey (Walstedt (1980)).

3. Rationale for Performance Audit

Even though it may be difficult to institutionalize these mechanisms, it may be possible to improve the decision-making process if there is a constitutional provision for a performance audit by an agency independent of the government.

> Even though conflicts cannot always be solved, they can be brought into the open to force decision makers to be confronted with several concrete choices. As there is no one principal but several tiers of agents, these agents can be forced to argue on choices to be made—and therefore implicitly on the goals—if independent "goal audit" is introduced, embodied in a broader comprehensive audit, as an integral part of the institutional design.[4]

Such an audit, if its results are published and disseminated widely, can illuminate the actual structures and processes of decision making and generate intelligent and well-informed public discussion, which may improve the policymaking process with respect to public enterprises.

Somewhat similar functions can be performed by a development bank, if the financing function is performed by such a bank rather than by the government, through the ministry of finance; a development bank with expertise in evaluating projects on the basis of social cost-benefit analysis and in monitoring the projects during their gestation, as well as operation, phases can illuminate and make explicit the structures and processes of decision making in the public sector (Bhatt (1972)). In the ultimate analysis, it is, of course, the nature and structure of the government and the socioeconomic groups which it represents that are the decisive factors regarding not only public enterprise performance but also

---

[4] See Aharoni (1982), pp. 72–73, and also Redwood and Hatch (1982), Chap. 8.

the pace and pattern of development. This, indeed, is a complex issue and relates to the theory of the nature and structure of the state and the society it represents (Reynolds (1983)).

VII. Ideology and Performance

For good performance, it is essential to have the type of decision mechanisms mentioned earlier. However, actual performance depends *on the spirit in which these mechanisms are operated* and the manner in which individuals and groups are motivated to identify their interests, objectives, and goals with those of the enterprise.

1. Role of Ideology

Commitment, a sense of belonging, and identification are easier to ensure if there is an enterprise ideology that motivates the individuals and groups within the enterprise and ensures the convergence of goals and expectations and active participation in tackling problems as they arise. Such has been the experience of Japanese enterprises (Morishima (1982)), as well as the most successful private enterprises in the United States (Peters and Waterman (1982)). In the successful enterprises in Japan and the United States, the nature of the enterprise ideology has enabled individuals and groups to relate their efforts and learning directly to the value system embodied in the ideology.

Such an ideology has generally the following characteristics: pride in the excellence of the product and consumer service; tradition of attention to and care for the overall well-being of individuals and their families and group solidarity; and a culture that (a) promotes healthy intergroup competition rather than competition among individuals; (b) provides stimulus through immediate attention to and recognition of group contribution rather than through fear of penalty or losing one's job; and (c) induces a spirit of improvisation, innovation, and learning for creative adaptation to a changing environment. The vitality with which an enterprise survives and grows depends critically on the enterprise ideology and its characteristics; effectiveness and efficiency and profits are the *by-product* of the motivation provided by the enterprise ideology.

2. Significance of Lifetime Employment and Continuous Training

Enterprise ideology is the creation of a strong leader in the top management team who initially is responsible for the success of the enterprise. The enterprise culture later on incorporates it in its value system. Its motivational significance depends on what the Japanese call "lifetime employment" and "continuous training" (Drucker (1974)). This Zen approach to continuous training emphasizes the fact that learning is a process and not a static objective, and that the learning process is a continuous process. This self-improvement through the process of continuous learning is institutionalized in the weekly training session, in which the workers of different skills meet and focus on the ways to improve total performance. This creates a habit of evaluating one's own performance and that of the group—which creates a sense of community, a sense of identification with the institutional or enterprise performance. Continuous training makes workers creative and receptive to innovative change; instead of cost centers they become output centers.

3. Public Enterprise and Development Ideology

It is easier for a public enterprise to evolve an enterprise ideology if the state and its policies are motivated by what Gerschenkron (1962) calls industrialization ideology.

> To break through the barriers of stagnation in a backward country, to ignite the imaginations of men, and to place their energies in the service of economic development, a stronger medicine is needed than the promise of better allocation of resources or even of the lower price of bread. Under such conditions even the businessman, even the classical daring and innovating entrepreneur, needs a more powerful stimulus than the prospect of profits. (p. 24)

VIII. Concluding Observations

In the final analysis, public enterprise performance depends on (a) political stability; (b) commitment of the state to socioeconomic development; (c) the capacity and willingness of the political and administrative apparatus to evolve learning mechanisms that promote creative adaptation of decision structures and processes to a changing environment; and (d) an ideology that provides a powerful motivation for group effort and learning through the convergence of goals and expectations. If these preconditions for performance do not exist, it may be desirable for the state to restrict its own role and activities merely to maintaining political and social stability; creating a favorable environment, through the development of social and economic infrastructure, for private entrepreneurial initiatives; and letting the capitalist spirit and motivation have free play.

References

Aharoni, Yair, "State-Owned Enterprise: An Agent Without a Principal," in *Public Enterprise in Less-Developed Countries*, ed. by Leroy P. Jones (Cambridge, England: Cambridge University Press, 1982), pp. 67–76.

Ayub, Mahmood Ali, and Sven Olaf Hegstad, *Public Industrial Enterprises: Determinants of Performance*, International Bank for Reconstruction and Development, Industry and Finance Series, Vol. 17 (Washington, 1986), p. 11.

Balassa, Bela, *China's Economic Reforms in a Comparative Perspective*, International Bank for Reconstruction and Development, Development Research Department, Discussion Paper No. 177 (Washington, April 1986).

Bhatt, V.V., *Employment and Capital Formation in Underdeveloped Economies* (Bombay: Orient Longmans, 1960), Chap. 6.

———, *Structure of Financial Institutions* (Bombay: Vora, 1972), Chap. 8.

———, "Decision Making in the Public Sector: Case Study of Swaraj Tractor," *Economic and Political Weekly* (Bombay), Vol. 13 (May 1978), pp. M-30–M-45.

———, *Development Perspectives: Problem, Strategy, and Policies* (Oxford, England: Pergamon Press, 1980), Pt. II.

———, "Institutional Framework and Public Enterprise Performance," *World Development* (Oxford, England), Vol. 12 (July 1984), pp. 713–21.

———, "Resource Mobilization in Developing Countries: Financial Institutions and Policies," *Economic and Political Weekly* (Bombay), Vol. 21 (June 1986), pp. 1114–20.

Dreyfus, Pierre, "The Efficiency of Public Enterprise: Lessons of the French Experience," in *Public and Private Enterprise in a Mixed Economy*, ed. by William J. Baumol (London: Macmillan, 1980), pp. 198–207.

Drucker, Peter F., *Management: Tasks, Responsibilities, Practices* (New York: Harper & Row, 1974), Chap. 20.

———, "The Changed World Economy," *Foreign Affairs* (New York), Vol. 64 (Spring 1986), pp. 768–91.

Escobar, Janet Kelly, "Comparing State Enterprises Across International Boundaries: The Corporación Venezolana de Guayana and the Companhía Vale do Rio Doce, in *Public Enterprise in Less-Developed Countries*, ed. by Leroy P. Jones (Cambridge, England: Cambridge University Press, 1982), pp. 103–27.

Gerschenkron, Alexander, *Economic Backwardness in Historical Perspective: A Book of Essays* (Cambridge, Massachusetts: Belknap Press of Harvard University, 1962), Chap. 1.

Goldsmith, Raymond W., *Financial Structure and Development* (New Haven, Connecticut: Yale University Press, 1969), pp. 131–35.

Haron, Mohmod Suffian, "Government Executive and Supervisory Controls Over Public Enterprises in Developing Countries: Malaysia's Experience," *Public Enterprise* (Ljubljana, Yugoslavia), Vol. 2 (No. 4, 1982), pp. 59–68.

International Bank for Reconstruction and Development, *World Development Report, 1983* (Washington, 1983).

Jones, Leroy P., "Introduction," in *Public Enterprise in Less-Developed Countries*, ed. by Leroy P. Jones (Cambridge, England: Cambridge University Press, 1982), pp. 1–13.

─────, and Edward S. Mason, "Role of Economic Factors in Determining the Size and Structure of the Public-Enterprise Sector in Less-Developed Countries with Mixed Economies," in *Public Enterprise in Less-Developed Countries*, ed. by Leroy P. Jones (Cambridge, England: Cambridge University Press, 1982), pp. 17–47.

Jones, Leroy P., and Il SaKong, *Government, Business, and Entrepreneurship in Economic Development: The Korean Case* (Cambridge, Massachusetts: Council on East Asian Studies, 1980).

Kaldor, Nicholas, "Public or Private Enterprise—The Issues To be Considered?" in *Public and Private Enterprise in a Mixed Economy*, ed. by William J. Baumol (London: Macmillan, 1980) pp. 1–12.

Khandwalla, Pradip N., *The Performance Determinants of Public Enterprises: Case Studies of Four Equipment Manufacturing Indian Public Enterprises* (Ahmedabad, India: Indian Institute of Management, May 1981).

─────, *Effective Management of Public Enterprises* (Washington: International Bank for Reconstruction and Development, 1985).

Kim, Hyung-Ki, *Decision Making in Public Enterprises: The Case of Pohang Iron and Steel Co. Ltd.* (Washington: International Bank for Reconstruction and Development, 1986).

Korea, Republic of, Economic Planning Board, *Economic Bulletin* (Seoul) (June 1984).

Kornai, János, *The Dual Dependence of the State-Owned Firm: Hungarian Experience* (Washington: International Bank for Reconstruction and Development, May 1985).

Kuznets, Simon, *Modern Economic Growth: Rate, Structure, and Spread* (New Haven, Connecticut: Yale University Press, 1966), pp. 352–53.

Lockwood, W.W., *Economic Development of Japan—Growth and Structural Change* (Princeton, New Jersey: Princeton University Press, 1954).

Marsan, V. Ajmone, "The State Holding System in Italian Economic Development," in *Public and Private Enterprise in a Mixed Economy*, ed. by William J. Baumol (London: Macmillan, 1980), pp. 138–57.
Morishima, Michio, *Why Has Japan Succeeded?: Western Technology and the Japanese Ethos* (Cambridge, England: Cambridge University Press, 1982).
Mufti, Abdul Majid, *Policy and Prospects of Public Manufacturing Enterprises in Pakistan*, paper presented at the International Seminar on Management of Public Manufacturing Enterprises, sponsored by the Indian Institute of Management at Bangalore, India, July 12–17, 1982.
Nyers, Rezsö, and Máron Tardos, "Enterprises in Hungary Before and After the Economic Reform," in *Public and Private Enterprise in a Mixed Economy*, ed. by William J. Baumol (London: Macmillan, 1980), pp. 161–93.
Okawa, Kazushi, and Henry Rosovsky, *Japanese Economic Growth: Trend Acceleration in the Twentieth Century* (Stanford, California: Stanford University Press, 1973).
Parekh, H.T., *Management of Industry in India* (Bombay: Vora, 1971), pp. 18–19.
Peters, Thomas J., and Robert H. Waterman, *In Search of Excellence: Lessons from America's Best-Run Companies* (New York: Harper & Row, 1982).
Ramachandra, K.V., *Case Study of an Indian Public Enterprise* (Washington: International Bank for Reconstruction and Development, 1985).
Redwood, John, and John Hatch, *Controlling Public Industries* (Oxford, England: Blackwell, 4th ed., 1982).
Reynolds, Lloyd G., "Spread of Economic Growth to the Third World, 1850–1980," *Journal of Economic Literature* (Nashville, Tennessee), Vol. 21 (September 1983), pp. 941–80.
Schumpeter, Joseph A., *Capitalism, Socialism, and Democracy* (London: Allen & Unwin, 4th ed., 1952).
Trebat, Thomas J., *Brazil's State-Owned Enterprises: A Case Study of the State as Entrepreneur* (Cambridge, England: Cambridge University Press, 1983).
Trivedi, Prajapati, "Evaluating the Evaluators: Performance of Bureau of Public Enterprises," *Economic and Political Weekly* (Bombay), Vol. 20 (August 31, 1985), pp. M-97–M-102.
Walstedt, Bertil, *State Manufacturing Enterprise in a Mixed Economy: The Turkish Case* (Washington: International Bank for Reconstruction and Development, 1980).

Comments

Muzaffer Ahmad

I congratulate Mr. Bhatt for presenting a large number of wide-ranging issues regarding the public enterprise syndrome. I shall attempt to present initially the propositions and issues contained in the paper, not necessarily in the same order.

According to my understanding of public enterprises, Mr. Bhatt makes the most important observation about public enterprises almost casually, toward the end of his paper. Public enterprises are creations of the state, and this can only be understood in relation to the nature of the state. Public enterprises, like any other public policy instrument, are conditioned by the nature of the social forces that coalesce in the government, and the functional performance in reality, despite the rhetoric, is critically dependent on the basic interests of the classes constituting the dominant groups in the government. Thus, the public enterprise in a bourgeois-dominant democratic regime performs qualitatively different functions from the public enterprise in a mass-based socialist state or in the intermediate regime à la Kalecki. While Mr. Bhatt has reported this, quietly, he certainly has not made much of it. In fact, he minimizes the importance of this fact when he uncritically accepts the Jones and Mason proposition that ideology of state does not matter. However, it should be noted that the ideology pronounced in the constitution, or even in the rhetorical chapters of the planning documents, does not necessarily portray the functional ideology of the state which is revealed through governmental operation where the coalition of social forces is most directly alive.

Mr. Bhatt has stressed the point that development is an important responsibility of the government in the developing countries, where the pace has to be faster, and greater direction needs to be given, compared with the historical situation of the developed countries of today. In this context, public enterprises have been used to initiate the economic transition involving structural change or adaptation. The intensity and extensity of the use of public enterprises in this context is directly related to the stage of a country's development. Mr. Bhatt refers to development in narrow economic terms and notes the often-repeated proposition that the role of the public enterprise is greater in economically backward countries in the sense that its share in gross fixed capital formation, industrial investment, and industrial gross domestic product is greater than in economically advanced countries. He leaves out altogether the compulsion of the nature of the state and such factors as the decolonization process.

The high visibility of public enterprises is due to the non-availability of competent domestic entrepreneurs, whose effective presence is a necessary, and is alleged to be a sufficient, condition for reducing the role of public enterprise in a free market or mixed economy. However, two other necessary conditions remain unstated. First, there has to be a social transition to identify and promote such talent, and, second, there has to be a political evolution that puts this group, or a group dependent on or coalescing with it, in power. In other words, the bourgeois democratic revolution on the completion of primitive capital accumulation needs to be completed in order to minimize the role of public enterprise in the developmental entrepreneurial activities. This is the second proposition of Mr. Bhatt's—that lack of entrepreneurial managerial tradition is the basic rationale for the imposed or induced importance of public enterprise.

How to fill this lacuna? The prescription is that public enterprise build, quickly and on a sound basis, physical and financial infrastructure, the cost of which has to be borne by the society, since development will benefit society. Public enterprise has been allotted another role—to assume responsibilities where the private sector is not yet competent to do so. Examples are areas where risk is high, projects that have long gestation periods, sectors that require sophisticated technology, and projects that are strategic to development but are low yielding. This is, as you would recognize, an extension of the infrastructure argument. What puzzles one is the fact that public enterprise is considered inevitable for such activities, even by those who are convinced of the inefficiency of public enterprise. The answer to the puzzle lies in the political economy and not in efficiency economics as such. Unless public enterprise performs these functions, private capital interest would not emerge as a dominant force. There is a third role that public enterprises play in the name of development: they provide key inputs—goods and services—for the growth of the private sector in the name of growth and development. The subsidy so provided is considered a cost of development and thus has to be borne by the people at large. The cost efficiency of such a subsidy game is rarely raised by public enterprise opponents.

This takes us to an interesting question. Public enterprises are required to assume risks, supply subsidized goods and services, and provide infrastructural facilities; but addressing externalities and creating inducements may not provide them with the opportunity to produce a surplus. They were created to produce "development" or "an environment for development." If the public enterprises have been operating efficiently in the technical sense (i.e., productivity is as good as it can be given the circumstances, and process wastage is not considerable), then the generatable surplus can only be dissipated through procurement, pricing, distribution, and compensation policies. If the dominant coalescing groups do not desire to see a surplus as a return to investment (in the revealed sense) for various reasons, then dissipation is allowed to occur through all or some of those policies. The mass-based proletarian coalition seems to have, at least theoretically, a compulsion to generate and extract such a surplus in an aggregative sense, but a bourgeois regime or intermediate regime may not have such a compulsion at all or may have it only in certain stages of development (e.g., capital accumulation) or in certain sectors. The entire discussion by Mr. Bhatt is based on the premise of poor financial performance of public enterprises and does not analyze the causes of this. He mentions elsewhere that there is no apparent reason for poor performance of public enterprises. However, it is assumed that causes lie in the government enterprise nexus which has made public enterprises "agents without principals." A poor financial performance has become critical for mixed-economy developing countries, particularly for those dependent on aid resources, because those resources seem to be constrained by the international economic situation. Mr. Bhatt repeats the assertion that the net resource inflow to developing countries will continue to decline. As public enterprises will have to continue a developmental role in many of the developing countries in terms of gross domestic capital formation, industrial investment, and industrial output, it has become necessary for public enterprises to operate efficiently in financial terms. However, Mr. Bhatt is conscious that performance criteria for public enterprises cannot be the same as those of the private sector. He seems to suggest that an agreed goal mix, with appropriate costing and weightage, could provide a single yardstick in financial terms for evaluation of the performance of public enterprises. A development role may, however, be adequately performed in the aggregate, through externalities and multiplier effects, even without a reasonable return on investment.

This, in fact, puts the public enterprise in the perspective of growth and adjustment—the theme of this seminar. The deficits generated by public enterprises are reducing available developmental resources, and thus the removal of deficits would be helpful in the mobilization of domestic resources. Mr. Bhatt recognizes two important factors in public enterprise inefficiency: first, the adversary relationship between enterprise management and government, and, second, the inappropriate selection and evaluation of projects and top management personnel. He wishes to eliminate the first through a creative dialogue between government and enterprise that identifies operational goals and strategy. He visualizes that if this can be done, then enterprise and government can enter into a management contract and eventually privatization will take place, reducing the responsibility of government in productive sectors. This can be done through institutionalizing the decision-making framework, including the selection of top management and such important things as choices of project, technology, and location. The second set of problems, he recommends, should be addressed by a development bank rather than a ministry. He assumes that a development bank does not assume the character of a public enterprise or become a part of the bureaucracy. However, Mr. Bhatt forgets that even in the United States, the failure rate of new or old private enterprises is quite high in normal times, despite any such constraints. Further, Mr. Bhatt suggests that public enterprises should grow over time in classical fashion, with acquisition, skill, performance, confidence, and innovation playing significant roles in extending the opportunity frontier. He concludes that financial viability will generate confidence and secure supportive assistance from government. In order to generate such success, it is necessary to induce competitive pressures on public enterprises. All these add up to one thing: making public enterprises emulate enlightened private enterprise culture. This is perhaps easier said than done, and private enterprise experience provides no guarantee of success.

Finally, Mr. Bhatt brings in the question of motivation and recommends *Theory Z* as a mode. But management is a culture-based phenomenon. What works in Japan may not work in societies with different social values and institutions. Can Theory Z be effective in an environment where Theory X produces the result?

The entire exercise on public enterprise, as presented by Mr. Bhatt, seems to be premised on the following: First, it has become necessary to transform public enterprise management culture from development to performance, since that would reduce the burden on the budget and make public enterprises attractive for divestiture. This seems to be an escapist view. Second, public enterprise performance is conditioned by political stability, commitment of the state to socioeconomic development, capacity, and a willingness of the political and administrative apparatus to evolve mechanisms that promote creative adaptation of the decision structure and processes to a changing environment. This is an ideology that provides a powerful motivation for group effort and learning through convergence of goals and expectations, which are difficult to find in developing countries, and hence public enterprises should be restricted. This is a defeatist view. Mr. Bhatt forgets the nature of the state wherein the coalescing forces may desire public enterprises in spite of the absence of such efficiency criteria if creation of these enterprises serves their class interests or if that is the immediate survival and growth route available. Further, it should not be forgotten that public enterprises and public institutions have been used, and can be used, for rapid, effective social transition under a committed leadership, as evidenced in the experience of such diverse economies as those of the Republic of Korea and China. The cost—suboptimal performance in financial terms—may simply have to be borne. In addition, the conditions enumerated for public enterprise are also relevant for private enterprise. Should the proposition for restriction of public enterprise apply equally to private enterprise?

T.L. Sankar

I would like to join Professor Ahmad in congratulating Mr. Bhatt for presenting a very balanced analysis of a wide spectrum of issues relating to public enterprises in developing countries.

Mr. Bhatt has rightly emphasized that public enterprise performance cannot be judged by the same criteria as private enterprises and has cogently listed a number of reasons for this—the more important among them being (a) the instrumental role that they have to play in a developing economy and (b) their size, structure, and technology, compared with those of the private sector. However, he has considered the capacity to generate surpluses as the principal criterion for judging their performance and for comparing their performance with that of private enterprises. The paper deals mainly with various structural deficiencies in public enterprise management that adversely affect the surplus-generating capacity of the enterprises. The public sector has to trade off the profitability of the enterprises, either in the short run or in the long run, for the sake of optimizing the total benefits likely to accrue to the nation or the society as a whole. Concerns for interclass equity and intergenerational equity which public enterprises have to reckon with in some cases are not of any significance to the private sector. It is therefore possible, and sometimes unavoidable, that some public enterprises will lose at the enterprise level (now or in the foreseeable future); these firms' losses may very well be acceptable, provided their contribution to social profitability is more than adequate to offset them. This point is fairly well recognized in the literature on the role of the public sector in economic development, while the management literature tends to overlook this aspect. Mr. Bhatt, in my humble view, has taken more of a management view.

In the plan documents of various developing countries, the rationale for investing in public enterprises has been set out clearly. The main reasons advanced, irrespective of the political ideology of the regime, are (a) to gain control of the commanding heights of the economy; (b) to provide critical development inputs of strategic value; and (c) to generate a surplus for sustaining a high level of capital formation. Needless to say, in Indian plans, in addition to the above objectives, public enterprises are also expected to contribute toward achieving self-reliance. It is therefore not surprising that a fairly large share of public investment has been made in areas of low profitability and/or high risk. The performance appraisals of the public enterprises should, therefore, take into account their contribution to social gain when analyzing their financial losses.

However, one cannot but agree with Mr. Bhatt that the surplus-generating potential of the public enterprises has not been fully realized, and it has become a constraint in financing the development plans. Any nonfinancial objective or socioeconomic constraint imposed on a public enterprise would no doubt erode, to some extent, its financial profitability. Under any given set of constraints there would nevertheless be an achievable level of profits which would be enterprise-specific and be determined with reference to the total objective functioning of the enterprise. The performance of the management of each public enterprise would have to be appraised against the specific anticipated surplus of the particular enterprise.

How, then, could such performance levels be achieved? Mr. Bhatt attempts to answer the question based on a small number of case studies of successful public enterprises in developing countries. He concludes that "there is no inherent reason for the poor performance of public enterprises in terms of their effectiveness and efficiency in relation to the major goals, provided certain key decision mechanisms are institutionalized." Mr. Bhatt has suggested a suitable institutional framework to reduce (or minimize) the influence of political and bureaucratic interference and ad hocism in the decision-making process. While there can be no dispute about the identification of the ills, the suggestion that by setting up institutional arrangements, we could overcome the problem appears to be facile and does not carry conviction. The creation of institutions is no doubt a necessary condition but is hardly likely to be a sufficient one. The Indian experience with institutionalization of decision making is a good example to show the limitations of Mr. Bhatt's arguments. Though the Public Enterprise Selection Board has been in existence for nearly two decades, there has been no perceptible change in the quality of top management. Further, as many as 15–20 percent of the public enterprises under the Central Government have remained "topless" for several months in recent times. The Bureau of Public Enterprises has been in existence for three decades. If there is an issue on which there is near unanimity among public enterprise chief executives in India, it is the need to curb the interference of the Bureau in their affairs!

The performance of a public enterprise depends on a number of factors, and it is difficult to isolate any of them as the primary one. In a recent study by the Institute of Public Enterprise, the public enterprises are classified in terms of (a) return on capital employed and (b) competitiveness of the environment, both based on their market shares. Out of the 158 central government enterprises (excluding 48 units which are taken over), 84 are in the competitive environment. Of these, 36 are financially successful (i.e., earn a return of 10 percent and above on capital employed). Similarly, in the noncompetitive environment, 38 out of 74 are financially successful. Since, according to the above analysis, there is no systematic association between competitiveness and financial performance, it is difficult to conclude that by merely providing a competitive environment the public enterprises would improve their performance. Therefore, one could argue that the performance of these enterprises would probably depend on their ability to cope with the intervention from "outside."

Mr. Bhatt's suggestion of entrusting the financial institutions with the investment decisions of public enterprises is also questionable. Anyone closely associated with the financial institutions would testify that they are not free from pathology, which afflicts the public enterprise system in general in India. Very often, behind their apparent profitability and professionalism, it is not uncommon to find sordid instances of favors done for particular firms and particular industrialists, mostly on the interference of politically powerful agents.

We therefore come back to square one and ask what, in the ultimate analysis, would contribute toward improved public enterprise performance. According to Mr. Bhatt, "In the final analysis, public enterprise performance depends on (a) political stability; (b) commitment of the state to socioeconomic development; (c) the capacity and willingness of the political and administrative apparatus to evolve learning mechanisms that promote creative adaptation of decision structures and processes to a changing environment; and (d) an ideology that provides a powerful motivation for group effort and learning through the convergence of goals and expectations."

If we agree on this, one should discount much of the emphasis on the structural improvement of managerial functions that has been dealt with in great detail in Mr. Bhatt's paper. If a government compromises the development imperatives because of distributional pressures, no amount of reforms or "institutionalization" could provide the remedies for the poor performance of a public enterprise. The time has come when the issue has to be faced squarely—in terms of the politics and economics of the development process.

As Professor Raj pointed out, "While there has been much verbal support for public enterprises . . . perhaps the most important reason why they have not been able to grow, in the manner once hoped and expected, was simply that there have not emerged any political forces in the country genuinely interested in making such enterprises yield adequate profits and savings of their own."[1] I submit, therefore, that we should not seek managerial solutions but instead should create a countervailing force to the political power of the regime by bringing together people who are affected by the performance of public enterprises. Finally, a centralized system at the one end, and the highly decentralized management system of the Yugoslavian type at the other, have to be studied closely in evolving totally new institutional arrangements to make—if a rhetorical expression is permitted—public sector enterprises really a "people's sector." Unfortunately, I have no clear proposals to suggest. But this much appears clear to me: a study that suggests that depoliticalization would lead to the better performance of public enterprises is like a study that concludes that "poverty is the cause and affluence is the solution."

---

[1] K.N. Raj, V.T. Krishnamachari Memorial Lecture, delivered under the auspices of the Institute of Economic Growth, New Delhi, on November 20, 1985. This has been published, in slightly abridged form, in *Mainstream* (New Delhi), Vol. 24 (December 14, 1985), pp. 7–10+ and (December 21, 1985), pp. 15–19. The above quotation appears on pp. 17–18 of the December 21 article.

6
Institutional Framework for Decision Making in Korean Public Enterprises: Some Implications for Developing Countries

*Hyung-Ki Kim**

I. Introduction

The appropriate institutional framework for decision making in public enterprises has been a theme for discussion in many countries, both developed and developing. Typically, this discussion revolves around issues related to political and public accountability of the operations of public enterprises, on the one hand, and to the degree of authority to be delegated to public enterprises and the manner in which the delegated authority is to be exercised, on the other. These discussions, not infrequently, move in a seesaw fashion, tilting now toward a "let the managers manage" orientation and now toward a stricter control of public enterprises.

The crux of this discussion hinges on how to establish the means of proper accountability while ensuring operational autonomy for the enterprise. Accountability should not only (a) prevent the abuse of delegated power but also (b) ensure that "power is directed toward the achievement of broadly accepted national [or corporate] goals with the greatest possible degree of efficiency, effectiveness, probity, and prudence."[1] More often than not, discussion merely emphasizes the need for establishment or reinforcement of the missing or weak accountability links of category (a). Such a development obviously tends to introduce greater control over public enterprises, often without providing for a commensurate delegation of authority, thereby limiting autonomous decision

---

*The views expressed in this paper are solely those of the author and should not be attributed to the World Bank.

[1] Canada, Royal Commission on Financial Management and Accountability (1979), p. 21.

making in public enterprises. Particular emphasis is put on accountability for financial administration as a means by which government authorities may exercise their power (by, for example, approving by-laws; appointing and removing directors, board chairmen, and chief executive officers; and issuing policy directives).

This paper illustrates, on the basis of the experience of the Republic of Korea, the changing character of the relationship between the government and public enterprises, as it emerges in tandem with overall structural adjustments in the economy designed to create greater stability and efficiency. A shift in the relative emphasis on accountability and autonomy of public enterprises characterizes the recent changes in the institutional framework for decision making in Korea. These changes have relevance for developing countries that experience a similar urgency for modifications in the structure of their policies.

II. Basic Setting of Public Enterprises in Korea

In the wake of the Republic's founding in 1948, two factors were responsible for the public ownership of key enterprises in Korea. First, the new government had to take over, upon liberation, public or private enterprises formerly owned by colonial powers. Many of these enterprises were divested by 1960. Second, and perhaps most important, the Government of Korea pursued interventionist economic objectives in various policy contexts, some of which stimulated the growth of public enterprises that formed "leading sectors" in order to spur growth in related sectors.[2]

Though Korea has recently been cautious in creating public enterprises, and indeed since 1968 has favored the privatization of many such enterprises, the role of public enterprises has been crucial, particularly in the first decade of rapid economic growth—

---

[2]The first Constitution of the Republic (1948) took an explicit socialist bent in regard to the public ownership of enterprises in such key sectors as transportation, communication, finance and insurance, electricity, irrigation, water works, gas, foreign trade, and others related to public welfare. The 1954 amendment to the Constitution, however, manifested a shift from such a line by, first, dropping the clause reserving specific industries for public ownership and, second, stipulating that "private enterprises shall not be transferred to state or public ownership except in cases specifically designed by law to meet urgent necessities of national life; nor shall the management or operation be controlled by the state or by juridical persons organized by public law." See Jones and SaKong (1980), p. 146.

the 1960s. As Jones and SaKong ((1980), p. 141) note, "A minor paradox of Korean development is that an ostensibly private-enterprise economy has utilized the intervention mechanism of public ownership to an extent which parallels that of many countries advocating a socialist pattern of society."[3] In 1984, total value added of public enterprises (90 enterprises at the central government level and 108 at the local level) amounted to US$8.1 billion, or about 10 percent of gross domestic product (GDP). In terms of employment, they represent 2.6 percent of non-agricultural employment, indicating the relatively higher capital intensity in public enterprises. Out of 90 public enterprises at the central government level, 5, with a 5.5 percent share in the nation's total value added and foreign debt, are under ministerial management (i.e., the Office of Monopoly of the Ministry of Finance, which produces cigarettes and ginseng, and the Office of Railroad Administration of the Ministry of Transportation, which runs the nation's railway system); 25, with a 23.4 percent share, are government-invested enterprises (GIEs) with over 50 percent direct equity participation by the Government; 54 are subsidiaries of these government-invested enterprises (which, by definition, have no more than 50 percent equity participation by the Government); and 6 are government-backed enterprises. (Tables 1 and 2 show the breakdown of public enterprises and the magnitudes of 25 government-invested enterprises.) Out of 25 GIEs, only 3 were created in the 1980s. They are (i) Korea Electric Power Corporation (KEPCO), which emerged as a GIE by buying out all the stock held by nongovernment stockholders to make KEPCO a wholly owned public enterprise, principally to provide long-term capital that nongovernment stockholders were unable to provide; (ii) Korea Telecommunication Authority, which was transformed from one of the monopoly ministerial operations under the aegis of Ministry of Communication into a wholly owned public enterprise; and (iii) Korea Gas Corporation. In contrast, several major public enterprises, such as the Korea Oil Corporation, were privatized during this period in accordance with the Government's policy of restricting the number of public enterprises. Those ceasing to exist as GIEs included the Korea Fisheries Development Corporation, the Dae Han Reinsurance

---

[3]Ibid., p. 141.

Table 1. Korean Public Enterprise, by Type As of December 31, 1984

Type	Characteristics	Number	Employment	Budget	Sales (1982)
			thousands	*million*	*U.S. dollars*
Government enterprises	Government department type (Office of Monopoly, Office of Railroad, etc.)	5	78	4,196	3,585
	Percentage share		37.9	15.3	19.1
Government-invested enterprises	Government holds at least 50 percent of stock (Korea Development Bank, Korea Electric Power Corporation, etc.)	25	134	14,625	8,952
	Percentage share		47.9	53.5	47.7
Subsidiary companies of government-invested enterprises	Indirect government investment through government-invested enterprises	54	41	2,849	2,402
	Percentage share		4.6	10.4	12.8
Other government-backed enterprises	Government holds less than 50 percent of stock	6	27	5,695	3,815
	Percentage share		9.6	20.8	20.4
Total		90	280	27,365	18,754
Percentage			100	100	100

Source: Republic of Korea, Economic Planning Board.

Table 2. Size of Government-Invested Enterprises As of January 1, 1985

Enterprise	Employment	Paid-In Capital	Budget	Primary Service/Product
	thousands	*million U.S. dollars*		
Korea Development Bank	2,010	706	1,027	Long-term loans, investment guarantees, and international banking
Small and Medium Industry Bank	7,494	190	445	Providing credit guarantees, loans, and discounts to small and medium industries
Citizens National Bank	10,314	68	527	Promoting household savings; expanding financing to small enterprises and low-income groups
Korea Housing Bank	7,137	41	424	Fund-generation financing for both public and private housing sectors
Korea Securities Exchange	347	4	9	Regulation of securities sales; review of new stock offerings
Korea Electric Power Corporation	23,789	1,937	6,599	Fund-generation financing for both public and private housing sectors
Korea Coal Corporation	14,230	105	393	Coal production
Korea Integrated Chemical Stock Company	83	106	8	Urea and chemical fertilizer production
Government Printing Office	554	10	32	Textbook production and supply
Government Mint	2,095	8	66	National mint
Korea Mining Promotion Corporation	430	90	26	Technical guidance, mine assessment, and mineral credit financing
Petroleum Development Corporation	402	27	23	Petroleum resource exploration and development, domestic oil supply, and demand stabilization

Table 2 (*concluded*). Size of Government-Invested Enterprises As of January 1, 1985

Enterprise	Employ-ment	Paid-In Capital	Budget	Primary Service/Product
	thousands	*million U.S. dollars*		
Korea Highway Corporation	2,519	150	262	Planning, construction, and management of expressway
Korea Housing Corporation	2,418	228	586	Low-income-housing construction
Industry Site and Water Resource Development Corporation	1,453	559	514	Industrial site and special regional development
Korea Land Promotion Corporation	999	259	306	Land acquisition and supply
Agriculture Promotion Corporation	1,841	12	167	Irrigation development and land reclamation
Agriculture and Fishing Development Corporation	539	12	39	Assisting processing and marketing distribution of agricultural and fishery products; research
Korea Telecommunication Authority	47,469	2,182	3,531	Dredging and filling
Labor Welfare Corporation	1,319	44	32	Providing industrial accident insurance, industrial safety/health-related services
Korea Trade Promotion Corporation	565	1	34	Overseas marketing and information services
Korea Tourism Corporation	593	34	66	Tourism
Korea Broadcasting System	4,627	91	430	Radio and TV broadcasting services
Korea Gas Corporation	466	28	185	Gas production and distribution
Overseas Development Corporation	226	1	5	Overseas labor supply services
Total	133,919	6,893	15,736	

Corporation, the Dae Han Salt Corporation, the Dae Han Dredging Corporation, and the Pohang Iron and Steel Corporation.

Table 3 presents a comparison of the values added by public enterprises and private enterprises. Wages account for a preponderant share of value added by private enterprises, followed by financing charges; while for public enterprises, the order is wages, depreciation allowance, and profit before taxes. In terms of linkages, 25 GIEs generally show greater forward linkages than private industries, indicating the former's strategic role in the overall industrial structure. Some enterprises have been transformed from the status of GIEs to subsidiaries by effectively reducing the Government's direct equity participation in order to give a greater degree of management independence to enterprises. A notable example in this category of public enterprises is the Pohang Iron and Steel Corporation (POSCO), the nation's largest integrated iron and steel mill, with over 11 million tons of annual production. In this case, the Government's equity share was lowered from 50.1 percent in 1975 to 41.6 percent in 1976. With its newly acquired autonomy in operation, POSCO has emerged as one of the most competitive steel mills in the world, according to the trade journal *Iron Age*, as well as the biggest corporate taxpayer in the nation for the last four years.

III. Framework for Control of Public Enterprises

In Korea, the institutional framework for control of public enterprises has undergone fundamental changes. Until 1962, when the Law for the Budgeting and Accounting of GIEs (with varying degrees of government ownership) was promulgated, public enterprises were generally under non-uniform, multiple layers of control in accordance with the laws by which they were established and the ad hoc decrees and other regulations that pertained to their sectors. The 1962 Law provided public enterprises with uniform procedures for budgeting and expenditures in an overall perspective of national economic management. This law was enacted during the first year of the nation's first five-year economic development plan and was presumably an attempt to ensure strict financial accountability for public enterprises' expenditures right at the

Table 3. Composition of Value Added by Public and Private Enterprises[1]
(In percent)

	Public Enterprises				Private Enterprises		
	Manufacturing industries	Construction industries	Service industries	Average[2]	Manufacturing industries	Construction industries	Service industries
Wages and salaries	26.7	35.8	36.3	35.8	48.4	63.8	67.6
Depreciation allowances	32.4	7.5	30.3	27.4	17.9	8.1	8.4
Gross profit before taxes	22.5	36.6	18.9	20.4	4.0	6.7	15.0
Financial charges	17.7	19.5	13.4	15.0	25.8	16.0	2.2
Duties and fees	0.2	0.3	0.9	0.6	2.0	2.0	3.8
Rentals	0.5	0.3	0.5	0.5	1.9	3.4	3.1
Total	100.0	100.0	100.0	100.0	100.0	100.0	100.0

Source: Bank of Korea (1983).
[1] Data for 1982. Details may not add to totals shown on account of rounding.
[2] Includes publicly owned financial institutions.

inception of highly interventionist economic development planning. It was essentially oriented toward expenditure; was based on the budget system for public administration; and gave little, if any, regard to the dynamism of enterprise management. As the 1962 Law covered finance and accounting only, leaving out supervision and exercise of stockholders' rights, a more comprehensive law for the management of public enterprises was introduced in 1973 to eliminate these shortcomings. It contained the following provisions:

(i) the establishment by the Government of the Management Committee for Equity Participation in the Ministry of Finance to act as the central body for the formulation of basic policies for public enterprises;

(ii) the detailed elaboration of the qualifications and the number of board directors and executives, and the manner in which they are appointed;

(iii) the imposition on the chief executives of public enterprises of self-evaluation of performance and the requirements for reporting upon their self-evaluation to the ministers concerned;

(iv) the introduction of annual management review of public enterprises by the Ministry of Finance and its designates;

(v) the standardization of the materials and commodities public enterprises use, as well as the categorization of those materials and commodities according to function, properties, and organizational units involved;

(vi) the requirement that chief executives of public enterprises formulate demand and supply plans for necessary materials and supplies so that procurements of any materials and commodities other than those listed in the plan be reported to the minister concerned and to the Ministry of Finance;

(vii) the requirement that chief executives of public enterprises conduct an annual inventory survey of materials and products; and

(viii) the establishment of a legal basis for conducting extraordinary investigations on inventories by the Office of Supply with the consent of the Ministry of Finance.

These and other provisions stipulated in the law greatly reinforced the *control aspect* of accountability at the expense of its *contributory aspect*, as they substantially encroached on the domain of operational autonomy.

The 1976 directives for the supervision of public enterprises that were issued by the Ministry of Finance, for example, had 41 items that required approval by, and reporting to, the Government, involving over 300 reporting documents a year.

For manufacturing enterprises, such stringent control by the Government was found to be cumbersome, particularly when those enterprises needed to make prompt decisions in order to adapt to change. In addition, the orientation of the Ministry of Finance's Committee for Management of Government Equity Participation turned out to be too narrowly focused on financial control issues rather than on the issues related to the attainment of corporate objectives in a wider and dynamic sense.

During the time the economy was on an upward spiral of growth, the gravity of poor performance of public enterprises was not properly appreciated. As the Korean economy began to suffer from stagflation in the late 1970s and early 1980s, however, the causes of poor performance of public enterprises emerged as a high-priority agenda item for action by the Government as an integral part of the Economic Stabilization Program and Structural Adjustment Programs (for which the World Bank lent a sizable amount of money).

Against this background, the Government of Korea introduced the Basic Law for the Management of Government-Invested Enterprises, promulgated on December 31, 1983. This law provides the following:

(i) ensuring autonomy of operation in GIEs by de-emphasizing control in an effort to help evolve a responsible management system;

(ii) establishing the Committee for the Performance Evaluation of GIEs in the Economic Planning Board (EPB)—the central planning and budgetary authority, created in 1962 by absorbing, among others, the Bureau of Budgets from the Ministry of Finance—to deliberate on matters related to the management of GIEs and to decide on formulation of basic guidelines for the establishment of management objectives and of common guidelines for budgeting and performance evaluation. This Committee is chaired by the Minister of Economic Planning Board (EPB) (who concurrently holds the nation's only deputy prime ministership), with the Minister of Finance and other concerned ministers, plus no more than five individuals, appointed by the President of the Republic on the basis of their intellectual and experiential background, as members;

(iii) establishing the GIEs Performance Evaluation Task Force, staffed mostly by nongovernmental experts, to undertake reviews of performance evaluation in accordance with the methodology approved by the Committee for the Performance Evaluation of GIEs;

(iv) requiring the EPB Minister, who acts as the Chairman of both the Economic Ministers Council and Roundtable (an informal consultative gathering), to issue basic guidelines for the formulation of management objectives by the *end of June* every year so that the chief executives of GIEs can submit, as required by law, their management objectives to the minister concerned. After review and adjustment where necessary, the minister must submit it, in turn, by the *end of September*, to the EPB Minister, who adjusts it, where necessary, and notifies the minister concerned and the GIEs before the *end of October*;

(v) requiring chief executives of GIEs to submit, by the *end of March*, to the minister concerned and the EPB Minister their own annual performance evaluation reports, which become a basis for the governmental review of GIE performance evaluation of GIEs;

(vi) requiring that the method of performance evaluation be developed by the EPB Minister and be amenable to objective performance measurement in terms of the public interest, achievement of management objectives, and efficiency;

(vii) requiring the EPB Minister to make review of performance evaluation of GIEs and to make a report to the President of the Republic on the results of the review by June 20;

(viii) empowering the EPB Minister to ask the minister concerned for corrective measures if such are found necessary, including the recommending of dismissal of members of the enterprise's board and requiring ministers concerned to take appropriate actions accordingly;

(ix) establishing boards of directors responsible for such decisions as annual budgets, adjustments to those budgets, and operational plans, while ensuring that no one can serve as chairman and chief executive officer concurrently, so that a check-and-balance system between policymaking and execution can be introduced;

(x) requiring GIEs to procure from the Medium and Small Industry Cooperatives products that the Minister of Trade and Industry determines that members of the Cooperative will produce, so that GIEs would help to promote the growth of the nation's small and medium industries; and

(xi) eliminating many of the control measures the 1973 Law had stipulated.

Since only two and a half years have passed since the enactment of the Basic Law for Public Enterprises, it is still too early to evaluate the results of the new approach. Some evidence has begun to emerge, however, pointing to both positive and negative aspects. These are discussed in the following section.

IV. Review and Implications of New Approach

First, the focal point for decision making for public enterprises has been effectively shifted from the Minister of Finance and the minister concerned to the EPB Minister. By virtue of his central planning and budgetary responsibilities, the latter can conceivably take a more comprehensive overview of the role and objectives of GIEs in making decisions relating to investment by them, as well as in evaluating their performance. For GIEs, the EPB has emerged as the super master, albeit in a *cooperative*, rather than an *adversarial*, relationship. The Bureau of Appraisal and Evaluation of the EPB acts as secretariat to the Committee for the Performance Evaluation of Government-Invested Enterprises, in addition to being responsible for monitoring major government projects, mostly concerning infrastructure. Since it relies heavily on the Korea Development Institute and other nongovernmental experts for professional expertise, instead of attempting to create its own professional expertise, the Bureau has assumed the nonthreatening posture of a "control agency."

Second, a considerable array of responsibilities has been shifted from the government to GIEs, particularly to Boards, which have yet to emerge as functioning policymaking units. Such delegation of authority exemplifies the Government's resolve to stay away from management of public enterprises by calling for little reporting on their routine operations.

Third, the new approach mandates that the chief executives of GIEs undertake their performance evaluations as a part of their managerial decision making, as well as the principal basis for EPB evaluation. The evaluation system creates both visibility (because evaluations are reported to the President and then made available to the public) and incentives, in the form of higher bonuses for *all* employees of GIEs that receive higher performance ratings. The imposition on GIEs of self-evaluation can contribute to improved accountability, through elaboration of a system of performance measurement, in order to achieve the desired goals with efficiency and effectiveness.

Fourth, the new approach tries to put emphasis on professional management by requiring that new employees be hired on the basis of demonstrated evidence of qualifications, thereby minimizing political influence in this regard.

Fifth, the new approach tries to introduce some kind of interactive and iterative processes between the Government and GIEs by allowing the apex committee—the Committee for the Performance Evaluation of Government-Invested Enterprises—to invite executives and employees of GIEs to testify or to make observations on matters of importance for the Committee's decision, as well as by incorporating the views of GIEs in the *Manual for Performance Evaluation* containing both the generic set of criteria applicable to all GIEs and those that are *sui generis* to particular GIEs.

V. Concluding Remarks

While the situation in Korea is obviously different from that of other countries, its experience in evolving an institutional framework for decision making in public enterprises sheds light on alternative solutions to similar problems faced by other developing countries. What the Government of Korea set out to accomplish through the introduction of a new institutional framework for decision making in public enterprises was to create synergism from what Mascarenhas (1982) has called the "policy efficiency" of the government, on the one hand, and the "operational efficiency" of public enterprises, on the other.[4]

Whether such "an exercise in artful government," as Musolf[5] has aptly called it, will culminate in a new institutional and policy framework for the enterprise system in Korea, with a fruitful balance between autonomy and accountability, remains to be seen. The basic policy postures the Government of Korea has adopted appear, however, to be very promising. These postures relate to (1) the renunciation of the role of managerial decision maker by reducing, rather than maintaining, reporting and approval requirements, and (2) the introduction of interactive and iterative processes between the Government and public enterprises in setting appropriate bases for performance evaluation. These profound changes in perspective are likely to provide greater autonomy to enterprises and to enhance their accountability.

The Economic Planning Board has now become the linchpin of the new institutional framework. This basic change should provide the public enterprise managers with a broader perspective within which to formulate their management policies and, at the same time, should make it possible for the EPB to make an informed judgment about the role and performance of the public enterprise system without demanding a great deal of operational information.

---

[4]Mascarenhas (1982), pp. 47–48.
[5]Musolf (1959), p. ix.

Bibliography

Bank of Korea, *Analysis of Enterprises' Management* (Seoul, 1983).

Bhatt, V. V., "Institutional Framework and Public Enterprise Performance," *World Development* (Oxford, England), Vol. 12 (July 1984), pp. 713–21.

Canada, Royal Commission on Financial Management and Accountability, *Final Report* (Ottawa: Canadian Government Publishing Center, 1979).

Jones, Leroy P., and Il SaKong, *Government, Business, and Entrepreneurship in Economic Development: The Korean Case* (Cambridge, Massachusetts: Council on East Asian Studies, Harvard University, 1980).

Mascarenhas, R. C., *Public Enterprise in New Zealand* (Wellington: New Zealand Institute of Public Administration, 1982).

Musolf, Lloyd D., *Public Ownership and Accountability: The Canadian Experience* (Cambridge, Massachusetts: Harvard University Press, 1959).

Wettenhall, R. L., "Acworth, Attlee and Now: One Hundred Years of Debate About Public Enterprise-Government Relations," *Political Science* (Wellington), Vol. 37 (December 1985), pp. 125–39.

7
The Asian Experience and the Role of Multilateral Institutions, Foreign Aid, and Other Financial Sources

C. Rangarajan

Japan excluded, the rest of Asia forms part of the developing world. For most of Asia, therefore, external financing has been of particular importance in its efforts for rapid development. In view of the heterogeneity of developing Asia, the magnitude and the sources of external finance have varied from country to country. The rates of growth in income achieved by countries have also differed significantly. The varied experience of Asian developing countries in respect of external finance, development, and adjustment should provide useful insights, not only for developing Asia but also for the developing world at large and financing agencies. Section I deals with some important developments in developing Asia in the context of the changes in the international economic environment. Major aspects of their external financing needs are analyzed in Section II. Some issues arising from discussions in these sections are brought together in Section III.

I. International Economic Environment and Asian Economies

The Asian experience needs to be looked at against the backdrop of international economic developments. For some time, growth in industrial countries has been sluggish while unemployment levels have continued to remain high. Among developing countries, external debt burdens, modest growth, and large external account deficits are a cause for concern. World trade growth has been less dynamic in the last ten years than in the previous two decades. Protectionism is on the rise, especially in the form of nontariff barriers in industrial countries. The volatility of foreign exchange rates and the uncertainties facing international banking are other aggravating factors.

The steep increases in oil prices of the 1970s, the worldwide escalation of inflation in the 1970s, and the deep and widespread recession of 1980–82 affected enormously the growth and trade of non-oil developing countries. Several among them incurred large external debt obligations to finance sudden and sharp increases in their current account deficits, and debt servicing became burdensome in terms of their export earnings. The budgetary deficits of the United States, its growing current account deficits, and the dollar's strength during 1982–early 1985 made adjustment more difficult because of the rise in international interest rates, the increase in debt burden in real dollar terms, and the diversion of investable funds to the United States. Recently, however, there have been some welcome changes, particularly in interest rates.

World trade (volume) growth has been modest since 1980, except for 1984. In 1985, it was 3 percent, and the growth rate may be the same in 1986. On the whole, the trade volume of developing countries has not risen as much as that of industrial countries. The sharp deterioration since 1982 in their trade performance is due mainly to the decline in the volume and prices of oil exports, the rather modest growth of industrial economies, the nontariff barriers in industrial countries' markets to imports from developing countries, and the generally depressed state of non-fuel primary commodity prices, which have recently been the lowest since the Second World War.

Development aid flows have reached a plateau. Bilateral and multilateral funds on concessional terms are under attack. *Net transfers of resources*—public and private—for supplementing the domestic savings efforts of a number of developing countries are now less than in earlier years because, while gross disbursements are rising slowly, debt-service payments have become substantial.

The developing countries in Asia,[1] by mid-1984, had a population of 2.4 billion, accounting for about one half of the world's population, and include two countries, China and India, with the largest populations in the world. In the same year, the gross

---

[1] Basically, the data used in the paper are from Fund and World Bank publications. The classification *developing countries in Asia* conforms to the Fund's *International Financial Statistics* coverage. The World Bank's classification of South Asia and East Asia and the Pacific has also been found helpful and is used extensively.

domestic product (GDP) of developing Asia was about $816 billion, forming roughly 7 percent of world income (excluding East European nonmarket economies). The Continent could be divided into two regions: (1) East Asia and the Pacific, with countries having relatively small populations, large per capita incomes, and high rates of per capita income growth and (2) South Asia and China, with large populations, low per capita incomes, and generally low rates of per capita income growth. The average per capita income of the East Asia and Pacific region was about $1,015, ranging from $540 in Indonesia to $7,260 in Singapore. The average annual per capita income growth over nearly two decades ended in 1984 ranged from 4.2 percent to 7.8 percent for six of the eight countries for which data are readily available. On the other hand, the per capita income of the South Asia and China region, with a population of over 2 billion, was about $280 and ranged from $130 in Bangladesh to $380 in Pakistan. Thus, the highest per capita income in this region was much lower than the lowest for the other region. The per capita annual average income growth over the period 1965–84 varied between 0.2 percent in Nepal and 2.9 percent in Sri Lanka. Only China from this group had a growth rate in per capita income of 4.5 percent, comparable with that for countries in the other group (Table 1).

Many developing countries of Asia have maintained steady and satisfactory real growth rates over a long period. The main contributory factors are relatively high investment/savings rates, a pronounced orientation of several Asian countries toward exports (including manufactures), and no serious debt-servicing problems. The investment rates were generally higher among countries in the region of East Asia and the Pacific than those in countries of the other region, except China. In the former region, in 1984, the investment rates generally ranged from 21 to 31 percent of GDP, with Singapore having a rate of 47 percent. In the latter, the investment rate generally varied from 16 to 26 percent of GDP; China, however, had a rate of 30 percent. The rates of growth in GDP in the region of East Asia and the Pacific were much higher and ranged generally from 6.8 to 9.1 percent per annum over the period 1973–84, as against 5–6 percent in the other region. The divergence in the growth performance of the two regions cannot be fully explained by the differences in their investment rates.

Table 1. Developing Countries in Asia: Selected Indicators[1]

	Population, Mid-1984 (millions)	GDP, 1984 (million U.S. dollars)	Per Capita GNP 1984 (U.S. dollars)	Per Capita GNP Average Annual Growth Rate, 1965–84	Gross Domestic Investment	Gross Domestic Savings 1984 (percentage of GDP)	Resource Balance	Real GDP Growth, 1973–84 (percent per annum)	Exports' Average Annual Growth Rate, 1973–84	Per Capita Aid, 1984 (U.S. dollars)
East Asia and Pacific										
Hong Kong	5.4	30,620	6,330	6.2	24	29	5	9.1	12.9	2.6
Indonesia	158.9	80,590	540	4.9	21	20	–1	6.8	1.4	4.2
Republic of Korea	40.1	83,220	2,110	6.6	29	30	—	7.2	15.1	–0.9
Malaysia	15.3	29,280	1,980	4.5	31	32	1	7.3	7.5	21.4
Papua New Guinea	3.4	2,360	710	0.6	31	16	–14	1.0	...	94.0
Philippines	53.4	32,840	660	2.6	18	18	–1	4.8	5.6	7.4
Singapore	2.5	18,220	7,260	7.8	47	43	–4	8.2	7.1	16.2
Thailand	50.0	41,960	860	4.2	23	21	–2	6.8	10.4	9.5
South Asia and China										
Bangladesh	98.1	12,320	130	0.6	16	4	–12	5.0	2.9	12.3
Burma	36.1	6,130	180	2.3	22	17	–5	6.0	3.2	7.6
India	749.2	162,280	260	1.6	24	22	–3	4.1	3.3	2.1
Nepal	16.1	2,290	160	0.2	19	10	–9	3.1	...	12.3
Pakistan	92.4	27,730	380	2.5	17	6	–12	5.6	7.4	7.5
Sri Lanka	15.9	5,430	360	2.9	26	20	–6	5.2	3.5	29.5
China	1,029.2	281,250	310	4.5	30	30	—	6.6	10.1	...

Source: International Bank for Reconstruction and Development, *World Development Report, 1986* (Washington, 1986).
[1] GDP denotes gross domestic product; GNP denotes gross national product.

Another important feature has been the much greater reliance of countries from South Asia on external finance. In 1984, all of them, except India, depended on external resources to the extent of about 25 to 75 percent of their investment. On the other hand, in Hong Kong and Malaysia, from the other group, savings exceeded investment, while others (excluding Papua New Guinea) depended much less on external resources for investment. However, it needs to be borne in mind that, considering the low income levels of countries in the South Asia and China region, the achievement of savings rates of about 20 percent and above in some of the countries in this group has been commendable (Table 1).

Countries of East Asia and the Pacific achieved remarkably high growth rates of exports in volume terms over a long period, 1973–84. Over the same period, the Republic of Korea, Hong Kong, and Thailand had growth rates of 10 to 15 percent per annum, while Malaysia, Singapore, and the Philippines had a 5.5–7.5 percent annual expansion in their exports. Only China from the other group attained an export growth of 10 percent, and Pakistan, 7.4 percent. The annual increase in exports of all others was in the range of 3.0 to 3.5 percent (Table 1).

The current account deficit of developing countries in Asia, which had declined to $8.7 billion by 1978, almost trebled within three years, following the second sharp increase in oil prices, to reach a peak of $23.7 billion in 1981. It steadily declined thereafter to $7.6 billion in 1984 but rebounded to $18.2 billion in the next year. Between 1982 and 1984, China enjoyed a sizable though declining current account surplus; in 1985, there was a sharp change, with a current account deficit of $11.5 billion. Excluding China, the current account deficit of developing Asia as a proportion of gross national product (GNP) rose from 2.9 percent in 1980 to 4.5 percent in 1982, but declined to 2.7 percent in 1984. These ratios have been generally well below those for other regions in the developing world. The decline in the ratio was aided by the strong growth in exports of the Republic of Korea, Malaysia, and Nepal in 1983 and 1984, and of Indonesia, Singapore, Thailand, Bangladesh, and Sri Lanka in 1984. In recent years, the reduced volume of oil exports and the fall in oil prices have, however, adversely affected export earnings of Indonesia and Malaysia and the decline in primary commodity prices—those of Sri Lanka, Bangladesh,

Indonesia, Malaysia, the Philippines, and Thailand. On the other hand, imports of Indonesia, Papua New Guinea, the Philippines, Burma, and Sri Lanka declined in 1983, as well as in 1984, while growth remained subdued in several other countries in one or both of these years. Thus, the trade deficit for developing Asia contracted markedly from $22.7 billion in 1981 to just $4.0 billion in 1984 because of import compression. The deficit balance on services, however, steadily increased from $4.0 billion in 1978 to $11.8 billion in 1985, if 1982 is excluded. In 1984, the services deficit was nearly three times the trade deficit and formed about 85 percent of the trade deficit in 1985. Private transfer receipts (workers' remittances) were an important source of exchange earnings for this region, meeting broadly 20 to 30 percent of the deficit on goods and services account since 1978. These receipts more than doubled between 1978 and 1983, to $8.5 billion, but declined somewhat thereafter with the fall in oil revenues in the Middle East (Table 2).

II. External Financing Needs and Sources of Finance

In the years from 1977 onward, external financing needs exceeded the deficit on goods and services and private transfers referred to in the previous section because of movement in reserves and errors and omissions. However, over nearly the decade ended 1985, by far the largest component of financing requirements of developing Asia, which reached a peak of $33.6 billion in 1981 from $7.7 billion in 1977, was the magnitude of the current account deficit (Table 3). Since 1978, the current account deficit constituted generally between 60 and 70 percent of financing needs, with the proportion going up to 98.9 percent in 1985, by which time the financing needs declined to $18.4 billion. Every year, except in 1985, reserves were augmented by countries of developing Asia as a group, with the rise ranging from $5.0 billion in 1978 to $9.3 billion in 1984. Apart from the uncertainties in the international environment, the growing debt-servicing obligations and the rise in international transactions necessitated an increase in their reserves. Throughout the period, errors and omissions were negative, with a peak outflow of $4.7 billion in 1982.

Between the two groups of Asian countries, net debt-creating

Table 2. Developing Countries in Asia: Current Account, 1978–85[1]
(In billions of U.S. dollars)

	1978	1979	1980	1981	1982	1983	1984	1985
Exports (f.o.b.)	93.5	122.9	155.9	170.2	163.0	171.1	198.6	197.6
Percentage change[1]		*31.4*	*26.9*	*9.2*	*−4.2*	*5.0*	*16.1*	*−0.5*
Imports (f.o.b.)	102.2	135.7	176.9	192.9	184.8	188.6	202.6	211.5
Percentage change[1]		*32.8*	*30.4*	*9.0*	*1.0*	*−3.2*	*7.4*	*4.4*
Trade balance	−8.7	−12.8	−21.0	−22.7	−21.8	−17.5	−4.0	−13.9
Services								
Receipts	21.6	27.4	34.5	42.3	46.7	45.9	46.7	48.0
Payments	−25.6	−34.0	−42.3	−50.2	−52.0	−53.9	−58.2	−59.8
Balance	−4.0	−6.6	−7.8	−7.9	−6.3	−8.0	−11.5	−11.8
Goods and services balance	−12.7	−19.5	−28.8	−30.5	−28.1	−25.5	−15.5	−25.8
Unrequited private transfers	4.0	4.4	6.9	6.8	7.9	8.6	7.9	7.6
Current account balance	−8.7	−15.1	−21.9	−23.7	−20.2	−17.0	−7.6	−18.2

Source: International Monetary Fund, *World Economic Outlook: A Survey by the Staff of the International Monetary Fund* (Washington, April 1986).
[1] Figures in italics show percentage change from the preceding year.

Table 3. Developing Countries of Asia: External Financing Needs and Sources of Finance, 1977–85
(In billions of U.S. dollars)

	1977	1978	1979	1980	1981	1982	1983	1984	1985
Deficit on goods, services, and private transfers	0.9	8.7	15.1	21.9	23.7	20.2	17.0	7.6	18.2
Use of reserves (+) or accumulation (−)	−6.0	−5.0	−6.0	−6.7	−6.7	−6.0	−8.8	−9.3	0.5
Errors and omissions	−0.8	−1.2	−0.2	−1.8	−3.2	−4.7	−2.3	−2.3	−0.7
Financing needs	7.7	14.9	21.3	30.4	33.6	30.9	28.1	19.2	18.4
Non-debt-creating flows (net)	3.5	4.9	5.5	6.5	8.7	6.8	6.8	7.3	7.3
Percentage of financing needs	*45.5*	*32.9*	*25.8*	*21.4*	*25.9*	*22.0*	*24.2*	*38.0*	*39.7*
Asset transactions (net)	−2.0	−0.2	−1.5	0.9	0.1	−1.9	−2.7	−3.9	−3.2
Net external borrowing	6.2	10.3	17.3	22.9	24.8	25.9	24.1	15.8	14.4
Percentage of financing needs	*80.5*	*69.1*	*81.2*	*75.3*	*73.8*	*83.8*	*85.8*	*82.3*	*78.3*
Long-term borrowing from official creditors	2.9	4.4	4.6	6.9	10.2	9.4	9.3	10.7	6.5
Percentage of financing needs	*37.7*	*29.5*	*21.6*	*22.7*	*30.4*	*30.4*	*33.1*	*55.7*	*35.3*
Reserve-related liabilities	−0.3	−0.2	−0.1	1.3	3.4	2.6	4.2	1.4	−3.6
Percentage of financing needs	*−3.9*	*−1.3*	*−0.5*	*4.3*	*10.1*	*8.4*	*15.0*	*7.3*	*−19.6*
Other borrowing	3.6	6.1	12.8	14.8	11.2	14.0	10.6	3.7	11.4
Percentage of financing needs	*46.7*	*40.9*	*60.1*	*48.7*	*33.3*	*45.3*	*37.7*	*19.3*	*62.0*

Source: International Monetary Fund, *World Economic Outlook: A Survey by the Staff of the International Monetary Fund* (Washington, April 1986).

flows of South Asian countries reached a peak in the 1980s of $6.9 billion, or 3.1 percent of GNP in 1982, and declined thereafter to $4.4 billion, or 1.8 percent of GNP in 1984 (Table 4). The peak for the group of countries from East Asia and the Pacific occurred in 1980 with net flows of $21.7 billion, or 8.2 percent of GNP; these steadily declined to $11.7 billion, or 3.7 percent of GNP (Table 5). The reliance of the latter group on external finance, both in absolute terms and in relation to GNP, was much higher than that in South Asia throughout the 1980s. As a result, by the end of 1984, outstanding debt of countries from East Asia and the Pacific formed 45.5 percent of their GNP, while this ratio was only 22.0 percent for countries in South Asia.

1. Multilateral Agencies

Among the multilateral financing institutions, the World Bank, the Fund, and the Asian Development Bank have been the major ones providing finance to Asian countries. These agencies have been playing an important role in the financing for South Asian countries. Net flows from them to this region ranged from $2.3 billion to $4.3 billion a year during 1980 to 1984 and formed as much as 47 to 72 percent of total debt-creating net flows to this region (Table 6). The trend in net flows from multilateral agencies, rising from $2.6 billion in 1980 to $4.3 billion in 1982 before declining to $2.3 billion in 1984, was largely influenced by the amount of assistance from the Fund and particularly by the drawings under the extended Fund facility arrangement with India. Net flows from other multilateral institutions were broadly stable at about $2 billion a year, with International Development Association (IDA) flows accounting for about two thirds of that amount during 1981–84.

For the group of countries from East Asia and the Pacific, the debt-creating flows from multilateral institutions fluctuated from $2.1 billion to $3.6 billion over the same period (Table 7). The annual variations in use of the Fund's resources were wider ranging, from $0.03 billion to $1.6 billion. The relative dependence of this region on multilateral agencies was, however, much less than that of South Asia, as reflected by the much lower ratio of net credit from multilateral institutions to total credit, which ranged from 10 percent to 27 percent for this region, against 47–72 percent

Table 4. South Asia, Net Flows, 1970 and 1980–84

	1970	1980	1981	1982	1983	1984	Outstanding Debt 1984
Total net flows (*million U.S. dollars*)	759	5,643	4,956	6,947	5,315	4,416	53,913
Total net flows as percentage of gross national product	1.0	2.7	2.2	3.1	2.2	1.8	22.0
			Percentage of Total Net Flows in Outstanding Debt				
Public and publicly guaranteed long-term debt—net flows	129.8	68.9	60.6	60.7	61.1	82.3	79.1
Official creditors	127.9	59.6	50.1	44.6	49.6	60.3	70.9
Multilateral	17.0	38.9	33.9	30.6	36.7	44.6	33.5
World Bank	5.1	1.5	6.7	3.5	7.7	4.5	4.5
International Development Association	11.1	16.5	22.4	22.3	24.2	30.1	22.9
Others	0.8	20.9	4.8	4.8	4.8	10.0	6.1
Bilateral	110.9	20.7	16.2	13.9	12.9	15.7	37.4
Private creditors	1.8	9.4	9.3	16.1	11.6	22.0	8.2
Suppliers' credits	1.1	−1.0	−0.6	−0.5	0.1	0.9	0.8
Financial markets	0.7	10.4	9.9	16.6	11.5	21.1	7.4
IMF (net)	−30.1	7.6	20.2	31.4	35.6	8.0	10.9
Private, nonguaranteed debt	0.3	3.4	6.9	5.4	7.0	11.9	5.0
Short-term debt (variation in debt)	—	19.9	12.3	2.5	−3.7	−2.2	5.0

Source: International Bank for Reconstruction and Development, *World Debt Tables, 1985–86* (Washington, 1986).

Table 5. East Asia and Pacific: Net Flows, 1970 and 1980–84

	1970	1980	1981	1982	1983	1984	Outstanding Debt 1984
Total net flows (*million U.S. dollars*)	1,271	21,739	18,433	18,975	13,640	11,730	142,940
Total net flows as percentage of gross national product	3.0	8.2	6.3	6.2	4.5	3.7	45.5
	\multicolumn{6}{c}{Percentage of Total Net Flows in Outstanding Debt}	
Public and publicly guaranteed long-term debt—net flows	61.5	33.1	50.3	56.7	86.1	76.3	57.1
Official creditors	51.7	13.0	20.8	20.0	32.3	31.5	25.4
Multilateral	6.3	6.5	9.8	11.6	18.7	18.0	11.7
World Bank	5.1	4.0	6.9	8.4	13.2	12.7	7.9
International Development Association	0.4	0.3	0.6	0.6	0.8	0.7	0.9
Others	0.8	2.2	2.3	2.6	4.7	4.6	2.9
Bilateral	45.4	6.5	11.0	8.4	13.6	13.5	13.8
Private creditors	9.8	20.1	29.5	36.7	53.8	44.8	31.6
Suppliers' credits	8.0	0.4	−1.5	0.9	2.0	4.0	3.7
Financial markets	1.8	19.7	30.8	35.8	51.8	40.8	27.9
IMF (net)	4.7	3.7	8.9	0.6	8.0	0.3	2.7
Private, nonguaranteed debt	33.8	9.4	16.7	12.3	19.8	23.0	16.7
Short-term debt (variation in debt)	—	53.8	24.1	30.4	−13.9	0.4	23.5

Source: International Bank for Reconstruction and Development, *World Debt Tables, 1985–86* (Washington, 1986).

Table 6. South Asia: Net Flows, 1970 and 1980–84
(In millions of U.S. dollars)

	1970	1980	1981	1982	1983	1984	Outstanding Debt 1984
Public and publicly guaranteed long-term debt—net flows	984.6	3,891.3	3,003.8	4,214.9	3,247.4	3,633.0	42,627.1
Official creditors	971.1	3,363.0	2,484.1	3,098.0	2,635.2	2,663.5	38,220.4
Multilateral	128.9	2,196.9	1,682.1	2,128.6	1,952.5	1,972.0	18,045.6
World Bank	38.6	87.1	333.0	246.0	407.4	196.5	2,424.7
International Development Association	84.1	931.6	1,113.1	1,548.0	1,287.6	1,332.1	12,350.7
Others	6.2	1,178.2	236.0	334.6	257.5	443.4	3,270.2
Bilateral	842.2	1,166.1	802.0	969.4	682.7	691.5	20,174.8
Private creditors	13.6	528.3	519.7	1,116.9	612.3	969.5	4,406.7
Suppliers' credits	8.3	−58.2	28.3	−36.0	3.3	38.4	441.9
Financial markets	5.3	586.5	491.4	1,152.9	608.9	931.2	3,964.8
IMF (net)	−227.9	427.5	1,000.1	2,182.0	1,892.6	351.9	5,919.9
Private, nonguaranteed debt	2.0	198.5	344.0	372.8	372.5	526.0	2,681.4
Short-term debt (variation in debt)	...	1,126.0	608.0	177.0	−198.0	−95.0	2,685.0
Total	758.7	5,643.3	4,955.9	6,946.7	5,314.5	4,415.9	53,913.4

Source: International Bank for Reconstruction and Development, *World Debt Tables, 1985–86* (Washington, 1986).

Table 7. East Asia and Pacific: Net Flows, 1970 and 1980–84
(In millions of U.S. dollars)

	1970	1980	1981	1982	1983	1984	Outstanding Debt 1984
Public and publicly guaranteed long-term debt—net flows	781.4	7,196.1	9,268.1	10,753.0	11,739.3	8,944.0	81,602.5
Official creditors	657.0	2,817.0	3,835.0	3,793.8	4,399.9	3,698.6	36,407.5
Multilateral	79.7	1,393.5	1,814.8	2,197.8	2,543.3	2,113.3	16,638.6
World Bank	64.8	863.9	1,278.8	1,599.5	1,806.4	1,484.7	11,238.7
International Development Association	5.1	60.1	102.3	110.4	102.4	83.3	1,203.6
Others	9.8	469.5	433.7	487.9	634.5	545.3	4,196.3
Bilateral	577.3	1,423.4	2,020.2	1,596.0	1,856.7	1,585.3	19,768.9
Private creditors	124.4	4,379.2	5,433.1	6,959.1	7,339.3	5,245.4	45,195.0
Suppliers' credits	101.6	103.6	−254.9	173.1	271.1	464.5	5,325.6
Financial markets	22.8	4,275.6	5,688.0	6,786.1	7,068.3	4,780.9	39,869.4
IMF (net purchases)	59.8	804.3	1,634.2	114.5	1,089.0	29.6	3,826.5
Private, nonguaranteed debt	429.7	2,043.1	3,076.2	2,330.2	2,694.5	2,694.0	23,804.2
Short-term debt (variation in debt)	...	11,695.0	4,464.0	5,777.0	−1,883.0	52.0	33,707.0
Total	1,270.9	21,738.5	18,442.5	18,974.7	13,639.8	11,729.6	142,940.2

Source: International Bank for Reconstruction and Development, *World Debt Tables, 1985–86* (Washington, 1986).

for the other region. Net credit from multilateral agencies other than the Fund, however, steadily rose, from $1.4 billion to $2.5 billion over the period 1980 to 1983, but declined to $2.1 billion in the next year. These flows, as a proportion of total debt flows, nearly trebled, from 6.4 percent in 1980 to 18.0 percent in 1984, largely because of the rise in non-IDA loans and the almost-steady decline in debt-creating flows. Debt flows to this region from multilateral agencies, excluding the Fund, exceeded those to South Asia in absolute amounts in four of the five years, the divergence in per capita flows being at least three times larger for East Asia and the Pacific. As would be expected, the IDA flows to this region were negligible, forming less than 5 percent of non-Fund credits from multilateral agencies.

Net credit from the Fund to Asian countries, which exceeded SDR 2 billion a year during 1981 to 1983, dropped to SDR 0.4 billion in 1984. There were net repurchases by this region from the Fund of the order of SDR 0.8 billion during 1985 and SDR 0.7 billion during the first seven months of 1986. Despite the need for balance of payments support, the reluctance of countries to approach the Fund for resources can perhaps be attributed to the members' perception of the conditionality attached to Fund programs.

2. Official Development Assistance

Net official development assistance (ODA) from all sources to Asian countries as a group declined in absolute terms from $8.3 billion in 1980 to $7.6 billion in 1982, despite a sharp increase in assistance to China, and hovered around that level during the next three years. In relation to their GNPs, the ODA flows to this group of countries contracted steadily throughout the period. It is difficult to know precisely what factors influenced this distribution among different countries and their relative importance. Several countries with higher per capita incomes have secured significantly larger per capita ODA than what became available to countries with much lower per capita incomes.

3. Direct and Portfolio Investment

Direct investment has not been an important source of finance among developing Asian countries, except in China, Singapore, and Malaysia. In Singapore and Malaysia the annual flows in recent years have remained broadly stable. The group of countries from East Asia and the Pacific, with significantly higher per capita incomes, have been generally more successful in attracting direct investment than those from South Asia. The important difficulties faced by them seem to be regarding an agreement on areas of investment from the point of view of both investors and recipients, and the uncertainty felt by recipient countries as to the period over which the funds would stay and the probability of withdrawals at short notice, which could cause problems for balance of payments management. Further, while in the short run, direct investment may be less costly in terms of exchange outgo for servicing the same, over the long run, the relative costs of direct investment may be greater than those of other forms of financing. One must therefore carefully assess the relative costs of the various forms of financing on a case-by-case basis.

Malaysia has been successful in attracting sizable portfolio investment for a number of years, though the net flows dropped sharply in 1985. There was a substantial step-up in portfolio investment during 1985 in the Republic of Korea, Thailand, China, and Singapore.

4. Official Transfers

Official transfers to developing Asian countries, another element of non-debt-creating flows and part of ODA, have remained generally stable, at about $2.8 billion a year, from 1980 onward. As they are in the nature of grants, they are obviously favored most by recipients, while the donors are generally reluctant to augment these flows appreciably.

5. External Borrowing

While the financing needs, as mentioned earlier, rose appreciably until 1981 and declined thereafter, non-debt-creating flows (mainly official transfers and direct investment) remained broadly stable, at least from 1980 onward. As a result, the gap in financing needs had to be met through external borrowing. The major source of external finance, as in other regions, was the net external borrowing (including that from multilateral institutions and the loan part of ODA), which from 1980 onward supplied roughly 75–85 percent of financing needs of Asian developing countries. The annual variations in total financing needs, therefore, generally got reflected in net external borrowing, which rose from $10.3 billion in 1978 to a peak of $25.9 billion in 1982 and steadily declined thereafter to $14.4 billion in 1985. On an average, a little more than one half of net external borrowing was from nonofficial creditors, banks, and others, the annual proportions ranging from 23 percent in 1984 to 79 percent in 1985. Resort to non-official sources of finance was mainly by the Republic of Korea, Indonesia, the Philippines, Malaysia, and Thailand from the East Asia and Pacific region and by India from South Asia. For most other countries from these two regions, this source of finance was available only to a limited extent, implying restricted maneuverability in their adjustment process for want of adequate financing of the desired nature. Several countries, notably Indonesia, the Philippines, Bangladesh, Burma, Nepal, and Sri Lanka, were forced to contract their imports or considerably slow down growth in imports in some years because of the financing constraints, with adverse effects on their overall economic activity.

While a very large proportion of financing had to be arranged through debt on terms and conditions that increasingly became harder, several Asian countries continued to enjoy a fairly satisfactory credit rating. They did not have to resort to severe adjustment programs and generally were able to cover continuing current account deficits. Many of those who relied much more on borrowing on commercial terms were able to achieve satisfactory growth in their exports. Knowing the financial constraint and their export potential, many South Asian countries were forced to limit their current account deficits, even at the cost of low output growth.

Developing countries in Asia, like their counterparts in the rest of the world, accumulated external debt and experienced a rise in debt-servicing obligations. The external debt position of Asian developing countries is, however, much less critical than that of those in Latin America and Africa, and their debt-service ratio is much lower. Thus, while the ratio of outstanding debt to the export of goods and services for all capital importing developing countries was 169 percent for 1985, it was only 99 percent for capital importing countries of Asia. Similarly, against a debt-service ratio of 24 percent for all capital importing developing countries for that year, it was only 13 percent for Asia.

In sum, net flows from multilateral agencies, including the Fund, during 1980–84 were not commensurate with the sharp rise in the financing requirements of the area. The richer region of East Asia and the Pacific was able to attract substantial net flows from private creditors, including banks, and was, therefore, more successful in reducing the net debt flows in relation to GNP and achieving higher growth. Poor countries from South Asia faced a severe constraint of financing both from multilateral and nonmultilateral sources.

III. Adjustment and Financing: Some Issues

In international discussions, "adjustment" secured ascendancy at the cost of development soon after the large and widespread imbalances on current account following the sharp increases in oil prices in 1973–74. While the developing countries consistently opposed the deflationary elements of adjustment programs, it was being argued by others that although such policies might have a deflationary impact to begin with, in the medium-to-long term they restored growth prospects. Besides, as a result of the preoccupation of the industrially advanced countries with rolling back the strong inflationary forces, "growth" as an objective suffered considerably. With the second oil shock, strong adjustment became the watchword. The strategy adopted in the early 1980s to deal with the world debt crisis averted financial collapse at the cost of a sharp decline in the growth rate and investment in the indebted countries. The time has come to change the strategy. There is a need to achieve a better balance between adjustment and financing.

"Adjustment" in countries with current account deficits denotes a reduction in such deficits to sustainable levels. This implies policies aimed at shifting resources to export-promoting and import-substituting sectors, as well as larger investments to achieve higher growth. Thus, the structure of aggregate demand and supply have to undergo changes to achieve higher growth rates while generating current account positions consistent with normal external resource flows. Experience has, however, shown that these changes require time, the extent of time required varying from country to country depending on the resource endowments, the extent of external imbalance, the financing that is available, and the international economic environment. Price incentives do not necessarily work when there are extreme rigidities on the supply side. There are no universal remedies applicable to all countries and in every situation. The guidelines on conditionality for the use of the Fund's resources and for stand-by arrangements rightly state: "In helping members to devise adjustment programs, the Fund will pay due regard to the domestic social and political objectives, the economic priorities, and the circumstances of members, including the causes of their balance of payments problems." What is required is adherence to this, both in words and in spirit, in designing and monitoring programs in furtherance of adjustment.

The need for adjustment is rarely disputed, although there are strong views about the speed of adjustment and the content of the adjustment policies. As economic strength and the ability to postpone adjustment varied considerably from one country to another, it was the weakest countries that had to undergo maximum adjustment irrespective of the costs involved. A global and cooperative adjustment strategy would have reduced hardships to many developing countries and at the same time would have promoted sustained growth of output and trade all around. Adjustment, to be meaningful, must be made by both deficit and surplus countries, as the obligations are mutual. It may be noted that a similar problem was experienced under the international gold standard system. While gold-losing countries had to contract, gold-gaining countries were under no compulsion to expand. This introduced a deflationary bias in the system, and this was one of the reasons for the collapse of the system. Even under the present scheme of things, the adjustment obligation applies almost wholly to developing countries, even though the success of adjustment in deficit countries very much depends on the international environment and the availability of finance on appropriate terms as the adjustment policies are implemented.

The Asian experience with adjustment shows that the relatively better-off countries of East Asia and the Pacific were generally in a much better position to withstand larger imbalances in the early 1980s. They also succeeded in reducing these imbalances over the medium term. On the other hand, the low-income South Asian countries generally had to restrict imbalances to low levels. They also found it difficult to achieve sustained progress in adjustment. This divergence of outcome owes much to the differences in the structures of economies and the availability of finance.

In recent years, many developing countries in deficit were required to adjust simultaneously, and the needed adjustment was of a large order. On the other hand, most industrial countries were concerned with anti-inflationary policies, with little regard for their impact on adjustment efforts of developing countries. Consequently, the developing countries in deficit had to bear the brunt of adjustment, in an inhospitable international environment. It was argued at one stage that if the international situation turned out to be worse than what was postulated at the time of the adjustment program, it was for the country under the program to strengthen its adjustment effort to compensate for the deterioration in the world environment. Happily, the situation has changed recently as reflected by the Mexican program, under which it has been stipulated that the developments in oil prices are to be reckoned with in assessing the implementation of the program. It is hoped, as urged by the Group of Twenty-Four, that the Mexican program will be the forerunner of similar programs in other countries.

The shift in resources called for under adjustment is facilitated if an economy has sizable resources and a diversified structure. From this point of view, again, countries in East Asia and the Pacific are in a more advantageous position than those in South Asia. The rates of saving and investment in the former group have been generally much higher than in the latter. This, together with the relatively high per capita incomes in the former, provides the necessary flexibility to pursue adjustment policies.

It is being increasingly recognized that in the present world situation, characterized by rigidities of various kinds, rising protectionism, and a large number of deficit countries under pressure for adjustment, the time span over which adjustment can be expected to be completed by an individual country would be longer. One would have thought that in this situation there would be a greater recourse to extended Fund facility arrangements and/or successive stand-by arrangements with the Fund. Actually, by end-August 1986, only one country (outside Asia) had an extended Fund facility arrangement, and only four countries from Asia had stand-by arrangements, in force. It is necessary that the Fund be seen as aggressively discharging its responsibilities as a supplier of balance of payments assistance to its members on terms and conditions that promote adjustment along with growth. A realistic assessment of the prospects of the international economy over the medium term and the particular circumstances of individual members must be built into any adjustment program. For playing an effective role in this regard, the Fund's own resources need to be augmented sufficiently and early through quota increases.

The Fund is in a position to assist participants in the SDR Department through a regular allocation of SDRs in amounts that would make the SDR the principal reserve asset of the international monetary system, as agreed under its Articles of Agreement. An allocation would lessen the need for developing member countries to build up reserves, through a costly process, and promote growth and adjustment. It is unfortunate that some countries have, however, succeeded in preventing an allocation for the past five years. Their strategy seems to be to postpone an allocation to the extent possible. In the process, a greater burden has been placed on the developing countries, who are under a compulsion to adjust.

There are some disturbing developments in respect of other multilateral financing institutions as well. The ability of these institutions to provide both concessional and nonconcessional flows is being severely constrained through a tight rein on their resources. Some strong economies with sizable external account surpluses find it convenient to hold back their support for augmenting the resources of these institutions. Japan has made an offer of SDR 3 billion to the Fund to augment Fund resources. It is hoped that, as the major capital surplus country today in the world, Japan would make a similar contribution to the eighth replenishment of IDA. There is some thought that the terms and conditions of concessional resources should be made much more stiff. The World Bank is also moving toward imposition of conditionality in its loan assistance. Further, while the stated policy has been that there would be no cross-conditionality between Fund and Bank assistance, in reality several members have experienced such cross-conditionality.

The United Nations (UN) General Assembly, in 1970, adopted the International Development Strategy for the Second UN Development Decade, which included a provision as follows:

> Each economically advanced country will progressively increase its official development assistance to the developing countries and will exert its best efforts to reach a minimum net amount of 0.7 percent of its gross national product at market prices by the middle of the decade.

By 1975, the ODA/GNP ratio for the group of Development Assistance Committee countries had reached only 0.35 percent, just one half of the agreed target. By 1984, nine years after the target date, the ratio moved up to only 0.36 percent. Had the UN target been achieved even by 1984, the external financing needs of all developing countries in that year would have been more than matched from this source alone. If the targeted ratio had been reached by 1975 and maintained thereafter, the adjustment problems of many developing countries would have been eased substantially and those of many others resolved completely.

It is distressing that almost no progress has been seen toward reaching the target ratio of 0.7 percent. Besides, the distribution of these flows seems to be influenced much more by factors other than the number of people suffering from absolute poverty. Visible progress toward the ODA target and adequate weight given to the distribution-to-poverty criterion—both the extent of poverty and the number of people suffering from poverty—is called for. The United States is the main market for some Asian countries—the Republic of Korea, Hong Kong, Singapore, etc.—which have achieved strong export growth. Nearly one fifth of the U.S. trade deficit of $150 billion in 1985 was with Asia, excluding Japan. Unless Western Europe and Japan increase their imports from developing countries and unless the improvement to be effected by the United States in its trade deficit is achieved largely by correcting its adverse trade with Japan and the Federal Republic of Germany, exports of countries like Korea and Singapore may be adversely affected. A number of large countries, particularly from the South Asian region, had a ratio of debt to exports of goods and services in the range of 200 percent to 465 percent. These countries would remain vulnerable to any hardening of the terms of lending, as well as to international developments adversely affecting their export prospects.

An exchange rate policy aimed at maintaining competitiveness of exports is generally advocated in furtherance of adjustment. The recent experience of the reduction in the misalignment of exchange rates of major industrial currencies has brought out clearly that, even in sophisticated economies functioning under market forces to a very large extent, it takes considerable time before the effects of exchange rate changes can be felt. In much weaker economies with inflexible production structures, the time required to have the favorable effects of exchange rates felt would be considerable. The time span is bound to increase in a situation when the spread and intensity of protectionism is rising and world trade is expanding at a relatively low rate.

There is no doubt that economies faced with severe balance of payments constraints must readjust their economic structures. Nations which have been living beyond their means must necessarily cut expenditures. "Growth" without "adjustment" is not sustainable. Equally, "adjustment" without "growth" lacks purpose. A program of adjustment that calls for a sharp and sudden decline in growth and investment may not even pave the way for long-run growth. Adjustment ultimately requires moving resources into the export sector in order to reduce current account deficits and investing more in general to accelerate growth. Both of these require time. The speed of adjustment will depend on the structural characteristics of the economy, and external flows will help to provide the needed time and also to avoid the adverse effects of sudden changes in policy that will otherwise be required. An optimal path of adjustment must therefore be chosen, bearing in mind possible adverse consequences, economic and social. The negative attitude toward the transfer of real resources to developing economies that exists currently must give place to a more positive approach. In this, multilateral institutions like the Fund have an important role to play.

Comments

Nimal Sanderatne

The author has discussed the international economic environment and its bearing on Asian countries in the first section of the paper. The slow growth of industrial countries, the escalation of inflation, the two oil price hikes, increased protectionism, and high interest rates are among the adverse international developments that affected the developing countries of Asia in the 1970s. Despite this international economic environment, many Asian countries have been able to achieve impressive growth rates. The countries of East Asia and the Pacific achieved higher growth rates.

Although the author's categorization into East Asia and the Pacific, and South Asia and China, brings out interesting contrasts in performances, the categorization focuses on the results achieved rather than the differences in policies pursued by the countries. Further, as in any broad categorization, within each group of countries there are widely different economies. In the East Asia group there are both oil exporters (Indonesia and Malaysia) and oil importers. Therefore, the oil price hikes had opposite impacts on these countries. In the South Asia and China group, India and China pursued different economic systems and hence their being lumped together is not very useful analytically. Perhaps China is best considered separately. Again, India is so large that it may not be comparable to its small neighbors, especially Nepal and Sri Lanka. While Sri Lanka may be placed with South Asia until 1977, since then its liberalization policies have been more akin to those of the East Asia group.

Any broad categorization of countries leads to difficulties. Yet the point I wish to make is that the structure of the economies and the differences in policies pursued were the factors responsible for the results achieved. The author's categorization is largely based on geographic and ex post results and highlights these, rather than the policy differences.

The higher investment rates of East Asian countries are no doubt an important reason for their growth. The issue that should be discussed is why their savings rates are higher. Is it because the initial economic conditions were better? Is it because of policies that encouraged savings? Is the higher savings volume related to investable opportunities—in other words, were savings investment-led and goal-directed? Is the pattern of income distribution an important factor? Are there cultural reasons? These are factors that should be discussed more fully if we are to understand the differences in economic performance among these countries. In the same context, the higher savings rate in India compared with its neighbors merits discussion.

The analysis of the investment-savings gap uses the data of a single year (1984). This could be somewhat misleading, since unexpected or abnormal price developments could change the ratio. It would have been more reliable if the average for a number of years had been used. The higher savings ratio in the South Asian region in 1984 may not reflect average conditions.

The high growth rates of exports of East Asian countries merit further discussion, since they are not only results of the policies pursued but are also an important factor responsible for the economic performance of these countries. The fact is that these countries pursued a policy of export-led growth in the face of adverse international developments. Further, the policy response of East Asian countries to the harsh international environment was one of liberalization, in contrast to the inward-looking policies pursued by South Asian countries. The export-led growth was possible in the former group of countries, owing to their trade-liberalization policies and structural adjustments of their economies.

In Section II, the author summarizes the overall experience of external financing for the two groups of countries. The external financing needs and sources of financing are, however, specific to the countries of Asia. The choice of policies and the policy mix in each country have an important bearing on external financing. Since foreign-funded adjustment programs are in fact complex packages and are geared to particular circumstances, it is difficult to aggregate the experiences of countries meaningfully. Only case studies of countries could elicit more useful insights on the resources for the types and quantum of external financing.

In Section III, the author is basically critical of adjustment policies. He has summarized the problems with and limitations of adjustment policies: their deflationary bias; preoccupation with short-term stabilization rather than long-term growth; lack of appreciation of rigidities in developing countries' economies, which do not make it realistic to attain the expected objectives with the adjustment programs; and the lack of appreciation of internal social realities and political constraints. Further, he points out that the burden of adjustment falls unfairly on the developing countries, and that for adjustment to be meaningful deficit and surplus countries must have mutual obligations.

The international experience so far provides evidence that adjustment policies have the potential and capacity to attain economic growth and, ultimately, economic development. Yet the burden of such adjustment tends to fall on the poorer groups in a society and consequently creates difficulties in pursuing these policies to their logical conclusion. Apart from this, long-run attainment of objectives is no answer to the deprivations and difficulties that sections of a community have to face in the short run. Further, these deprivations may affect the quality of life and affect the quality of human capital in the future. As the author points out, while this position is generally agreed, in fact the formulation of adjustment policies in most cases has not given adequate attention to this aspect. In fairness it may also be pointed out that the lack of concern with maintaining human capital investments may not necessarily be an imposition of the Fund but may be considered a condition by countries making their adjustment programs. It is not very clear whether in negotiations between the Fund and developing countries there is an insistence on curtailment of social expenditure or whether countries implementing adjustment policies interpret the Fund's stance as requiring such curtailment. This is an area which merits discussion at this seminar.

In this connection, it may also be argued that if the financial discipline that is a condition of Fund programs is adhered to, then this would, itself, release adequate resources for human investment. For instance, in many countries the wastage in government expenditure and losses incurred by public corporations would release more than adequate funds for needed social expenditure. In any event, if adequate investments are not made in human capital, long-run economic growth surely cannot be a reality. It is, therefore, very essential that adjustment programs be neither undertaken at the expense of such expenditure nor conceived of as requiring the curtailment of essential investment that would permit long-run economic growth and development.

In analyzing the effects of externally supported adjustment programs on the level or rate of growth of output, it is important first to consider the circumstances in which such programs were introduced. Typically, the need for a stabilization program, whether supported by the Fund or any other agency, arises when the country experiences an imbalance between aggregate domestic demand (absorption) and aggregate supply which is reflected in a worsening of its external payments position. Many countries in Asia experienced such situations and resorted to foreign financing with a view to undertaking structural adjustment programs. As pointed out in the paper, it is true that in many cases external factors, such as the deterioration in the terms of trade and rising foreign interest rates, have been responsible for the basic demand-supply imbalances. Yet often, this imbalance can also be traced to inappropriate domestic policies that expand aggregate domestic demand too rapidly in relation to production in the economy, thereby leading to distortions in relative prices. If foreign financing is available, the expansion in domestic demand can be extended over a period, albeit at the cost of a widening current account deficit.

Many types of imbalances can give rise to the need to implement adjustment programs, but by far the most common is the emergence of an adverse balance of payments position. Disruptive inflationary pressures are also a reason for adopting an adjustment program. In many Asian countries, the Philippines in particular, the two problems were encountered simultaneously, resulting in a loss of creditworthiness that triggered the need for implementation of an adjustment program.

In Sri Lanka, for example, the fourfold rise in energy prices during 1973/74, the weak performance of the industrial countries and hence the lower demand for exports, and the second oil price hike during 1979/80 were the factors that resulted in a persistent adverse balance of payments position. The international output, weaker demand-management policies, restrictions on trade and payments, and the dual exchange rate policies pursued prior to 1977 contributed to the loss of competitiveness and added to balance of payments difficulties.

The criticism that external financing programs are in some sense inimical to growth can be decomposed into two specific areas.

First, a number of policy recommendations contained in externally financed programs, in particular the Fund programs, relate to the restraint on aggregate domestic demand and to alterations in the exchange rate. These are thought to interfere with economic growth and the level of activity. Second, policy recommendations are unduly harsh, leading to a greater worsening of the performance of the economy than is, in fact, necessary to secure the objectives of the stabilization effort. Therefore, the basic issues that arise with respect to adjustment of finances would be the following:

(1) What are the short-run effects of externally funded adjustment programs on the level or rate of growth on output in the countries concerned?

(2) Are these effects larger than they need to be to achieve the principal objectives of the programs and, in particular, are they significantly larger than the effects that would result from an alternative set of policies?

(3) What are the effects of externally funded adjustment programs on the long-run rate of growth of the economy, and how do these relate to the short-run effects?

Perhaps the discussion could deal with some of these issues.

The availability of empirical evidence is limited on each of these issues. Although there are some studies, done both by the Fund and outside agencies, the comparison of the programs and the policies would have to be based explicitly on the disequilibrium that the country faced at the time the stabilization program was introduced. Similarly, the alternative set of policies against which to compare a given externally funded program would have to be precisely defined. This is important because this alternative could presumably differ in the mix of policies consistent with the same objectives (more emphasis on demand management or on structural policies) or in terms of policy instruments (controls and imports versus devaluation).

Little empirical evidence exists on the long-run effects of the externally funded programs, and most of these studies do not analyze the effects of stabilization policy on economic development. While many countries in Asia have achieved both price stability and high growth by adopting prudent financial policies, others managed to combine a high rate of inflation with strong rates of growth for extended periods of time. At the same time, many countries have experienced high inflation and low rates of growth.

The external position of Sri Lanka deteriorated over the decade prior to 1977 owing largely to the worsening of the terms of trade and the stagnation of the export-oriented agricultural sector. Rapid expansion in monetary aggregates and rising inflationary pressures moved domestic real costs out of line with levels in international markets. Similar economic conditions have been experienced by many Asian countries.

Illustrative of an adjustment program in South Asia was the fundamental shift in Sri Lanka's overall development strategy in November 1977. The basic objective of the policy package was to lay a foundation for rapid and balanced economic growth. The initial adjustment package, therefore, included the dismantling of direct and indirect controls on prices, imports, and external payments; retrenchment of government operations in processing and distribution of basic commodities; provision of adequate incentives to producers; unification of the exchange rate at a depreciated level; and the introduction of a flexible exchange rate policy.

The adjustment of current account deficits to sustainable levels sometimes ignores the adverse international effects. Thus, while adjustment is supposed to take account of the circumstances of the (developing) countries, it does not give adequate weight to the transmission of balance of payments problems, owing to the policies followed by industrial countries. For instance, the influence of persistent budget deficits in drawing reserves away from Europe and reducing the demand for developing countries' exports has not been given adequate weight. In fact, deficits in developing countries are the counterparts of surpluses in developed countries. There is, therefore, a need to stress the need for more responsible international fiscal/financial discipline when adjustment measures are recommended.

Concerning the role of the Fund in adjustment, it is necessary to stress the revolving character of the Fund's reserves, the temporary nature of its financial support based on quotas, and the linking of that support to policies designed to correct payments problems over the short-to-medium term. However, countries facing balance of payments difficulties have adopted measures that have been insufficiently vigorous and comprehensive, leading to larger adjustment periods and more extended use of Fund credit. The report of the Group of Twenty-Four concluded that the Fund had not been successful in developing countries and that program periods had been too short, the amount of financing inadequate, and insufficient consideration had been given to the effects of adjustment measures on growth, income distribution, and short-term inflation. Too much attention is given, in Fund programs, to demand restraint and too little attention to structural policies needed to address the underlying payments disequilibria in developing countries.

This paper has been successful in raising a large number of issues that require detailed discussion. Owing to the differences in resource endowments, initial conditions, and policies pursued, it is difficult to be conclusive about the impact that adjustment policies and external financing have had on the economic development of Asian countries. Adjustment policies could, if pursued logically with the required financial discipline, lead to economic growth. Yet formulators of such policies should be mindful of political realities and social goals, which are themselves extremely important for the long-run development of Asian countries. Further, the burden of adjustment should be borne by both developed and developing countries, and international institutions should endeavor to assist developing countries both in coping with their short-run problems and in achieving long-run economic and social development.

8
Surpluses for a Capital-Hungry World[1]
Paul Streeten

The high growth rate of Japan has been held up as an example for the more tired economies of the United Kingdom and the United States. While Japan's gross national product (GNP) grew by 4.3 percent annually between 1980 and 1985, the average annual growth rate of other industrial countries was only 2.2 percent. The U.S. growth rate declined from 6.6 percent in 1984 to 2.3 percent in 1985.

Some say that the key to Japan's spectacular growth performance is exporting. Japan's surplus on its current account was $80 billion in 1986. It was largely the result of a highly competitive economy, helped by the U.S. twin deficits—the gigantic deficits that the United States ran in its budget and in its foreign balance—and the drop in the price of oil. Most observers—including the President of the United States—would agree that these two deficits must be reduced. What, then, would be the fate of the Japanese surplus? If the United States were to reduce its twin deficits without a corresponding expansion anywhere else, Japan's exports and growth would decline. This would give a powerful deflationary impact to the world economy, which already is suffering from high unemployment. The conventional recommendation is that Japan expand its economy, appreciate the yen even more, import more, and raise consumption and investment at home. As the *New York Times* put it in the headline of an editorial, "Japan Should Eat More, Not Sell More."[2]

But an attempt to absorb the whole of this surplus domestically is neither desirable nor possible. It is true that Japan's housing

---

[1] This paper draws on an excellent paper by Saburo Okita, Lal Jayawardena, and Arjun K. Sengupta entitled "The Potential of the Japanese Surplus for World Economic Development" (unpublished, United Nations University, Tokyo, April 1986). This study was subsequently published under the same title as No. 1 in the Study Group Series of the World Institute for Development Economics Research (Helsinki).

[2] *New York Times*, Vol. 135 (July 6, 1986), Sec. 4, p. 12.

conditions are poor and that investment in more and better housing is desirable. The share of residential building in total reproducible fixed assets is only 25 percent in Japan, compared with 35 percent in the United States. But housing and some other parts of the infrastructure apart, the absorption of the whole surplus could be achieved only by lowering the Japanese growth rate and, with it, the growth rate of other parts of the world economy. And, in a world that needs capital desperately, preaching high consumption to a nation that combines the work ethic with the saving ethic borders on the immoral.

Let us look at very rough orders of magnitude in the world's current account balances in 1986.

Deficits		Surpluses	
	billion U.S. dollars		
United States	140	Japan	85
Developing countries	50	Fed. Rep. of Germany	35
Of which: Oil exporters	(25)	Other industrial countries	20
			140
		Errors and omissions[1]	50
	190		190

[1] The missing billions are largely caused by capital flight from the developing countries to U.S. and Swiss banks.

The first question to ask is whether the Japanese surpluses are likely to continue. It has been argued that these large surpluses are a temporary aberration, resulting from overadjustment to the rise in the oil price in the 1970s and that, with falling oil prices, they will automatically disappear. If that were to be so, it would be a cause not for rejoicing, but for regret. In a capital-starved world, we should be grateful for any country whose production grows rapidly and that attempts to save more than it invests at home, as long as the deflationary impact of these excess savings can be avoided. The Japanese saving rate has been running at 27 percent of GNP, and some economists have maintained that this high propensity to save is "structural"—that is, it is deeply imbedded in Japanese tradition and culture. Others have argued that it is the result of a peculiar age distribution. On a life-cycle theory of saving, the young save in order to live on their savings in their old age. Japan has a higher proportion of young workers to both old people and to dependent children than other Organization for Economic Cooperation and Development (OECD) countries. If this interpretation is right, the saving rate will decline over the next 15 years.

If the Japanese were to attempt to divert the whole surplus to domestic use, by raising either consumption or domestic investment, they might have to accept a lower growth rate and higher unemployment. The world economy would also suffer from deflation. If, on the other hand, the surplus were likely to continue, a good source of foreign investment and markets other than the United States would have to be found. Here, an opportunity for a major positive-sum game would arise, in which the OECD countries (including the United States and Japan), the developing countries of the Third World, and the global economy would all benefit.

A recycling, on commercial terms, of these excess savings to the developing countries, instead of the U.S. market, would have the following advantages: Japan would find safer returns for its foreign investment; the OECD countries would find a larger market for their exports of capital goods and other goods to the Third World; the developing countries would find a source of capital for their development needs; and the global economy would resume higher growth and employment. Three now-underutilized pools of resources would be combined, to good effect: the surpluses of the excess savers, which need to be channeled into safe investments; the underutilized industrial capacity and unemployment of the developed countries; and the largely idle or low-productivity manpower of the Third World would be brought together in a happy union.

Some have argued that Japan should give more aid to low-income countries. In fact, Japan has made a beginning in this direction with its increased contributions to the World Bank and the International Monetary Fund. But though Japan should give more aid, the reason is not its large current account surpluses, but rather its high income. By the same criterion, the United States and the United Kingdom also should give more aid. Japan's surpluses are a reason for it to undertake more long-term foreign investment on commercial terms. If we say that a surplus is a reason for giving more aid, deficit countries will soon argue that their deficits are a reason for giving less. But that would be rather like a man who found himself with temporary liquidity problems, and then cut first his contribution to Oxfam. The proper criterion for aid-giving is income per head; for lending commercially or investing abroad, it is the size of the current account surplus.

At this time, we lack appropriate financial institutions to provide lenders or investors with what they want, while on-lending to borrowers on acceptable terms. It is not difficult to envisage an international investment trust or a fund that would combine security for the lender with acceptable terms for the borrower. Now, the Japanese invest in a currency that has been depreciating, and whose value will drop further as soon as U.S. inflation starts again. A multilateral guarantee against devaluation and inflation should be welcome to the Japanese in return for a steady, but somewhat lower rate of return than they have been enjoying.

An important difference between the Organization of Petroleum Exporting Countries (OPEC) surpluses in the 1970s and the Japanese (and the German) surpluses now is that while the former consisted largely of government loans, the present surpluses are from private lenders. Japanese private banks can mediate in the bank lending, and in portfolio and equity investment of some of the private savings. Japanese private direct investment also can make a contribution. But, although the Japanese banking system has been quite remarkably adaptive and has developed the capacity to channel international loans, financial innovation may be required, because a multilateral institution is better suited to providing the guarantees and to accomplishing at least part of the task. The World Bank and its affiliates, the International Finance Corporation and the International Development Association, also may not be able to accomplish the whole task, though they could contribute to a solution. It is for debate how multilateral these institutions should be, how much of a government guarantee is needed, and whether the loans should be guaranteed against currency depreciation and inflation.

An additional imaginative step would be to graft an interest-subsidy scheme onto the recycling mechanism, for the benefit of the low-income countries. Contributions to this should not be made according to the size of the surplus on current account, but instead according to income per head, preferably in a progressive fashion, so that the percentage contribution would rise with rising incomes per head. The cost-effectiveness of such aid would be quite high, because a small interest subsidy would make it possible for large investment funds to be recycled to the poor countries.

Some observers advocate that the Japanese and German (Fed. Rep.) surpluses should be used to refinance and relieve debt, mainly that owed by Latin American countries. Such is, for example, the proposal by two members of the U.S. Congress, Representative David R. Obey and Senator Paul S. Sarbanes.[3] Similar ideas were expressed by Felix Rohatyn and Paul Volcker at a meeting organized by the Overseas Development Council in Washington in 1986. If such proposals were accepted, the result could be a scheme to aid industrial country banks rather than to foster productive investment in poor countries. It might amount to rewarding greedy lenders and profligate borrowers. This outcome is not at all inherent in the proposal espoused in this paper. However desirable it might be to deal with old debt in such a way as to restore creditworthiness in Latin America and to resume world growth, the fact remains that there are large areas of the world, such as South Asia, which have no debt problem, have carefully husbanded their resources, and could make excellent use of these scarce funds.

Another objection that has been raised to recycling proposals is that as long as the U.S. budgetary deficits continue, the reduction or elimination of the Japanese surpluses will exert pressure on world capital markets, which might have adverse repercussions on Latin American debtors. The reply to this objection is that the U.S. deficits are, in any case, unsustainable and that recycling surpluses to the developing countries would raise their demand for U.S. exports and contribute to the reduction or elimination of the U.S. deficit. This is surely a better way of stimulating the world economy than either the present exhortations to Japan and the Federal Republic of Germany to buy more from the United States or, in the absence of expansion abroad, further contraction in the United States. In addition, monetary expansion in Japan and Europe might rekindle inflation, while continuing U.S. deficits might lead to a

---

[3] " 'Recycling' Surpluses to the Third World," *New York Times*, Vol. 136 (November 9, 1986), Sec. 3, p. 3.

collapse of the fairly open trading system. The recycling of the surpluses to the Third World offers a solution that yields better returns for the Japanese; a reduction in the deficit without restriction of the domestic economy to the United States; much-needed resources to the developing countries; and an expansionist, non-inflationary solution for the world economy.

Biographical Sketches

Bijan B. Aghevli serves as Assistant Director in the International Monetary Fund's Asian Department, where he heads a division covering Japan, the Republic of Korea, and Tonga. He received his doctorate in economics from Brown University (Providence, Rhode Island) and subsequently joined the Fund. During 1975–76, he was a Research Fellow at the London School of Economics, where he taught international finance and carried out research. Mr. Aghevli has published various papers in the general area of international and monetary economics.

Ehtisham Ahmad, a Pakistani, serves as Director of the Development Economics Research Programme at the London School of Economics (LSE). Before assuming his present position, he was Deputy Director of the Development Economics Research Center at Warwick University and a Lecturer at Quaid-e-Azam University (Islamabad). He has directed, jointly with Professor Nicholas Stern of the LSE, a project on the Indian fiscal system and another on tax reform in Pakistan. Mr. Ahmad holds a doctorate in economics from the University of Sussex and has published numerous economic articles.

Muzaffer Ahmad, a Bangladeshi, serves as Professor of Economics and Management at Dhaka University. Previously, he worked as a corporate planner with the East Pakistan Industrial Development Corporation and as Development Planner with the First Planning Commission of Bangladesh. He has served on various expert groups; on official committees and commissions related to industry, taxation, finance, and planning; and as a consultant to many international organizations. Dr. Ahmad has also taught at U.S. universities in Chicago and Boston. He has published extensively on economics and management. His most recent book is *State and Development* (1987).

V. V. Bhatt, an Indian, serves as Senior Training Officer in the Economic Development Institute of the World Bank. Before assuming his present position, he served the World Bank as Chief of the Division of Public Finance. He also served as Chief Executive of the Industrial Bank of India, Economic Adviser to the Reserve Bank of India, and as Development Economist at the United Nations Asian Institute for Development and Planning. Mr. Bhatt holds a doctorate in economics from Harvard University and has published extensively on development problems, strategy, and policies. His most recent book is *Development Perspectives* (Pergamon Press, Oxford, England, 1980).

Hyung-Ki Kim, a Korean, serves as Adviser, Institutional Development at the Economic Development Institute of the World Bank. Before assuming his present position, he held positions in the World Bank's Education, Industry, and Projects Policy Departments. He also held various positions in the Government of the Republic of Korea, including Senior Policy Analyst on the President's Economic and Scientific Council, Director General of International Technical Cooperation, Director General of Policy Planning and Development in the Ministry of Science and Technology, and Vice Minister of Education. Mr. Kim holds a master's degree in engineering economics from Columbia University and has been a Fellow at Harvard University's Center for International Affairs.

Insu Kim, a Korean, serves as Economist in the Financial Relations Division, Treasurer's Department of the International Monetary Fund. At the time this seminar was held, he was an Economist in the Fund's Asian Department working on India. He holds a doctorate in economics from the Graduate Institute of International Studies (Geneva).

R. N. Malhotra, an Indian, serves as Governor of the Reserve Bank of India. Before assuming his present position in February 1985, he was an Executive Director of the International Monetary Fund; financial adviser to the Fund in Indonesia, Tanzania, and at its Washington headquarters; and Secretary, Economic Affairs in the Indian Government. He began his career in the Indian Administrative Service in 1951. Mr. Malhotra holds B.A. and M.A. degrees, as well as a Bachelor of Laws with a diploma in international law, from the Punjab and Lucknow Universities.

K. M. Matin, a Bangladeshi, serves as Research Fellow at the Bangladesh Institute of Development Studies (Dhaka). He has worked as a consultant to United Nations organizations and to Bangladesh's Ministries of Commerce and Finance and its Export Promotion Bureau. He has also served on expert groups organized by the United Nations Conference on Trade and Development. Mr. Matin holds a B. Phil. degree from Oxford University and an M. Phil. degree from Columbia University. His research and publications have been primarily in the areas of trade policy and stabilization policy.

Azizali F. Mohammed, a Pakistani, serves as Director of the External Relations Department in the International Monetary Fund. Before assuming his present position in 1980, he was Advisor to the Saudi Arabian Monetary Agency, Senior Advisor in the Fund's European Department, Secretary to the Technical Group on the Transfer of Real Resources of the Committee of Twenty (Committee on Reform of the International Monetary System and Related Issues), and Economic Adviser to Pakistan's Ministry of Finance. He holds a doctorate in economics from George Washington University (Washington, D.C.).

Sang-Woo Nam, a Korean, serves as Senior Fellow at the Korea Development Institute (Seoul). He is currently on leave from the Institute, working as an Economist in the Country Operations Division of the World Bank's Asia Country Department No. 2. Before assuming his present position, he held various research positions with the Korea Development Institute and served as Counsellor to the Deputy Prime Minister of the Republic of Korea. Mr. Nam holds a doctorate in management from the Sloan School of Management, Massachusetts Institute of Technology. His research interests are in money and banking and macroeconomic modeling.

Hubert Neiss, an Austrian, serves as Deputy Director of the Asian Department in the International Monetary Fund. Before assuming his present position in 1980, he served in a variety of positions in the Fund's European and Asian Departments, as Advisor (Resident Representative of the Fund) to the Government of Indonesia, and as Economist with the Austrian Institute of Economic Research (Vienna). He holds a doctorate in economics from the Hochschule für Welthandel (Vienna).

Wilhelm G. Ortaliz, a Filipino, serves as Executive Director of the Philippine Council for Foreign Relations (Manila). Before assuming his present position in April 1987, he served the Philippine Government as Assistant Minister of Trade and Industry and as Director of the Bureau of Industrial Development. In the latter position, he played a leading role in the formulation of policy and program reforms that formed the basis of the Industrial Restructuring Program launched in the early 1980s.

C. Rangarajan, an Indian, serves as Deputy Governor of the Reserve Bank of India. Before assuming his present position, he was Professor of Economics at the Indian Institute of Management (Ahmedabad). Dr. Rangarajan is also currently a Member of the Economic Advisory Council of the Prime Minister of India. His research interests are in monetary theory and financial institutions, industrial economics, and planning.

Nimal Sanderatne, a Sri Lankan, serves as Chairman of the Bank of Ceylon. Before assuming his present position, he served in a number of positions at the Central Bank of Sri Lanka, including Director of Economic Research and Director of Statistics. He has also been a consultant to the World Bank, the Asian Development Bank, and the United Nations Children's Fund (UNICEF). Mr. Sanderatne holds a doctorate in economics from the University of Wisconsin and has published a number of articles in journals and books. He was a joint author of *Sri Lanka: The Social Impact of Economic Policies in the Last Decade* (UNICEF, Colombo, 1985).

T.L. Sankar, an Indian, serves as Director of the Institute of Public Enterprise (Hyderabad). During his 30 years of service in the Indian Administrative Service, he specialized in development administration, with particular reference to public systems and public enterprise management. Since 1971, he has been involved in India's energy policy formulation and implementation. Mr. Sankar holds master's degrees in chemistry and development economics. His current research interests are in public policy analysis, with particular reference to public systems and energy systems.

Sunanda Sen, an Indian, serves as Professor of International Economics at the Centre for Economic Studies, Jawaharlal Nehru University (New Delhi). She has been a Visiting Fellow at Clare Hall, Cambridge University and a Directeur d'étude at the Maison des sciences de l'hommes (Paris). She has also been a visiting faculty member at research institutions and universities in Boston, Binghamton (New York), Cambridge (England), Oxford, Paris, Heidelberg, and the Hague. Ms. Sen has published numerous articles in books and journals. Her most recent research work includes a study in economic history, *Tributes, Transfers and Spoliation in the Age of Finance Capital: India 1890–1914*; a paper on women in India, Bangladesh, and Pakistan; and an ongoing study of the Third World and international finance in the 1980s.

Paul Streeten, a citizen of the United Kingdom, serves as Director of the World Development Institute at Boston University. Before assuming his present position, he was Special Adviser to the Policy Planning and Program Review Department of the World Bank and Director of Studies at the Overseas Development Council (Washington, D.C.). Until 1978 he was Warden of Queen Elizabeth House, Director of the Institute of Commonwealth Studies, and a Fellow of Balliol College, Oxford. Mr. Streeten was also Professor of Economics and Director of the Institute of Development Studies at the University of Sussex and Deputy Director-General of Economic Planning at the U.K. Ministry of Overseas Development. He holds a D. Litt. degree from Oxford University and has published widely in economic development.

Charan D. Wadhva, an Indian, serves as Research Professor of Political Economy at the Centre for Policy Research (New Delhi). Before assuming his present position, he was Director of the Indian Council for Research on International Economic Relations (New Delhi), Reserve Bank of India Chair Professor at the Indian Institute of Management (Ahmedabad), and as Economic Adviser to Bharat Heavy Electricals Limited. He has been a consultant to the United Nations and several other organizations. Mr. Wadhva holds a doctorate in economics from Yale University and has published several books and numerous articles in professional journals.

Arshad Zaman, a Pakistani, serves as Chief Economist and Ex-Officio Member of Pakistan's Planning Commission. Before assuming his present position in March 1987, he served as Economic Adviser and Additional Secretary in Pakistan's Ministry of Finance. From 1970 through 1982, he was with the World Bank, where he served as Senior Economist in both the Country Programs Department, and the Office of the Vice President, of the Europe, Middle East, and North Africa (EMENA) Region. Mr. Zaman holds a doctorate in economics from Michigan State University and has published numerous articles.

Seminar Participants and Observers*

I. Participants

K.B. LALL, *Seminar Chairman*
    Chairman
    Indian Council for Research
      on International
      Economic Relations
    New Delhi

PAUL STREETEN, *Seminar Moderator*
    Director
    World Development
      Institute
    Boston University

Bangladesh

MUZAFFER AHMAD
    Professor of Economics and
      Management
    Dhaka University

K. M. MATIN
    Research Fellow
    Bangladesh Institute of
      Development Studies
    Dhaka

India

SHANKAR ACHARYA
    Department of Economic
      Affairs
    Ministry of Finance
    New Delhi

V.K. BHALLA
    Reader
    Faculty of Management
      Studies
    University of Delhi

---

* The titles and affiliations listed for participants and observers are those they had at the time of the seminar (December 1986).

K. L. Deshpande	Adviser Department of Economic Analysis and Policy Reserve Bank of India Bombay
A. M. Khusro	Chairman National Institute of Public Finance and Policy New Delhi
Sudipto Mundle	Professor National Institute of Public Finance and Policy New Delhi
C. Rangarajan	Deputy Governor Reserve Bank of India Bombay
T.L. Sankar	Director Institute of Public Enterprise Hyderabad
N. A. Sarma	Consultant Indian Council for Research on International Economic Relations New Delhi
Sunanda Sen	Professor of International Economics Jawaharlal Nehru University New Delhi
S. K. Verghese	Professor National Institute of Bank Management Pune

CHARAN D. WADHVA   Director
                          Indian Council for Research
                            on International
                            Economic Relations
                          New Delhi

Indonesia

MOHAMMED SADLI   Professor of Economics
                          University of Indonesia
                          Jakarta

SANJOTO SASTROMIHARDJO   Chief Editor
                          Business News
                          Jakarta

Korea, Republic of

SANG-WOO NAM   Senior Fellow
                          Korea Development
                            Institute
                          Seoul

Malaysia

STEPHEN C. WONG   Fellow
                          Institute of Strategic
                            International Studies
                          Kuala Lumpur

TAT WAI TAN   Consultant
                          Bank Negara
                          Kuala Lumpur

Maldives

ADAM MANIKU   General Manager
                          Maldives Monetary
                            Authority
                          Male

Nepal

SURESH BABU SATYAL — Senior Officer
Nepal Rastra Bank
Kathmandu

Pakistan

EHTISHAM AHMAD — Co-Director
Development Economics
  Research Programme
London School of Economics

JAVED HAMID — Director
Lahore Business School

ZAHID HUSSAIN — Senior Reporter
Herald
Karachi

ASHRAF JANJUA — Economic Adviser
State Bank of Pakistan
Karachi

ARSHAD ZAMAN — Economic Adviser
Ministry of Finance
Islamabad

Philippines

MARIA CECILIA GONZALES — Economist
International Finance Affairs
  Office
Ministry of Finance
Manila

WILHELM G. ORTALIZ — Assistant Minister of Trade
  and Industry
Manila

Sri Lanka

MANIK DE SILVA — Editor
Ceylon Daily News
Colombo

NIMAL SANDERATNE — Director of Economic Research
Central Bank of Sri Lanka
Colombo

Thailand

KRIRKKIAT PHIPATSERITHAM — Vice Rector for Academic Affairs
Thammasat University
Bangkok

International Monetary Fund

AHMED M. ABUSHADI — Senior Information Officer
External Relations Department

BIJAN B. AGHEVLI — Assistant Director
Asian Department

AZIZALI F. MOHAMMED — Director
External Relations Department

HUBERT NEISS — Deputy Director
Asian Department

World Bank

V. V. BHATT — Senior Training Officer
Economic Development Institute

HYUNG-KI KIM — Adviser, Institutional Development
Economic Development Institute

II. Observers

India

B. N. ADARKAR   Former Governor
                          Reserve Bank of India
                          Bombay

B.S. BHATNAGAR   Director
                          Tata Exports Ltd.
                          Bombay

R. C. MURTHY   Bureau Chief
                          Business Standard
                          Bombay

KIRIT PARIKH   Director
                          Indira Gandhi Institute of
                             Development Research
                          Bombay

D.R. PENDSE   Economic Advisor
                          Tata Industries Ltd.
                          Bombay

UDAY SEKHAR   Manager
                          EXIM Bank
                          Bombay

MANU SHROFF   Editor
                          Economic Times
                          Bombay

PHILIP THOMAS   Executive Director
                          Industrial Development
                             Bank of India
                          Bombay